# ENDORSEMENTS

"Losing a loved family member or friend is one of the most devastating experiences that anyone will face in life. Psychologists call the emotional response to loss, grief. Grief is a necessary journey in the face of loss, but it is not a one size fits all process; it is complex and different for everyone. Thom Johnson has written a raw and honest account of his journey through grief after the loss of his beloved wife, Amy. In his book, *Good Grief*, Thom does more than simply tell his story, he serves as a guide, helping his readers understand the reality of grief and its significance in the healing journey. Thom's story is filled with transparency, humor, hope and faith and will inspire you to see grief in a new light. I know this to be true because I had a front row seat to Thom's story. I not only validate the message, I validate the authenticity of the messenger."

**Pastor Randy Remington**, former pastor of Beaverton Foursquare Church, current President of The Foursquare Church denomination

"*Good Grief* isn't a 'how-to' manual on processing loss; instead, it's a sacred invitation into a vulnerable experience as one family mourns the death of a cherished wife and mother while they each seek to find their footing again, collectively heralding the message that there is life after excruciating heartbreak. Having known the Johnson family for over two decades, I am deeply invested in the powerful story you are about to read because I have had a first-hand view as it has unfolded. I have no doubt that these pages will be tear-stained by the time you're finished reading while you will be simultaneously inspired by the profound and wise insights they share. This is one of the best books I have ever read on suffering, and though none of us may ever describe grief as good, in and of itself, one thing is clear in this redemptive story: When we walk through the fire without bypassing the messy, unscripted, and painful process, we come out like gold. I attest to the reality that the Johnson men are pure gold."

**Michelle Watson, PhD,** radio host of *The Dad Whisperer*, and author of *Let's Talk* and *Dad, Here's What I Really Need from You*

# GOOD GRIEF

One Husband's Journey from Incapacitating
Fear to Overwhelming Joy

*Gary & Char –*
*Thank you both so much for your friendship, love, prayers, & support through the years. I pray this book brings you joy.*

**Thomas Michael Johnson**

*Thomas Michael Johnson*

WestBow
PRESS®
A DIVISION OF THOMAS NELSON
& ZONDERVAN

Copyright © 2020 Thomas Michael Johnson.

All rights reserved. No part of this book may be used or reproduced by any means, graphic, electronic, or mechanical, including photocopying, recording, taping or by any information storage retrieval system without the written permission of the author except in the case of brief quotations embodied in critical articles and reviews.

WestBow Press books may be ordered through booksellers or by contacting:

WestBow Press
A Division of Thomas Nelson & Zondervan
1663 Liberty Drive
Bloomington, IN 47403
www.westbowpress.com
1 (866) 928-1240

Because of the dynamic nature of the Internet, any web addresses or links contained in this book may have changed since publication and may no longer be valid. The views expressed in this work are solely those of the author and do not necessarily reflect the views of the publisher, and the publisher hereby disclaims any responsibility for them.

Interior Image Credit: Leah O'Connor, LC Photography LLC

Scripture quotations marked (ESV) are from the ESV® Bible (The Holy Bible, English Standard Version®), copyright © 2001 by Crossway, a publishing ministry of Good News Publishers. Used by permission. All rights reserved.

Scripture quotations marked NIV are taken from The Holy Bible, New International Version®, NIV® Copyright © 1973, 1978, 1984, 2011 by Biblica, Inc.® Used by permission. All rights reserved worldwide.

Scripture quotations marked NLT are taken from the Holy Bible, New Living Translation, Copyright © 1996, 2004, 2015 by Tyndale House Foundation. Used by permission of Tyndale House Publishers, Inc., Carol Stream, Illinois 60188. All rights reserved.

ISBN: 978-1-9736-9508-0 (sc)
ISBN: 978-1-9736-9510-3 (hc)
ISBN: 978-1-9736-9509-7 (e)

Library of Congress Control Number: 2020912549

Print information available on the last page.

WestBow Press rev. date: 7/27/2020

# DEDICATION PAGE

This book is dedicated first and foremost to Abba God who has walked me through the Valley of the Shadow of Death without ever leaving my side.

Second, to the memory of my late wife Amy Standley Johnson and the nearly twenty years our lives shared through dating and marriage on this third rock from the sun. I will miss her greatly. She was my partner and the mother of my three boys. Amy taught me how to live and love in ways I had never before imagined. Her wit, wisdom, and willingness to put others first will stay with us, continually teaching and guiding us for the rest of our lives.

Third, to my three boys who have walked through the Valley of the Shadow of Death with me and Jesus and have risen to the challenge of living and not just existing. This story couldn't have been told without your help and the lessons you have learned alongside me. Your mama would be as proud of you as I am, if not more so.

Fourth, to "The General" and her incredible husband. Without their insight, wisdom, loving correction, and service to me and my boys, I would have burned out trying to do too much *for* Abba God instead of asking what I was supposed to be doing *with* Him. Words do not do their sacrifice, help, and friendship justice.

Lastly, to The Mom Mafia, an incredible group of prayer warrior moms who stepped in to "be mom" when Amy was called heaven-ward. These fearless women, with full plates of their own, were called of God and ordained with specific, intentional, spiritual giftings to speak uniquely into each of my boys, and often to me. They were sent by Abba God to be His hands, His heart, and His helpers to continue the healing process He had already begun within the walls of our home.

# CONTENTS

Preface ............................................................................................... ix
Acknowledgment ............................................................................ xiii

| Chapter 1 | The Beginning............................................................. 1 |
| Chapter 2 | In the Shadow of Death............................................. 4 |
| Chapter 3 | First Encounters ........................................................11 |
| Chapter 4 | "For a Lifetime"..........................................................18 |
| Chapter 5 | Three Miracles and a Worry Monster ....................24 |
| Chapter 6 | "You Only Have Ten Years…".................................37 |
| Chapter 7 | The Diagnosis.............................................................46 |
| Chapter 8 | Holding onto Fear with a Death Grip ....................53 |
| Chapter 9 | In Search of Joy.........................................................67 |
| Chapter 10 | The Darkness ............................................................81 |
| Chapter 11 | The Telling ................................................................91 |
| Chapter 12 | The Numb .................................................................98 |
| Chapter 13 | Where's the Dress? ................................................. 108 |
| Chapter 14 | Doing Life with Others.......................................... 117 |
| Chapter 15 | "So It's Not My Fault?"......................................... 124 |
| Chapter 16 | A Final Goodbye.................................................... 137 |
| Chapter 17 | Returning to Life.................................................... 160 |
| Chapter 18 | Celebration and Thanksgiving?............................ 172 |
| Chapter 19 | Three Months of Christmas................................. 180 |
| Chapter 20 | New Year's Scare ................................................... 191 |
| Chapter 21 | The Romance Lives On......................................... 196 |
| Chapter 22 | Ordinary Days........................................................ 207 |
| Chapter 23 | The Mom Mafia ..................................................... 219 |
| Chapter 24 | "If I Had a Time Machine…"................................ 243 |

| Chapter 25 | Parenting Without the Autism Whisperer | 255 |
| Chapter 26 | From Caretaker to Child | 276 |
| Chapter 27 | The Story Continues | 284 |
| Chapter 28 | Lessons from Camp | 295 |
| Chapter 29 | From 5 to 3 in 12 | 305 |
| Chapter 30 | Returning to Spring | 318 |

About the Author ... 323
End Notes ... 325

# PREFACE

So, you've picked up a book on grief. Either the title sounded catchy, or you were trying to figure out how to deal with a giant pink elephant standing on your emotional lungs. Am I close?

The book jacket probably gave it away, so you won't be surprised in chapter 10 when you find out that my wife, the love of my life, left this earth bound for Heaven on September 6, 2016. At the time, it was a shock, although the Holy Spirit had been dropping many clues along the way. Following her death, I spent countless nights grieving and staring at Facebook, wondering what I could handle posting online in black and white. There were many people at church and at work, friends and family, who wanted to know how my three teenage boys and I were doing. After months of posting on social media, a few of my close friends and family began to encourage me to gather it all together and write a book. I said, "No. I can't do that. There's not enough time in my day anymore…and I don't think I can emotionally handle it." That's when God stepped in and changed my perspective.

When a writer sits down to write a book…well, let's make this personal… when THIS writer sits down to write, I usually try to map out a book from beginning to end in just a few sentences and then get to writing. I don't always know what is going to happen in the book (especially since I usually write fiction) but this experience has been altogether different.

This book is a labor of love that, at first, I never wanted to write. The day Amy died, I posted a simple goodbye message on Facebook. There were so many responses; I continued to post the next night, and the next, and for many months after that day. I posted pretty regularly about the lessons my boys and I were learning in grief and the challenges autism brought to the process. After about four months, I started getting personal messages, phone calls, texts, and responses to my Facebook posts challenging me to begin to write a book. I did what any sane person in my position would have done: I said, "No!" Grief is hard work and exhausting work and sometimes seemingly never-ending work, and…(I think you get my drift.) The whole idea of carving time away from my hurting boys and my needy students piled on the guilt. *How could I deign to write a book about grief? I am no expert.* Except that, when it came to my boys and me, I *was* the expert.

As I prayed, asking God how to lead my boys with a broken heart, He began to show me how He had been at work through my brokenness–not just in my own home with my boys, but in the lives of countless family, friends, Facebook connections, and church contacts who were watching and hoping for another update.

As the months moved on and people continued to encourage me to write, I began to pray. A near instantaneous response from Abba God was met with outright indignation and worry. I found myself fighting with God for almost two months before I finally surrendered, praying, *Okay, God! I'll write the book!* And in the way only God does, He met me with a plan. I noticed it one day when I opened up Facebook and began scrolling through my feed. God had already orchestrated the book for me to begin writing.

My first concept for this book was to look at a short window of time, God showed me He had been preparing me for this road since I was very young. I'm sure it was long before the age of thirteen, but that is where this particular book begins in my heart.

I have wanted to be a writer since I was in the sixth grade. I never thought of myself as a nonfiction writer, a Self-Help writer, or a writer to offer strangers the story of my brokenness; I always assumed my first published book would be a novel. But when I sat down at the computer and found the skeleton of what this book has become, I realized that it was not just my friends and family bidding me write; Abba God was bidding me to bare my soul.

This book was written from the inside out. The most difficult chapter I could fathom writing was the one about the day of my wife's death. I can still remember that morning with vivid recollection as if it had just happened minutes ago. I knew it would be the hardest to write. I knew it could be the stumbling block that could take me down. Ultimately I knew if I didn't begin with that day as my starting point, I wouldn't be able to finish the book. God walked me through writing chapter 10 first. Then He gave me the other chapters on either side of that dark day.

As the book began to take shape, I noticed God had given me a message about overcoming fear and dealing with grief while on a quest to find joy. As I sat in retrospect, I realized that I'd been bound by the incapacitating fear of death since I was a very young boy. All of my decisions and actions were rooted in that fear. That did not change as I grew up, married, and had children. Six weeks before her death, God miraculously released me from the incapacitating fear.

As this book progresses, you'll find the incredible journey God and I took together, starting long before I knew the pit-stops and the destination. This book shows the honest conversations I had with Amy and with God. What you have in your hand is a labor of love resulting from two years of blood, sweat, and tears. I couldn't have completed this book without the help of my nearest and dearest family and friends who have continued to encourage and support me every day. They have been my Aaron and Hur holding my arms up in praise through the battle. It's been quite a ride.

I pray this book touches you in a way that only God could make happen. I also pray it helps you see how to overcome a possible fear in your own life or walk through grief that looks a little different than everybody else's in the days, weeks, and years ahead. My final prayer over this book is that God would use this act of worship—my story—to change your story.

Thank you for taking this journey with me by reading my book.

# ACKNOWLEDGMENT

This book would not have been possible without the help of many individuals.

Two of the chapters are written by two of my three sons, Micah and Isaiah. I felt that the book was incomplete without their point of view since grief interacts with each person a bit differently. My middle son, Gabriel, worked patiently with me while I interviewed and then wrote chapter 24 "for him," having tried to use as many quotes as possible while weeding through his challenges presented by autism in order to tell a complete story.

There have been five champions—Chris Baidenmann, Lisa Braun, Carolyn Johnson, Kathy Johnson, and Susie Sirovatka—who have read and helped me edit this work before it was submitted to publishers. These wonderful women all helped me organize my sometimes random and confusing thoughts into something that made much more sense. They even looked for the grammatical mistakes this Language Arts teacher was unable to find on his own.

I could not have published this work without the help of my friends who have already published: Dr. Michelle Watson, PhD, (a.k.a. The Dad Whisperer) and "Mama" Mindee Hardin (all around entrepreneur and inventor of Boogie Wipes). Their wisdom, advice, encouragement, and help were invaluable. Without their gentle and persistent goading, coupled with the time they spent leading me through the process, this book would not have become what it is.

This book would not have been possible without the cheering of my family and friends who continuously encouraged me to collect all my posts from Facebook, arrange them into a complete story, and then publish. I am eternally grateful to them all for the late nights, early mornings, random emails, and tear-stained conversations. There is an army who helped to encourage and pray for this work to be completed. Each of you know who you are. Thank you.

## CHAPTER 1

# The Beginning

Grief is like autumn. There are beautiful things all around to look at as you ponder the beauty and majesty of the divine. But autumn indicates life will be coming to an end…a close. The beauty and tragedy of autumn is overwhelming. As you look around, you can be so taken by God's majesty and wonder, and yet be overwhelmed by the toil and work you'll need to expend to clean up the leaves and dead branches.

That's what the death of my wife has been like for me.

Writing this book has helped me to see God's hand and His direction as I have raked the beautiful leaves, put them into piles, and sent them away in a recycling bin, only for new leaves and more dead branches to fall later, causing me to start over and deal with the fallen debris of grief. Would I do it again? Would I marry the wonderful, strong, amazing woman—the mother of my three children—again? Would I give myself to such a painful end for the blessing of having known and been known by a woman who challenged me, to be better than I thought I could be? In a heartbeat. My wife's life taught me many things; her death taught me what it truly means to wrestle with darkness and let God *be* God during the beauty and pain of autumn.

Autumn gives way to winter, the cold, hard truth of death and a time of contemplation, a hibernation of the soul. However, when winter gives way to spring, new life is brought forth, and there is new beauty to behold and new adventures to tackle. Life is a never-ending cycle. But the work of grief itself, the autumn of the soul, is something that is not often talked about in polite society. People who are so overwhelmed they cannot deal with everyday tasks disappear. Others try to press on, fighting to ignore the pain responsible for rending their hearts. And still others are blindsided by the dangers in front of them that they are desperately trying to avoid.

As you read the following pages, know that this is a work of worship and healing, from one broken heart to another. If these words encourage you, I give God all the glory. I could not do this without His amazing love, patience, encouragement, and strength.

While dealing with my own grief and the grief of my boys, I realized that not many Americans are schooled in the emotion of grief. There were many clinical and how-to resources, but none fit what I was looking for to help my boys and me in our specific situation, with autism in the mix. Many find themselves at a loss to know what to do when they encounter one who is grieving. Often, people have the right motives, but because the situation is awkward, their words get in the way. Our society doesn't do well schooling us about death either. In our earliest memories, we were fearless and dauntless. We thought we would live forever. Often, when people are introduced to their own mortality, their family and friends, and sometimes the whole world, get to witness a significant breakdown or shutdown. Is that wrong? Is it right? I've learned that no one walks through the darkness of grief along the same path; it's different for everyone. God has shown me, however, there are similarities that do pop up every once in a while. Those similarities can teach us how to move through grief, how to wrestle with our own mortality, and eventually, how to expect the angel of death when he comes knocking.

The bigger message, the one that God has been trying to teach me for many years, is found in my quest to find *true* joy. When your life is overwhelmed by fear and grief, joy—true joy—is difficult to find. It took me a long time to understand the difference between happiness and joy. Happiness is fleeting. Joy is from the throne of God. It's a state to dwell in, no matter what is happening in the tornado swirling about us. I learned to find joy amid the pain, amid the confusion, and amid the numbness.

My prayer as you walk through these pages with me is that you will be blessed, challenged, and healed by the words God used to heal me, my boys, my friends, and my extended family. When you find yourself in the autumn of life, God will meet you in very personal and profound ways. Lean into Him. Let Him lead you through the grove of colorful trees and the beauty and work they represent. Each leaf, each color, each tree will teach you about the Creator of the universe. His desire to walk with you through the toil and beauty memorialized in the autumn of life will become your own unique journey to one day write about so you can help others heal.

My journey from incapacitating fear, through grief, to find joy started in 1986, when I was only thirteen years old.

## CHAPTER 2

# In the Shadow of Death

I was thirteen. The knocking on the door startled me. My mother was almost two hours late. She was supposed to pick me up and take me to mow a new client's yard. My grandmother's lawn care business just couldn't keep up with the demand. She made me promise that I would do the very best job I could because I was representing her. Here I was, nearly two hours late, knowing I was disappointing my grandmother. I didn't know what was going to happen when she found out I had not completed what she was relying on me to do. I knew the person at the door was not my mother; she wouldn't be knocking.

"Thom," my pastor's wife said when I opened the door, "your mom's at my house. She asked me to come and get you."

"Are you taking me to my lawn job?"

"No, Thom. You're coming with me to my house."

I followed my pastor's wife to her car and we sat in near silence for the two- to three-mile car ride. I was confused. I couldn't figure out why I was on my way to my pastor's house, especially since I was supposed to be mowing a lawn.

"Is everything okay, Sue?" I finally asked.

"Your mom just needed to talk with Jim. Now she needs to talk with you at our house."

In just five short minutes, I was sitting in my pastor's living room, opposite my pastor, next to my mother.

"Thom, I've got some bad news for you," my pastor began. He had always been very straight with me. "Your grandfather has died."

"Which one?" I asked. At the time, I had two living grandfathers.

"Grandpa Lamb," my mother said, indicating my great-grandfather.

"No," I said, shaking my head. "I just saw him two weeks ago. He can't be dead."

"I'm sorry, Thom," my pastor said, placing his hand on my knee to console me.

My world began to crumble. Great-Grandpa Lamb's was the first death I had encountered in my life. I had spent the entire summer living on my great-grandparents' sheep ranch. I helped out wherever I could, learning many things about ranching, about my crazy extended family, and about my great-grandparents. It was a summer I'll never forget. It was October, just days after I had turned thirteen—the news was too close on the heels of the best summer I'd ever experienced. *He can't be dead* was all that kept running through my head. I don't remember the rest of the conversation. I don't remember the drive home. Nor do I remember how my sister, Zenina, found out the news. My brain turned off because of the pain. I walked through the rest of the day numb, not really realizing what was happening around me or to me. The next thing I remember is standing beside my bed three days later, packing a suitcase. We were heading to White Swan, Washington, a small town on the edge of the Yakima Reservation, in the foothills of the mountains separating Western Washington from Eastern Washington.

We often traveled to White Swan during the night, so leaving in the late morning was an odd experience for both of us kids. The trip took four-and-a-half-hours, and we usually slept through it. However, this time neither of us slept, and we were both surprised when we arrived in downtown Yakima, since it had seemed little time had passed since we left the house.

"Where are we?" my sister asked. I checked my watch. It was just after one o'clock in the afternoon.

"We're at the funeral home where Grandpa Lamb's body is for the service. There is a viewing today," my mother answered. Neither of us knew what that meant, so we followed our mother into the building. She asked the staff member who was patrolling the lobby a few questions and then pointed my sister and me toward a room down the hall. She followed us with my sister in the lead. Since neither of us knew what a viewing was, we were not prepared for what was waiting for us in the viewing room.

My sister walked into the room, turned on her heel immediately, and bowled right into me and our mother. Picking myself up off the floor, I looked into the room and realized why my sister had bolted. My great-grandfather was lying in a brown and bronze casket at the back of the room with his arms folded over his chest, crossed at the wrists, with his fingers near his collar bone. His eyes were closed. He looked as if he were just asleep, ready to wake up any minute.

It was a surreal moment for me. I had been living for days with the knowledge that my great-grandfather—the man who had become one of my mentors over the summer—was dead and I wasn't going to see him again. But there he was, right in front of me. When my brain caught up with the definition of *a viewing* and realized that the man in the coffin was my great-grandfather, but was also a corpse, I found myself unable to move into or out of the room. A war was being waged in my head. I loved this man with all of my heart. I didn't want to say goodbye. I had never before seen a dead body. I never wanted to see another dead body. But I loved this man.

While I stood stock still just inside the doorframe of the viewing room, my mother took my sister outside the room and talked with her. She returned a minute later without my sister. She squeezed between me and the door frame. I'm not sure whether she said anything to me or not. I couldn't hear a thing except the screaming of the silence and the war in my brain. I watched in wonder as she walked over to the casket and stood next to it. Then I watched her mouth move with her head bent down, as if she was talking to my great-grandfather, the corpse in the room. My brain registered that she couldn't have really been speaking, because I couldn't hear a word of what she was saying. Then I watched in horror as she reached down and grabbed ahold of my great-grandfather's hand. The final volley of war in my brain erupted and the side that was afraid of death won. I bolted from the room with more vigor than my sister had. I found her sitting on a pew in the hallway, sipping from a bottle of water. She offered it to me as I sat down next to her. I shook my head and we sat in silence for a long while. When my mother's cousins came through the front door of the funeral home and were directed to the viewing room, we watched as my mother exited the room and closed the door, forbidding any family from entering.

When my mother returned with a member of the funeral home staff in tow, they entered the room and closed the door. Moments later she emerged, talked with her cousins who were rather upset by this point, and stepped out of the way for them to enter. We followed our mother to the car.

"His hands were in the same position that Grandma Lamb had found him in," my mother said. "She would not have wanted to see him like that. I asked the funeral home director to fix it before it upset anyone in the family." Zenina and I were trying to recover from the events at the funeral home. We accepted the answer and sat in silence for the hour-and-a-half drive from downtown Yakima to the ranch, on the other side of White Swan.

When we arrived at the ranch, Great-Grandma Lamb was in the kitchen amidst the ingredients for a feast, some of it in process, some of it completed. She didn't react when we entered the back of the house. It was as if we'd been there all day. That wasn't like Great-Grandma Lamb. She and Great-Grandpa Lamb usually met us at the gate to the yard, having seen our dust plume as we drove down the half-mile long lane from the road. When she realized who was walking into the house, Great-Grandma Lamb was all business.

"I've got bread in the oven, a cake waiting to be frosted, a salad waiting to be made, and some dishes that need washing. Zenina, you and your mom can help me in here. Thom, you've got chores to get to." It was as if the summer hadn't ended, as if I hadn't gone back home with my sister and mother.

"Yes, ma'am," I uttered without a thought. "What would you like me to do with the luggage?"

"Your sister'll take care of it. Chores haven't been done since dawn. I expect those animals will be mighty hungry by now. Now git."

Over the next two days I walked around the ranch like a robot, performing the chores I had been doing all summer long. I did not think about what needed to be done; it just happened. While my body worked apart from my head, my brain tried to make sense of the oddity I was feeling. Around every corner, I expected to run into my great-grandfather. I expected to find him in the tool shed, or the sheep pen, or the shearing shack, or out by the dog kennel, or even near the hay stacks. But each time I walked around the corner, or opened a door, or even called out to him like I had that summer, I was instead met with disappointment.

The night before Great-Grandpa Lamb's funeral, my grandfather—his son—arrived, along with Grandma Nancy and my youngest aunt, Carrie, who was only two years older than me. A few other people arrived as well.

Carrie and I stayed outside; she followed me as I tended to the chores. After I finished, we sat next to each other on the hay stack, out of sight of the farmhouse. We sat there in silence, crying. After sunset, my grandmother came out to find us, and what a sight we were. Both of us were sitting on the hay, our pants covered in briars, our faces covered in streaked dirt from the chores and tears.

"There you are," Grandma Nancy said as she found us. "It's time for dinner."

"Do we have to come in?" Carrie asked.

"What are you waiting for?" Grandma Nancy asked, a little puzzled but a lot kind.

"Grandpa Lamb to come in from the back pasture," I whispered.

My grandma looked at me, then she climbed up on the hay stack between Carrie and me. Wrapping one arm around each of us, she hugged us tightly.

"We can wait a few more minutes," she whispered as she kissed me on top of the head.

The funeral was terrifying and stuffy. We were all packed into a very large chapel, yet for my extended family that seems to have no end, it was small. The service happened. I don't remember anyone who spoke, nor do I remember anything that was said. When everyone who was set to speak was finished, my grandfather escorted his mother out of the family room and up to the casket. His sister and brother followed closely behind them. Great-Grandma Lamb took a long time standing next to her husband's casket. I couldn't hear what she said. She stepped aside and my grandfather stepped up to pay his respects. When he finished, Great-Grandma Lamb took his arm and he led her back towards the family room. He stopped half-way back when my great-aunt stepped up to the casket.

It was as if everyone blinked at the same time. One moment my great-aunt was standing next to her father's casket. The next, she had flung herself across her father, wailing. My grandfather, his brother, and two of my great-aunt's daughters rushed to pull her off the coffin and help her into the family viewing room. The room held its breath.

When the sobs of my great-aunt could no longer be heard through the closed door of the family room, the minister announced, "It is time for you all to pay your last respects." People stood up in rows and began a line that traveled up past the casket. I watched as many of my relatives and some of my great-grandparents' friends filed past the coffin. It had been open for the entire service and I had sat watching it, hoping, praying Great-Grandpa Lamb would sit up and say something.

When it was my turn, I reluctantly stood and took my place in line. As I neared the casket, the bile in my stomach began fighting with my breakfast and my sense of courage. I was overwhelmed and just wanted to run. My aunt was in front of me. She paused at the casket to pay her respects. With so many others watching, I knew I couldn't run, I would just add to the chaos that I had just witnessed. I walked past the casket, paused briefly, stared at a button sewn into the middle of the batting of the interior casket lid for a count of three, and then walked on at a more significant pace. I thought I was going to pass out.

I walked to the far aisle and then glanced back. My mother was at the casket with her hand on top of Great-Grandpa Lamb's hand. I leaned on the wall praying I could get out of the room without an incident.

That was my first encounter with death. Thirty-one years later, I can still remember it as if it had just happened yesterday. Going back to the ranch was terrifying and when I was there, it seemed hollow. A few years later, my great-grandmother would leave the ranch for the last time, move closer to her oldest son, and then end her days living in the house where I grew up, under the care of her oldest granddaughter.

I walked away from that experience with a number of deep seated fears, ones I wouldn't realize were even a part of me until it was a problem too large for me to handle without God and counseling. From that time on, up until the Summer of 2016, I had a profound fear of losing someone I loved. When a friend or family member, and later my wife, were supposed to meet me somewhere, or call, or come home at a certain time, and they didn't show, my brain began going through the list of things that could be wrong, but the list was always extreme.

> *He's probably angry at me…*
>
> *I bet she wrecked the car, and now she's sitting along the road somewhere with no one to help her. She might die!…*
>
> *I know he's not picking up the phone because he thinks I'm a terrible person and really doesn't want to be my best friend anymore…*
>
> *There might be someone in the house. She's in danger. I should probably leave work and go home right away!…*

Each missed appointment/date/phone call drove me into a frenzied panic. It would be many many years until God healed me from those wounds and fears. Unfortunately, there were a few more significant deaths and my own bout with mortality I would have to face in order to realize that God was truly in charge. Nothing I did nor could do would change that.

Fast forward to college, fall of 1993. I fell while goofing around on campus one night. When I woke up, I couldn't move my right arm at the elbow and the level of pain in my right shoulder was nearing ten when I moved it. Because of my fall, my doctor ran some seemingly unrelated blood tests on a hunch. He treated the severe sprain and he paid for the blood tests he was ordering since he had no confirmed medical reason to order them. Sure enough, his hunch was right. To make a very long story short, I was diagnosed with acromegaly, a growth hormone disease usually stemming from a pituitary tumor. Since the growth plates are fused already but the body is still creating a significant amount of growth hormone, the extremities (hands, feet, and head) continue to grow. The disease also affects the internal organs causing them to continue growing as well, sometimes to dangerous sizes.

"Thom, people can live with this disease for sixty years, six years, six months, or even less. It is very hard to say. By my educated guess, you're probably looking at six months."

Those are not comforting words from a doctor. I was a sophomore in Bible College. Needless to say, once my test results came back, I was no longer focused on saving the world. I sounded more like the children of Israel during the Exodus: *Why did you bring me this far just to let me die, God?*

During that year of my life, I wrestled with my salvation and I wrestled with death. After three separate miracles—one financial (all medical bills were paid with a grant) and two physical (I was healed of the pituitary tumor and later my growth hormone levels suddenly returned to normal)—I realized God wasn't done with me yet. I began focusing again on saving the world. When it came to death, I was finally willing to trust God with my life, but I wasn't sure He could be trusted with the lives of my loved ones. I became a super-worrier. If there were an Olympic event in worrying, I would have the world record in gold medals.

CHAPTER 3

# First Encounters

"Is that a good book?"

It was an unexpected question while I was sitting outside the gym my college used for P.E. It was almost 8:00 p.m. and I had gone outside to read a text book for which I had to write at least a five-page essay by Friday. It was Monday and I had just started reading the book a few days prior. Being a slow reader and highly distractible made reading very difficult for me in a loud gymnasium. My volleyball team was participating in a round-robin event and we were sitting out the current round awaiting a winner. I had asked my teammates to come and get me when it was nearly time for us to play again.

"Huh?"

"Is that a good book?" the feminine voice asked again. I looked up to find a beautiful blonde looking down at me. I didn't know her name. She was on one of the opposing volleyball teams, and I had seen her around campus, but I didn't really know who she was.

"It's fine," I said. "I've just started reading it and I have an essay due on the entire book by Friday." It being Monday, I thought I had dropped a pretty important hint.

"It looks interesting," she said as she sat on the steps next to me and arrested the book from my grip. I cringed. I didn't know what page I was on in the book. Finding it would take precious time.

Realizing that this girl who I didn't really know was going to stay and chat, I decided to swallow my frustration and try being civil.

"My name's Thom," I said.

"I know. My roommate's Temple." I had gone to school with Temple for three years, but I didn't really know her well, and we were not part of the same social circles. This conversation wasn't starting out well. "I'm Amy."

We talked about random things for about ten minutes and then my teammates came to get me. Amy followed me inside. As it turned out, my team was playing her team. Since I was frustrated about losing ten quality minutes of reading (yes, I was being that petty), I decided that I would play hardball. In college, I was a pretty good volleyball player. Other intramural teams hated playing us because we worked well together and I had a wicked serve. I never started as server—we didn't think that was fair. I was usually the third or fourth to serve. By the time I was standing on the line, ball in hand, I'd realized that this girl who had interrupted my study time was not very good at fielding a serve, especially a powerful serve. I aimed right at her. As the ball rocketed toward her, she squealed and ducked. Her teammates dove to try and recover the ball, but their efforts were in vain. I kept serving. Most of the time, I aimed right at Amy. To throw the team off, once I dropped a serve right over the net, and another time I drilled the back foul line. Amy was standing in the back of the court, a little afraid of the ball, waiting for her teammates to field the serve before she would get in the fray. She never did. My serves were not ever returned, and my team dominated the game, 21 to 0.

Two days later, while walking between classes, I passed Amy in the hallway.

"That was a really good book," she said, stopping right in front of my path.

"What?"

"The book you were reading on Monday. I got a copy from the bookstore yesterday and read it last night. It was fantastic!" I had been reading the book since Saturday and I wasn't even halfway through it yet. The frustration began to build. It probably was visible, I'm not sure.

"I'm glad you liked it," I managed while trying on a fake smile. "I gotta get to class. I'm running a little late." As I said, I am a painfully slow reader. So far, from what I had read of the book, I agreed with her. But who does that? Who goes out and buys a new 275-page textbook, a month from the end of the school year, for a class they're not even taking and then reads it in one night? Those two encounters with Amy began to burrow under my skin. When I talked with my roommate that evening about it, he just listened, grinning.

"Sounds like Thommy has a crush!"

"You know I hate that," I said flushing blood red.

"Yep, it's a crush all right," one of my roommates began, laughing.

"Why would you say that?" I asked emphatically, a little perturbed.

"You didn't deny it," he answered.

I threw my pillow at him and went back to reading the same textbook. It was a long two nights as I finished reading the book and then writing the essay.

One month later, two days before my graduation, I was coming out of the lobby of the girl's dormitory, headed for my dorm room. It was just after 10:00 o'clock at night. Curfew was less than an hour away. When I crested the top of the stairs into the parking lot, a car pulled in and parked right in front of me. Two girls popped out of it. One was a Freshman girl who lived in the dorm, the other was Amy. I waved and she beckoned me to come over to talk. I was holding a novel I had just started reading on a famous conspiracy theory.

When I stopped next to her car, she nodded and pointed to my book.

"Is that a good book?"

I laughed

"So far. I just started reading it."

"Do you have to write a paper on it?" I could tell her voice was coy. She was playing with me. I guess my frustration in our previous exchanges had been a bit more obvious than I would have liked to admit. I grinned sheepishly.

We stood in the parking lot talking until 2:30 a.m., three and a half hours past curfew! We talked about life after school. I was graduating with a four-year degree; she had just come to take a one-year Bible and Business course, and then she was returning home to a suburb of Portland, Oregon. I was unsure of where I was headed, not having heard the results of my interviews the previous week. We talked about movies, plays, high school, and the future. Nothing was off limits.

No one bothered us the whole time we talked. Amy's friend had found the boy she wanted to flirt with and they were nowhere to be found. When the campus security guard passed us for the umpteenth time, I guess I was getting nervous.

"It's way past curfew," I said, not really wanting to break away from this girl I wish I had met the first week of the school year.

"What are they going to do, hold onto your diploma?" There was that coyness in her voice again. I felt as if I were the great tactician, Odysseus, who'd lost his wits at the sound of Siren Song.

"Shouldn't that be my line?" I asked with a grin.

"Do you have something to write on?"

I handed Amy the 3x5 index card I had been using as a book mark. She scrawled her name, address, and phone number on it before handing it back.

"If you end up near Portland, look me up." I took the card and grinned. Amy turned, ducked into her car, and was gone before I realized what had happened. I tucked the card back into the book and slowly headed for the men's dorm. My roommates, who had been standing outside on one of the walkways, saw me coming and ran to our room giggling. When I arrived, all three of them were posed as if they hadn't just been caught spying.

Our dorm rooms were divided into two living areas, each with two bunks, separated by a common bathroom. I lived in the back cubicle, but had to enter through the front and go through the common bath area to get to my room. When I entered, the two roommates who lived in the front were lying on their bunks, pretending to read a book while trying to stifle the giggles. My roommate was seated on a chair opposite the bunks, also "reading a book."

"What's her name?" Josh asked.

"Oh, shut up!" I said, not stopping on the way to my room. My roommate followed me into the back. Once we were both in the room alone, I locked the door. I slumped into my desk chair, leaned back, and propped my feet on the desk.

"I'm going to marry that girl," I whispered.

"Oh really?" he asked, trying to keep himself together.

"Yup. I'm going to marry that girl. Mark your calendar. June 5, 1996. I'm going to marry that girl."

Eight months later the phone number was a distant memory. I was working as a part-time youth pastor and part-time school bus driver in a very small town down the Columbia River Gorge, seventy-two miles from a certain Portland suburb. The day was coming to a close and it was about time for me to head home when there was a knock on my office door.

"Come in."

"Thom," the Senior Pastor's wife began, "I forgot to tell you about a phone call I received a week ago. It was really weird. A girl named Amy called the house. Apparently she thought she was calling the church, but instead called the parsonage. She was very confused. She asked for your address. I told her I didn't feel comfortable giving out your address, so I gave her the church's address instead."

"Amy?" I asked. "Did she give you her last name?"

"I can't remember it. You didn't get a letter from her? It sounded like she was going to mail you a card or something. She said she was a friend of yours and that you had her number if you wanted to call her back. Sorry for not telling you sooner."

"I know seven different Amy's!" I was very frustrated with the pastor's wife. I began listing off last names and then it hit me.

"It's in the book!" I shouted, startling her a little.

"What's in the book?"

"I gotta go!" I grabbed my keys and made a bee-line for the door. Twenty minutes later I was at home searching for the book I had been reading in the parking lot that night. I tore through the spare bedroom—which was doubling as my writing den—until I came across the only box I hadn't unpacked since moving from college. The box was marked "Catch All." I cringed. If the book wasn't in this box, it was back in my office at the church. *How foolish of me not to look before I ran out the door!* As I reached to remove the tape, my breath caught. *What if it's not her? What if I call her and she isn't the Amy who tried to call me?* Sitting atop the pile of catch-all items was the novel I had been reading when I graduated college. Poking its head out from between the pages was the 3x5 card carrying Amy Standley's phone number. I yanked it out of the book and headed for the phone in the kitchen. I set the card down next to the phone and picked up the receiver. As the dial tone announced itself, fear crept a little further into my thoughts. *You know it wasn't Amy Standley. Why would she call you?* I set the receiver back in its cradle and walked away from the phone.

Amy's number sat next to the phone for four days.

"Hello."

"Hi, is this Amy Standley?"

"Yes, Thom it's me. I wondered if your pastor's wife ever told you I called."

That phone call lasted six hours! And at a time of corded phones and expensive long distance calls, I didn't care. I was talking with a beautiful girl and she was talking to me! All throughout college I was the proverbial third wheel. All my friends were dating and then married; I was the lone wolf, trying to find that perfect girl. I'd convinced myself that it wasn't going to happen for me. "Ring by spring or your money back" was the unofficial motto of the Bible College. I was the only one of the guys in my close group of friends to make it to graduation unattached—and not for a lack of desire. There I was on the phone talking with a girl who was truly interested in me.

When I crawled into bed, the digital alarm clock announced that it was just past 2:00 a.m. I would be getting up in three and a half hours to drive school bus. I didn't care. I just talked with the most wonderful woman in the world.

Jeremiah 29:11-13 always comes to mind when I ponder those first few encounters with Amy.

> "For I know the plans I have for you," declares the LORD, "plans to prosper you and not to harm you, plans to give you hope and a future. Then you will call on me and come and pray to me, and I will listen to you. You will seek me and find me when you seek me with all your heart." (NIV)

God knew my heart, and although I had given up hope of ever finding true love, He also knew His plans for me. After freshman year in Bible college, I told God I would stay focused on Him. I wouldn't date. I wouldn't be distracted. I wouldn't pursue anyone until I had completed His directive and graduated. There were times I wanted to break that vow. There were even times when my heart and my head warred with each other because of a desire not to be alone, especially since my closest friends in college were all dating or married.

What I didn't know at the time was that God's plans to prosper me, to give me hope and a future, would not be easy. His plans would not be filled with only the interesting, the joyful, and the affluent. God's plans to prosper me—as I'm sure to prosper all His children—included learning to be strong, learning to be obedient, and learning to handle difficult things and difficult people.

During the summer I lived on his ranch, my great-grandfather taught me a tremendous lesson that continues to come back to me. Three months before Summer, my Great-Grandpa Lamb had a team come out and dig 35 sizeable holes in a 7x5 pattern. Then he and my Great-Grandma went into town and purchased thirty-five fruit trees. We planted those trees during Spring Break. It was a lot of work. When I returned to the ranch for the Summer, one of my jobs was to build a fence for the new orchard, to keep the deer from eating the leaves off the trees, and to care for each tree.

"Now, twice a week, you'll come out here with the hose and fill in the shallow indentation near each tree trunk. When you're done watering each tree, take this here broom handle and give each tree a solid whack. On the days you don't water the trees, you need to give each tree a good whack in the morning and at night." I looked at Great-Grandpa Lamb confounded.

"Why?" I finally managed to ask.

"These trees won't be alive next Spring if they don't grow strong. Hitting the trunks makes them harder, stronger. The roots will grow deeper and the branches will grow thicker. They'll know how to withstand the harsh winter if we don't coddle them."

I must have looked at him as if he needed to be admitted to the nearest psych ward.

"I'm serious, Thom. Now git to it." He handed me the broom handle and left me standing by the hose in process of watering the trees.

Years later when we moved Great-Grandma Lamb off the farm, all thirty-five of those trees had taken root and were growing strong. My great-grandpa had a plan for those trees, even though he didn't get to live long on this earth with them. He knew each tree needed to experience a little buffeting in order to overcome the harsh summers and frigid winters in eastern Washington and grow strong. God's plans for us are similar. He allows turmoil and heartache to cross our path, not to harm us, but to prosper us, to give us hope and a future.

# CHAPTER 4

# "For a Lifetime"

Three months before Amy and I got married, I finished penning a song for our wedding. "For a Lifetime." I mixed the traditional wedding vows with my hopes and dreams of our future marriage to create a vow I intended to never break. "I'll always be right here for you, in sickness and in health, holding tightly to your hand in poverty and wealth. For a lifetime." I had never before experienced love like the love I had with, for, and from Amy.

November 21, 1997, exactly nine months after our first date we became Mr. and Mrs. Johnson. I was the luckiest man alive. God had made good on a promise He gave me in a vision I'd had soon after the acromegaly scare. I was supposed to have a wife and a son. I was half-way there. No more broken heart. No more love lost. All I could think of was the incredible, overwhelming, and freeing love that God had given me, which much outweighed what I had previously thought I wanted. I had tried to force those feelings once before; this time, the relationship was organic, free, and unforced. I learned a lot about God's will during those nine months of dating. I had finally found someone who didn't make me work hard to be someone I wasn't. It was just natural. I had truly found love, real agape mixed with romantic love. My head didn't come out of the clouds for a long time after our wedding.

# GOOD GRIEF

Mr. and Mrs. Thom Johnson
Wedded Bliss

Some of my favorite memories center around food. Whether it was a birthday party, a family reunion, or a romantic getaway, the food—its smells, flavors, and overall experiences—tend to be the first triggers of great memories for me.

One of my favorite memories with Amy happened while I was eating a French pastry on a bustling street full of French, English, and other European speakers yammering away at one another in their various dialects. I stood there, one hand holding a fresh, warm cruller…well, a half-eaten cruller to be exact. The sugary glaze was slowly covering my hand; the warm, freshly baked dough melting in my mouth along with more of the sweet, semi-liquid coating; and the mingling scents of other pastries flooded the air. It was simply magical.

My other hand was busy as well. You see, it was the third day following our wedding. My new bride and I were holding hands, as we had been for much of the past three days. I'll admit, it was a new sensation, having lived seventy-two miles apart while we dated, and I enjoyed it thoroughly. Just intertwining our fingers brought warmth—inner and outer warmth—and a smile to my face. Mixed with the incredible pastry, I was in wedded bliss.

That evening, we were on a different street, full of many different languages again, but this time, we were eating authentic Chinese food prepared by people who truly know how to cook Chinese cuisine. As I looked around me at the imperial red and gold roofs that hearkened back to the Tang Dynasty in Ancient China, I was caught up in the grandeur of this new life together with the only woman I had met who perfectly completed me.

Later that evening, we stole away to a small shop that prided itself in unique cookbooks from around the world. Amy collected cookbooks. I chose one for her to help us remember the entire day. Handing it to my new blushing bride, I said, "We need to remember to come back here in twenty-five years." She smiled back at me.

Taking the book, she replied, "I agree, but in the meantime, we can use this cookbook and the memories of our honeymoon to inspire every room in our home." Home. It had a nice ring to it. Yes, we had a house that stored our earthly possessions, albeit a rented house, but a house is not always a home. This beautiful lady wanted to create a *home* with me! I grinned much bigger than I had already been grinning.

As we left the shop, dreaming of what our home would look like, I asked a simple question: "Do you want to head to the waterfront for the fireworks, or head over to Italy for some more Gelato?"

Looking around me now, each room of our home has been touched by that trip to Disneyworld, and each time I look at a cruller, I smile, making a mental note to begin planning my return trip to Disneyworld...alone.

No one thinks of the end of their spouse's life while they are on their honeymoon (unless they are marrying someone with a terminal illness). It's just not part of the expected things to accomplish while falling blissfully head-over-heals down the rabbit hole into Wonderland. Twenty years ago, almost twenty-one, I had not a care in the world. I had a good job, actually two good jobs. My bills were caught up with money in the bank to spare. The cupboards were completely full (mostly of Campbell's soup, but that's a story for another time). The car I drove was reliable and I owed nothing on it. Oh... AND God had seen fit to answer my heart's desire to start a family with Amy Standley. She had said, "Yes." What's incredibly amazing about the whole thing is that her parents had said, "Yes," even before she had (although I had it on good authority that Amy was also ready before I asked her parents).

In less than a month, Wonderland would be shattered. My boss at the time was very difficult to work for and his expectations of a part-time youth pastor required nearly full-time office hours. Amy and I didn't see much of each other since she had a good job in Beaverton, Oregon, while my two part-time jobs were up the Columbia River on the Washington side, some seventy miles apart. Amy left for work at 5:00 every morning, and arrived back at home around 7:00 p.m.

Little things like squeezing the tube of toothpaste in the middle of the tube created large blow-out arguments. The dinner I prepared for her on our first evening home after the honeymoon was Eggplant Parmesan, ala *L'Originale Alfredo di Roma Ristorante* in Epcot's Italy. It had been the first meal we had eaten together in Epcot Center. Mine didn't taste anything like the meal we'd loved so much; it tasted like failure.

One night, while trying to figure out why we felt like we were butting heads all the time, why things didn't seem to work out in our favor at all, and why it seemed like God had gone silent, I blurted, "I knew I should have resigned this youth pastorate before we got married."

"Wha..." Amy's response wasn't even a complete word, but complete thought nonetheless.

I inhaled as much courage as my lungs could find.

"I'm pretty sure we aren't supposed to be here. Three different people told me that they thought I was supposed to resign from the church so that we could spend the first year of our lives focusing on building a strong marriage before I began working on a path to become a teacher. I began praying about it and thought that I heard the same message from God, but I was really nervous to tell you since you had said, you 'felt called to marry a pastor.'" At the last word, my lungs let go of the remaining oxygen they contained and I deflated, standing in front of a new bride who just found out that she might have married a fraud. It had all come out rapid-fire. No breaks. No stopping for breath. No pausing for punctuation. It was just staccato bullets driving their way through our concept of Wonderland.

After an uncomfortable pause, Amy quietly said, "I've known you were supposed to resign the youth pastor job for a couple of months, but I kept thinking, 'Who am I to ask him to give up his calling?'"

I was the one now standing in stunned silence. I would never have guessed those words would come out of Amy's mouth, even if there were $20 million riding on it.

"Thom? Are you...going...to say...anything?"

I got the giggles.

"What's so funny?" This question was not inquisitive as the previous one had been; this question was shrouded in pain. Amy thought I was laughing at her.

I opened my mouth to speak, but the fit of giggles doubled, then tripled, and I found myself on the floor, turning deep reddish-purple and squeaking for lack of oxygen intake.

Many minutes later (it really felt like a lifetime happened in that space of time) I looked up from my seat on the floor while gasping for oxygen to fill my lungs.

"Honey," I lifted my arm in an effort to encourage her to come sit next to me, "We both knew, but were afraid to tell each other! Don't you see the irony in that?"

"Not really," she offered as she sat next to me, our backs against the narrow hallway wall.

"You thought I would break off the engagement if you told me, and I thought you'd tell me I wasn't worth it if I told you. So instead, we both sat in silence, letting what may come, come. In reality, we both, who love the LORD God with all our hearts, we both, who love each other and want what's best for each other to come to fruition...we both kept quiet. It's a bit comical to me that we're standing here, or rather sitting," which brought a short giggle out of Amy, "wondering what's wrong? Why isn't anything seeming to work out around us? It's just a week past Christmas and we've been talking about attending two different churches—you, in Beaverton, and me up here. Why? In order to try and get along? Or better yet, so that I can keep my two part-time jobs that pay less than one-third of your salary, so that I can feel *fulfilled* and *obedient to God* when He's the one who told me to leave in the first place?" (That first month back in ministry was the hardest I've ever endured, and I've worked in Christian schools for two-thirds of my twenty-two year teaching career.)

Amy looked at me sheepishly, "No. I was afraid you'd marry me and be unhappy for the rest of our lives because I'd asked you to resign your job at the church." I smiled a weak, wan smile, but still a smile.

"Amy, we both know beyond a shadow of doubt that God moved heaven and earth to cross our paths, from two completely different worlds. We both knew that night on the phone, three weeks before our first date that 'this was the one.' Promise me we'll never keep what God is telling us a secret from each other ever again."

"I promise."

Sadly, we didn't completely learn that valuable lesson on that late December evening in 1997. It wouldn't be until January 2014 before we truly learned what God had been trying to teach us. We had gotten so far away from trusting God with all of our finances and life events, it would take me being fired from a Christian school in the middle of the school year for God to remind us that He was ultimately in control.

# CHAPTER 5

# Three Miracles and a Worry Monster

"Were you going to tell me, or just let me figure it out in a few months," I asked, holding the pregnancy test I found in the bathroom garbage.

"What?" It was very early in the morning and Amy was just stirring in the bed. I had been getting ready for work.

"I said, 'Were you going to tell me the results of the pregnancy test or not?'"

"It was false," Amy replied.

I looked at the indicator window.

"Pretty sure two lines is a 'Yes,'" I replied. Amy shot out of the bed and crossed the room in seconds. She snatched the pregnancy test from my hand and stared at it.

"I took the test in the middle of the night so that you wouldn't be anxious," she began, a bit shaken. "I waited the five minutes it said and nothing happened so I threw it away and came back to bed."

"Well, now it says you're pregnant!"

"I'm sure it's a false positive, Thom." I could hear the tremor rise in her voice.

During my year with acromegaly, I learned the fate of my future family.

"The disease stems from a tumor on the pituitary gland and it messes up your chances of fathering children. Don't get your hopes up; you probably won't be able to have kids," doctors had said.

Shortly after we were married, the nurse in Amy's physician's office broke the news that Amy was diabetic.

"I wanted you to know, Amy, before my last day. When I found out the doctor has known for almost two years that you have diabetes and he hadn't told you, I was furious. He said he was trying to help you by controlling your diet and lowering your weight and cholesterol, but that's not good enough for me. He's playing with your life. You've got to get a new doctor. My last day is tomorrow."

We were stunned. Upon seeing a new doctor—one who immediately took charge of getting Amy's blood sugar in control—we learned that the disease had been very hard on Amy's body.

"You probably won't be able to have children," was the news one specialist gave us. We were devastated and angry. Then we asked God to take away our anger and give us children to love anyway.

We began looking into adoption, planning for five years of wedded bliss before bringing children into the family.

Here we were, eleven months after getting married, arguing in a tiny apartment bathroom over the results of a pregnancy test.

Amy had been sickly for the previous week and I'd had a gut check. I thought she might be pregnant. "Two negatives make a positive," I jokingly said as I purchased a pregnancy test kit containing two test strips.

"It's a waste of money," Amy argued.

"I don't care," I retorted, not really paying attention to the pain in Amy's voice. She hadn't healed from the painful news of possibly never having children. I was getting her hopes up, or at least she was afraid I was. I was usually the positive, head in the clouds optimist. Amy called me a "dreamer." She was not a dreamer. Amy was practical and pragmatic. I jokingly called her a "pessimist" once. She replied, "I'm just a realist. Deal with it."

It was five hours later before I recognized the pain in Amy's voice while we had been standing in the bathroom that morning, arguing over the pregnancy test. She took the second test reluctantly. When it almost immediately indicated she was pregnant, I was ecstatic! It was the morning I turned twenty-five and I had just found out I was going to be a father!

"What do doctors know?" I hollered, wrapping my arms around Amy. She pushed away from me, without any excitement.

"It could still be a false positive. You know what the doctors told us."

"Yes, but I also know God. He likes to confound doctors!"

There was a lengthy pause.

"We can't tell anybody," Amy finally whispered, trying not to get excited, even a little.

Five hours after Amy took the second pregnancy test, she came home.

"Why are you home so early?" I puzzled. I was just about ready to head to work for my second school bus run.

"I went to the doctor on my lunch break today. She kept me longer than I expected. When she was finished, I called my boss and told him I needed to come home immediately to talk with you." Amy's face was ashen, her eyes downcast, her voice brittle. Amy wiped at her cheek. She'd been crying.

"And..." I said it like it was a three syllable word. My heart was falling. I knew what she was going to say before it came out of her mouth. I felt awful; just that morning I had given her hope.

"The doctor said..." Amy paused, digging into her purse. "She said...I'm a month pregnant!" Amy jubilantly pulled her hand from her purse. In it, she held a pacifier. "You're going to be a dad!"

Two months later, we were moving out of our small apartment and into a three-bedroom house. One month after that, Amy was in more pain than she had ever previously experienced. Sitting in the high risk pregnancy specialists' office was nerve wracking.

My worry kicked into gear. *I got her hopes up. I shouldn't have made a big deal out of this. The doctors said...*Over and over the messages spiraled in my head. When the doctor entered the room, I was not expecting his report.

"Amy, as you know, you have two and a half times more amniotic fluid than most pregnancies, and although we know you are only four months pregnant, your baby is measuring almost six weeks larger than the average pregnancy. The weight is causing your spine to separate."

Amy was put on immediate bed rest. I had to fireman-carry her anywhere she needed to go, slinging her carefully over my shoulder. We even borrowed a wheelchair because she wanted to go to church on Sundays.

Just three days after eight months of pregnancy, the doctors performed an amniocentesis. The baby was measuring thirteen pounds. The doctors were concerned to let the pregnancy go much longer. Since the test returned with good results, it was decided that Amy would undergo a cesarean section in the morning.

It was a long night of making sure everything was ready. The nursery was all in place; we lacked nothing in the diaper supply arena. Amy's bag was packed. We were ready...we thought.

An hour after I followed the baby from the surgical room and into the neo-natal intensive care ward, the surgical nurse came to get me. Amy's vitals were not normal, and the doctors were concerned. Her heart was racing, then pausing, beating irregularly. She'd spiked a fever, and they couldn't keep her awake. I raced into the recovery room and pulled up short when I saw her. Amy's skin was bluish white. She was lying on her side, trying to say something. I knelt on the floor next to the bed, reached up and took her hand.

"Honey, I'm here." I paused. "Honey...?" There was no response. "God," I began again, this time turning to a different conversant, "I can't do this alone. Please heal her. Show the doctors what's wrong."

I had only been in Amy's room for twenty minutes when I was paged back to the NICU. Alarms were going off all around the heated infant bed. My son lay under the heating lamps screaming.

"What's wrong?" I asked the nurse.

"We've given your son almost two full doses of glucose and his blood sugars are still dangerously low. We've paged the doctors. They're coming to meet with you." The worry began rising in my throat. I stepped next to my son's bed and bent down to kiss his forehead.

"Micah Gene," I whispered, "Daddy's here. You're okay." Instantly, Micah stopped screaming. With his eyes still closed, his right hand shot out toward the sound of my voice. I intercepted his arm and he latched onto my finger, unwilling to relax his grip. "Daddy's right here. Mommy's in the next room getting better. You'll get to see her soon."

For the next three hours, I bounced between the NICU, the recovery room, and the waiting room. Loved ones were gathered, anxiously waiting to meet the brand new addition to our family. Godparents, grandparents, and friends alike held a prayer vigil. Once Micah's blood sugars began to normalize, I was allowed to bring family—two by two—into the NICU to meet him. Each time I left, he screamed. Each time I returned and Micah heard my voice, he grabbed my finger and stopped crying.

I have often pondered that experience. God made it evidently clear to me that babies need their daddies. He also showed me, once again, His miraculous healing power. Nine hours after the C-section, Amy was wheeled out of the recovery room and into a regular room. Thirty minutes later, a wonderful NICU nurse wheeled Micah into the room in a warming bed. The nurse deposited him into Amy's waiting arms and apologetically announced, "You only have about ten minutes. He needs to return to the NICU for more monitoring. We haven't been able to get his blood sugars to stay in the normal range." Amy nodded and the nurse stepped back to monitor from the wall.

My best friend Travis and his wife Jenny, who are also Micah's godparents, stood on one side of the bed while I stood on the other. Without ceremony, and without waiting for any of us to speak, Amy began to pray.

"God, thank you for this beautiful baby boy. Thank you for loaning him to us. Help us to raise him the way you intend us to and help us to guide him and grow him into the man of God we know he's been called to be."

We originally wanted to have five children. Three boys with two girls born in between the brothers. It took almost three years to get pregnant the second time.

In August 2002, we were about 4 hours from home attending the Standley family reunion, when Amy's pregnancy—already in the care of the high risk pregnancy doctors again—hit a scare. Returning from the restroom with panic etched in her face, Amy shot me a terrified look and made a beeline for her mother, the prayer warrior of the family. Seeing her trajectory, I met her at Susan's side, Micah toddling behind me.

"Dad, can you take Micah?" she asked. Her mom started to pray, not knowing why, but knowing God was needed. Gary picked up Micah and walked a few paces away from the rest of us. Amy turned to us with tears in her eyes.

"I'm bleeding...a lot."

"I'll get the first aid kit," I offered, missing Amy's implication.

"No, we need to go to the hospital." Her voice wasn't raised, but the tremors in it told me everything I needed to know.

"Can you guys keep Micah while we go to the ER?" Amy asked.

Susan nodded.

"You'll need the car seat," I added, already heading for the car. An hour later we were being rushed into a room at Sacred Heart Hospital in Springfield, Oregon. After three hours of tests and waiting, our nerves were brittle. We were nearly convinced the pregnancy was over when the doctor came in with a fetal heart monitor.

"Well, our initial observations and monitors show a healthy pregnancy. We're not sure why you're bleeding, Amy, but it doesn't appear to be at the peril of the baby." We exchanged relieved nods. "I brought the fetal heart monitor with me so you could hear for yourself." Within minutes we heard the baby's heartbeat. It was strong and steady. We were released shortly after that and told to enjoy our family vacation on the Oregon Coast. The doctor saw no reason why we shouldn't continue our trip. "Just check in with your doctor when you get back home. I'm sure everything will be fine."

And it was...until it wasn't.

Two weeks later, I was at work preparing for students and the beginning of a new school year, and Amy was at home. I was working at a Christian school at the time. During my devotions, God led me to Luke chapter one. He made it clear to me that the name Amy and I had chosen to name our unborn son was not the name He had chosen. Honing in on Luke 1:19, it was clear that our son's name was meant to be Gabriel.

"The angel said to him, 'I am Gabriel. I stand in the presence of God, and I have been sent to speak to you and to tell you this good news'" (NIV).

I inherently knew what God was trying to say to me: *I am sending your son, Gabriel, to be a bearer of good news.* It was very clear. I stopped reading, bowed in prayer and asked God directly if I was hearing Him. Minutes later, I was trying to get ahold of my wife via phone. That was back before call waiting and I got a busy signal. I hung up and tried again. Four or five times I was blocked by the aggravating busy signal. Beginning to get frustrated, yet realizing that the news I was going to share was not meant to be delivered with irritation, I waited for a beat, took a deep breath, and then reached for the phone. Before I could pick it up, it rang. I answered, and to my surprise, it was Amy. She'd been trying to reach me; God had shared something with her in her devotions she needed to tell me! After a comical battle for airtime, I relinquished the line.

"Thom, God told me we've picked the wrong name for our son," Amy said as I began to tear up on the other end of the line. "When I sat down to devotions, my Bible was already open, so instead of looking up the next part of our devotional series, I just looked at the page that was already open."

"Was it Luke 1?" I asked, already spilling rivers of tears down my face and knowing the answer to my question. There was a short pause in conversation.

After a beat, Amy said, "How did you know that?"

"It was just a guess," I covered, not wanting to steal Amy's revelatory zeal.

"Oh...while I was reading, God told me that He's picked a different name for the baby than we did."

"Let me guess, Gabriel?" I asked, barely able to speak.

There was a pregnant pause on the line.

"Amy, are you still there?"

"How...how did you know that?" she asked, completely baffled.

"I've been trying to call you for the last couple of minutes. I kept getting a busy sound each time I tried. I wanted to tell you what you just told me. I was also reading in Luke 1 this morning."

Never before had God spoken to both of us at the same time, about the same exact thing. We were both stunned and ecstatic. We were unaware of the plans God had for us, plans that would strengthen our faith, strengthen our marriage, and strengthen our resolve.

One week later, Amy became very ill with the flu. I helped her up off the bathroom floor and into bed. It passed through her system in about a week and everything seemed to be going well. Two weeks later, Lisa, Amy's sister, joined Amy for her next sonogram. Being a high-risk pregnancy, Amy had an ultra-sound every two to three weeks. Micah was with his grandparents, so I decided to work a couple of extra hours grading papers and writing lesson plans.

When the phone rang, I was expecting Amy. It was Lisa.

"Thom, I'm at your house with Amy. You need to come home now."

"Is everything okay?" I asked a bit puzzled since my sister-in-law is anything but demanding.

"You just need to come home now. I'll stay with Amy until you get here." Then the phone went dead. Lisa had hung up the phone. She didn't wait for a reply. No salutation. No explanation. In a fog of fear, I drove home. Lisa exited the front door as I entered the house through the garage. Amy was seated on our bed, waiting to give me the scariest news I'd ever received.

"The ultrasound didn't go well." I could tell she'd been crying, but her voice was strangely calm. "Basically..." she paused, I imagine to collect her courage, "my water broke a couple of weeks ago when I had the flu." I had cleaned up the floor after helping Amy to bed that day. I thought her bladder was having trouble with the pregnancy and the vomiting combined. I hadn't thought anything about it at the time.

"What?" It was a nervous response. I had heard her, but my brain wasn't keeping up with the conversation.

"My water broke. They call it 'dry baby' syndrome. The doctors sent me home with three options to talk over with you. I've got to call them back in a little bit to let them know our decision."

"Options? Are you okay? Is the baby okay? Are you in labor?" My brain was trying to calculate the pregnancy weeks.

As Amy spelled out the three different options, my brain finished the math. She was only nineteen weeks along! My mind started to tunnel. My vision began to fade—not to black, but to just colors. Bright colors.

"Thom!"

"Huh?" I stammered as I was snapped out of a daze of fear.

"Do I go to the hospital tonight and stay for the duration of the pregnancy—however long that will be—or do we wait until twenty-eight weeks and then enter the hospital? They said, there's not much they can do but monitor me at this time."

My heart was numb. I was chilled. My breath was erratic. Amy reached over and took my hand.

"Thom, are you okay?"

*Why is she asking me if I'm okay? This is happening in her! What am I doing?*

"I'm fine," I finally managed. "I guess we pray, prepare for the worst and hope for the best."

About fifteen hours later, we were sitting in our living room with our families and a few of Susan's prayer warrior troop. In the middle of that concert of prayer, God reminded me of the story of Hannah, a barren woman in First Samuel chapter one who desperately wanted a child. Then I remembered Amy's prayer over Micah when she first held him in her arms.

"God, you know our hearts," I'd begun. "You have seen fit to give us another child. We will love him for as long as You let us borrow him. We will raise him as You direct us to. As Hannah offered her son to You before he was even born, we offer our son to you as well. Help us to see the good news that You've sent him with, no matter how long that may be."

Amy was hospitalized at twenty-four weeks' gestation. I instantly became a single dad. My days started at 4:30 a.m. I got ready for work and prepared two lunches before waking my toddler up at 5:30. After getting Micah through the bath and breakfast, I was headed out the door by 6:30. I had to drop Micah off with a family member or friend by 7:00 a.m. in order to be at work by 7:30, where I taught high school English until 4:00 p.m. After work, I picked up Micah and headed to the hospital. Due to rush hour traffic, we'd usually arrive at Amy's room between 5:30 and 6:00. We'd have dinner with mommy, and then head home at about 8:00. I'd put Micah in bed, move laundry around and then land in the recliner with four scoops of Rocky Road ice cream while I watched something that would numb my brain. I often woke up in the recliner the next morning.

Halfway through that month of Amy's hospitalization, I sat next to her bed in tears. Micah was kept busy with one of the VHS tapes we'd brought with us.

"Honey," I whispered to her, "I can't do this alone. Promise me you won't leave until our youngest graduates from high school." It became our joke. I would say it to Amy often during our marriage, usually praising her abilities as a mother while proving I lacked basic mothering intuition and skills.

On Monday, November 4, 2002, Micah and I entered Amy's room like clockwork. We were surprised by a room full of people. Amy's parents had come to the hospital for a visit. There were also two nurses in the room, poking and prodding Amy's pregnant belly. Something was wrong, very wrong. Amy's body had gone into labor. Just a few hours later, our second son was born. It was both incredible and terrifying at the same time.

Gabriel was twenty-seven weeks and two days gestation at birth. He only weighed 2 pounds 6 ½ ounces.

The first time I had to leave the NICU after Gabriel was born, I said something to him that has since given me pause many times. I leaned down and kissed his head. Immediately, Gabriel reached out and grabbed my finger with all the might he could muster. I snapped a picture with my cell phone because it was so startling to me. The doctors had said Gabe "would be a vegetable." Those were their exact words. They had also told us he would never walk or talk his entire life, and that he wouldn't have control of any of his muscle groups. God was sending a much different message through His tiny new messenger: God was in control and Gabriel would be used to baffle not only the doctors but countless people who would come in contact with him. With him still holding my finger, I leaned down again and whispered, "Gabriel Ryan, you hold on to Jesus because He's holding on to you." It became my parting instruction to him each time I had to leave the hospital. I've even spoken it over him many times since he was released from the hospital.

On Thanksgiving Day, the NICU called me. "We've had to stop feeding your son," the nurse said. "We think you better come as quickly as you can." We raced to Gabriel's bedside to learn that each time they fed him, he stopped breathing and his heart slowed to a dangerous pace.

There were numerous phone calls with concerning information. My worry grew so much through that time that it became an ever present state of being. Each time the phone would ring, panic would erupt. *What if Gabriel's had another problem? What if he isn't thriving? What if they tell me he's dead?* It was a very long eighty days in the NICU.

Fourteen days after Gabriel came home on oxygen and a heart monitor, he popped a groinal hernia. A surgery date was set for two weeks later. I was past worry and panic at this time. My baby was going back to the hospital for surgery.

A week before the surgery, Gabriel began showing cold and flu symptoms. Amy called the doctor while I was feeding him his evening bottle. She was packing for a hospital stay before she hung up the phone. As she was relaying the doctor's decision to me, Gabriel began to cough and choke. I removed the bottle and turned him over to release any formula on which he might be choking. Instantly he stopped coughing and his body went rigid. I turned him back over and realized he had stopped breathing. Amy dialed 911 as I lept for the kitchen table to perform CPR. In the preemie CPR class we took before Gabriel was released from the hospital, we were told to inform the local dispatch and fire station that we were bringing home a preemie. This meant that when our number registered in the system, an ambulance was immediately dispatched. We lived only blocks away from the nearest fire station. Just seconds after starting CPR, Amy opened the door and six paramedics poured into our tiny dining room.

Gabriel spent a week in the hospital due to RSV, a disease that presents as the flu or a common cold, but is deadly in preemies.

A year later, Gabriel gave us another scare. When I turned on his bedroom light to wake him from a nap, I saw his lips were dark purple, and his hands and feet were blue. Gabriel wasn't moving. I picked him up out of the crib and uttered a panicked prayer: "God!" It was the shortest prayer I've ever uttered. I didn't have time for more, and I believed Abba God knew the rest of that desperate plea. I turned Gabriel over in my hands, gave him a decent pat on the back and dropped to the floor to perform CPR. When his head touched the carpet, Gabriel inhaled deeply, arched his back, and let out a siren worthy wail.

I spent another three days in the hospital with him. This time he had twenty-seven leads glued to his head. The doctors were concerned he had epilepsy. At the end of the three days, the doctors were baffled. They couldn't find a distinctive cause for the episode. I was exhausted having not slept much. Trying to keep an active one-year-old from playing with the ponytail of wires attached to his head was an exhausting job.

With each scare (and there were many others), my worry doubled. Yet with each scare, God intervened, showing us once again that He was truly in control.

Shortly after Gabriel was born, our family gave us an ultimatum. No more! Amy's body had been through two difficult pregnancies and they were concerned about what another pregnancy might do to her. Amy and I wrestled with that edict. It had taken over three years to get pregnant a second time. We'd been told we couldn't have children at all, and now we had two. We turned to prayer since our hearts ached for a third child.

"God, we're going to honor the family and set Thom's surgery date. If it be Your will, give us another child before the vasectomy."

I never had the surgery. A month before the date, we found out Amy was pregnant a third time. She was due in February 2004! This pregnancy seemed to have fewer problems than either of the other two. However, just after Christmas 2003, Amy came down with something that put her in bed for days. I was getting worried. She was not improving, even though we'd done everything the doctors had told us.

One afternoon Amy was very lethargic and was having difficulty walking. The Worry Monster reared its head. My innate fear of losing her kicked into high gear. I dropped my boys off at my sister-in-law's house and headed for the hospital. On the way to Lisa's house, the forecasted freezing rain began. It was a long and harrowing journey to the hospital that night. When we finally reached the doors to the ER, Amy was not responsive. I'd tried to keep her awake during the trip, but I wasn't successful. Two nurses helped me get Amy into a wheelchair. An hour later I was standing in the ICU at the foot of Amy's bed talking with the doctor.

"You did the right thing coming here," he said. "If you had waited only another thirty minutes, we wouldn't have been able to save your wife nor the unborn baby."

Amy's diagnosis: severe ketoacidosis, related to her diabetes. Once she was medicated and the NICU nurse whose job it was to monitor my unborn son was seated next to Amy's bed, I left the hospital. I knew if I didn't go home then, I wouldn't be able to get there at all due to the freezing rain. As it was, by the time I arrived home, after picking up the boys from Lisa, the roads were nearly impassable. Once parked in front of the house, the car didn't move for nearly a week. Once again I was a single dad, trying my best to take care of an infant and toddler. I spoke with the hospital two or three times a day. After four days, Amy was finally able to talk with me on the phone. The sheets of ice we once called roads, however, were not passable. Amy was in the hospital for another two days. When I picked her up she was a welcome sight. The boys were thrilled to see Mommy again. I was relieved she was coming home. I honestly thought I was going to lose her and the baby this time.

While I lay next to her in bed that night, I whispered, "I can't do this alone. Promise me you won't leave until our youngest graduates from high school."

Isaiah Bradley was born five weeks later. He too would spend time in the NICU, but only because of jaundice. We were done having children. We made sure the doctor took care of that issue during Amy's C-section. We were glad God answered our prayers and gave us three boys. We were a little bummed that we didn't have any girls and that we were stopping short of our goal of five, but we knew better than to try a fourth time. God and everyone this side of Heaven made sure we knew we were done.

Amy's favorite picture of being a mom
Picture courtesy of Leah O'Connor, LC Photography LLC

Sadly, I had become numb to the worry that lived in me at high levels by this point. Two years later I would begin having heart palpitations and other stress induced issues. When I found myself in an ambulance, fearing a heart attack, I knew it was time to deal with the worry monster (as Susan liked to call it).

The doctors found me to be in atrial fibrillation, or a-fib. It was not a heart attack. Basically, my heart had moved into a mal-rhythm and it needed immediate correction. A-fib can cause serious problems, even death.

"Mr. Johnson, we're going to have to shock your heart into a healthy rhythm. Usually things go as planned. However, there will be a crash team in the room when we do the procedure in case something goes wrong."

From my vantage point looking at the doctor, I could see Amy out of the corner of my eye. I saw the blood drain from her face; I knew that look of worry, that look of panic. When the doctor left to prepare for the procedure, Amy leaned over and kissed me on the cheek.

"I can't do this alone," she whispered. "Promise me you won't leave until our youngest graduates from high school."

That episode scared me into eating healthier and taking better care of myself. Within a year, I was seeing a counselor in order to deal with my worry and fears.

CHAPTER 6

# "You Only Have Ten Years..."

The night of our wedding rehearsal, I sat down in the foyer of the church to soak in the reality of what was happening. When my thoughts turned to prayer, I was not expecting the interchange God and I would have. After a few minutes in prayer, my soon-to-be sister-in-law and her husband entered the church for the rehearsal. At the time, they were living in southern California. I knew that Amy's mother missed having her daughter close, and that knowledge, coupled with the news the Lord had just shared with me, made my conversation with her husband, Dale, necessary. Taking him aside, I recounted what had just happened when I sat down to pray.

"Dale, God just told me we will only have ten more years with Susan before He takes her to Heaven." To be honest, I don't recall Dale's initial reaction. "If you and Lisa are still considering a move back here, I think now would be better than later." Dale and I hardly knew each other. I felt awkward in that conversation for many reasons. The gravity of it stuck with me, and I didn't share that information with anyone else for a very long time. But the countdown in my head never ceased to remind me.

Dale and Lisa moved back to the Portland area about a year later.

During our sixth year of marriage, shortly after the birth of our youngest son, I finally told Amy of the conversation God and I had the afternoon before our wedding. I was really nervous to tell her and felt guilty for not having talked with her about it after it first happened. I had kept the information from her for six years. Now that her mother's health was really beginning to decline, I felt I had to tell her.

When I sat Amy down and talked with her about what had happened the night before our wedding, I was shocked to find her at peace and not angry. She took the news better than I could have imagined. From that day on, we were very intentional to make sure our children had every opportunity to spend time with the matriarch of the family. We wanted all three of them to have their own memories of Grammy, as they called her, not just the memories we would tell them.

On March 7, 2006, Amy called me at work with a family emergency: her mother was in the hospital. A heart attack was to blame. Five minutes later, the phone rang again. This time it was my mother.

"Grandma Lamb died this morning." Already overwhelmed with the previous news, I began to hyperventilate. I had been very close with my great-grandmother until about a year after my great-grandpa died. Great-Grandma's memory began to wane then, and she started calling me by the wrong name when I talked with her. Each time I was with her, it was clear that I was losing the woman I knew. My great-grandmother had spent most of her time in bed the past two years, unable to recognize anyone. This phone call gave me some finality. However, piggy-backed on the news that my mother-in-law was in the hospital, I began having a panic attack. I remember finding my way to the school office and telling the office staff that I needed to go.

I must have not looked well. The secretary asked me to have a seat. She was going to get me some water. There was a blip in time that I couldn't account for, and then Amy was standing in the office. She received the call from my mother that Great-Grandma Lamb had died just after she hung up from talking with her father about her mother's heart attack. Amy told my mother she would give me the news after my class was over. Amy ended the call and bolted for her car, knowing that both pieces of information would be too difficult for me to handle at the same time by myself. Her intent was to pick me up on her way to the hospital and give me the news about my great-grandma after I was in the car.

For one reason or another, my mother decided I needed to know sooner rather than later. Amy was angry. She had intended to ease me into the information so that I wouldn't find myself in a tailspin.

When we arrived at the hospital, we headed straight for the ICU. My father-in-law was talking with the doctors, and Susan was asleep, alone in her cubicle. A couple minutes after we arrived, Susan's eyes fluttered open.

"Hi...when did you get here? Aren't you supposed to be at work, Thom?" Then looking over at Amy she added, "Where are the boys? Are they okay?"

"Mom, the boys are fine. We're here to check on you. Dad said you... were here." Amy didn't know if her mother knew why she was in the hospital and didn't want to give her any emotional distress.

"I had a pretty big heart attack, Amy, but I'm going to pull through it," she slurred. "They say we caught it early..." Susan's voice trailed off without finishing her thought. She was having a difficult time speaking since she was so weak.

Amy talked with her mother for a few minutes and then stepped aside, indicating it was my time to talk. Susan and I had a very close relationship. Upon asking Amy to marry me, I began automatically calling her parents "Mom and Dad." My relationship with my own parents was distant. I was instantly loved and part of this new family.

I will never forget the day I became a son in this family, not just the son-in-law. Months after Amy and I were married, a friend of the family had been in a near deadly skiing accident and we went over to pray for his recovery. I had the opportunity of witnessing Susan's determined style of prayer for the first time. It was also the first time I used her Bible. It had been her Bible for over fifty years. In it I found notes, prayers, hopes, and questions scrawled in the margins. A few of the pages needed to be reattached to the binding. It had been rebound twice; it had lived through the birth of her two children, the deaths of loved ones, both of her daughters' weddings, and the births of five grandchildren. It had also lived through some of the most dangerous spiritual warfare imaginable, the kind that many of us have never witnessed, and sadly for which many would be ill-equipped. I felt an instant connection to Susan's Bible and to her in a way I had never before felt.

When the night was over, I stammered a question out of both respect and fear.

"Mom, can I have your Bible when you're done with it?"

I knew what I was asking for and so did she.

Susan turned to me and said, "Today you have truly become my son. I won't be able to give it to you because I won't be finished with it until Jesus calls me home, but I'll leave a note." She hugged me and we cried together—Mom, because she gained a son, and me because I was stepping out in faith asking for a spiritual blessing. She was my Elijah, and I was her Elisha, asking for a double portion of the spiritual mantel that she wielded so well.

Standing in front of Susan's bed in the ICU, I was overcome with peace and urgency.

"You know, Mom," I started, "it's not your time to go." She smiled as I dug up all the courage I could find. "I still need your spiritual blessing before you go so that I can pass on your prayer warrior legacy to your grandchildren and their children."

Without saying a word, Susan reached out her hand and took hold of mine. She gently tugged and I stepped closer. Holding my hand in both of hers, she raised it to her lips and gently kissed the back of my hand.

"Son," my breath caught—she'd only called me that once before— "you have my blessing. God and I've already talked about that a couple of times."

We stayed and talked for a couple more minutes and then we left.

Susan lived another eighteen months. Nine months after her first heart attack, she had another. In order to prolong her life, the doctors decided it was time for Susan to begin dialysis. It was an emotional roller coaster for both Amy and me. Amy spent as much time with her mother as possible, often going to the dialysis center and playing cards with her during her four to six hour treatments.

September 22, 2008, at 3:15 a.m., the phone shocked me out of a deep sleep.

"Thom, you need to wake Amy and meet me at the hospital." I could tell by Gary's voice that something was terribly wrong. It took us a few minutes to get in touch with someone who could come over and stay at the house while the kids slept. On the way to the hospital, Amy was very quiet. I was praying. I knew what we were walking into when we arrived. I'm sure Amy did as well, but we didn't talk. When we arrived at the E.R., we were ushered into a small room set aside for grieving families. Amy's dad was in the room alone. One look at his face confirmed everything.

"No, Dad!" Amy whispered. "No! We just talked last night."

I put an arm around Amy and walked her to Gary. He stood there holding his daughter in an embrace. She wept. He was numb. It was obvious he'd cried earlier, but he was being strong for Amy. Moments later the door opened and Lisa walked into the room.

It was an odd moment for me. Susan had become a strong mother figure in my life. The story of my parents is a tale for another time. Suffice it to say, when I needed motherly advice, Susan was the person I called. When we needed the prayer of a righteous warrior, Susan was always ready to do battle. Having only been a part of the family for ten years, I felt a little odd wrestling with the deep loss I was experiencing. I chided myself for the way I was feeling and tried to be the husband Amy needed at that point. I packed my emotions away, fully intending to deal with them later.

After Gary told us about what had transpired in the few hours after I last spoke with Susan, there was a moment of silence. Lisa finally cleared her throat.

"Can we go see her?"

We were led to the room in the E.R. where Susan lay on a gurney. Her whole body was covered with a white sheet. Gary uncovered Susan's face. Amy and Lisa both stood on either side of their mother. Having not been in a room with a dead body since my great-grandfather, I stood back, away from the bed. Amy and Lisa both took their mother's hands and wept. Her hands were the instruments of blessing, of prayer, and of love. I watched both of them weep, and the fear and pain from my childhood crept up my throat. I became lightheaded. I took another step back, away from the bed. I was afraid I was going to pass out. Everything in me wanted one last touch from Susan's hand, but I let my fear overwhelm me.

After about ten minutes, Lisa bent over and kissed her mother's forehead. She whispered her goodbye. Amy whispered one as well. Then we all returned to the small room down the hall. It was nearly six o'clock in the morning and there was a looming issue we had to deal with in light of the situation.

In just a few hours, the daughter of Gary and Susan's close friends was getting married. We all had a part to play. Lisa was scheduled to take Micah to his double-header soccer games. Our youngest two were with a babysitter. Amy and I were catering the wedding. Gary and Susan had duties to perform as well, and Susan's job could not go unfilled. They were loaning their white, 1969 Chevrolet Impala convertible for the bride and groom to use in their wedding pictures. Susan was also supposed to drive the wedded couple away from the church after the reception in the convertible.

When the door to the small family room closed behind us, Gary took charge.

"We tell no one," he said in a fatherly tone. "The wedding's in a couple hours and your mother would not have wanted to detract from the bride on her special day. We tell no one."

"What do we say if someone asks where Mom is?" Amy asked.

"She's at Home. That's all you tell them. All of our friends will be at this wedding. They know your mom's been sick for some time. They'll understand."

"I don't know if I can do this, Dad," Amy replied.

"We can do it," I said, with my arm around my wife. "I'll run the food out to the buffet. You can stay in the kitchen." We were switching roles, but it was the only way.

"We don't say anything until tomorrow," Gary repeated.

"Can we tell the kids tonight after the wedding?"

"Yes, but nobody else."

We had our marching orders.

No more sleep was had that morning. Amy and I began catering a large wedding event with less than ten hours of sleep combined.

Heading into the church I mustered a very simple, crude prayer: "God, we can't do this without You." I couldn't think of anything else to say.

When I first walked out onto the reception floor with food during the party, I wrestled with Gary's decision. I do not like lying. It's the number one rule in our home: Do not lie. I paused the first time someone asked me the fateful question, "Where's Susan?" In the back of my mind I remembered hearing Susan say once, "I can't wait until Jesus takes me Home and I don't have to live with this pain." I silently thanked God for the memory and said, "She's at Home." Sometimes people would press; most did not. It was an exhausting thing to put aside grief, to honestly work to ignore it, while taking care of my grieving wife and a room full of hundreds of happy wedding guests.

When the wedding reception was over, Amy and I headed to our house to break the news to our boys. We chose to tell eight-year-old Micah first. He crawled up onto our bed and sat between us, facing us.

"Micah…" I paused, searching for words. I knew Amy could not even begin to tackle this parenting task. "Honey, Grammy went to be with Jesus early this morning."

It took a long minute for the information to register, then he broke into sobs. Micah and Susan had a special bond. They had been nearly inseparable. Being the oldest, he had the most time and memories with Susan. As we helped him grieve, my mind began to race. *What am I going to say to a three and four-year-old? How do I tell them?* Again, a crude, but silent, prayer escaped me. This time it was even shorter.

"God," I whispered, as Micah left our room and his brothers entered. That was my whole prayer. The reality that Susan was really gone and that I could now grieve hit me at that very moment. "God," I repeated.

"Daddy, what's wrong. Why you crying?" Isaiah asked me.

"Sweetie," I said, pulling him into my lap while Amy corralled Gabe in her arms, "This morning, Jesus came to get Grammy." Those words never crossed my thoughts. They just came out of my mouth.

"Is He bringing her back?" Gabriel asked.

"No..." Amy started and then shook her head.

"No, boys, Grammy will not be coming back. When you go to Heaven, it's for good. You don't get to come back to earth. You don't want to."

"Can I go?" he asked excitedly.

"Yes, Gabriel, you can go to Heaven when Jesus comes to get you, but not before." I grinned. Such innocence and simplicity. I thanked God again for speaking through me to my little boys.

That night, Gary took the whole family out to Red Robin. No one had enough energy to think about cooking, let alone actually cook. As we walked out of the restaurant, a gust of wind gripped the balloon Isaiah had been given as he left the restaurant. He was no longer holding it. As it floated away, he giggled.

"Jesus, can you give my balloon to Grammy?"

I breathed a sigh of relief. My boys would miss their grandmother immensely. However, they understood the finality of death a lot better than we realized they would.

Before she died, Susan had asked me if I would do her eulogy. At the time I said, "Yes, Mom, I would be honored." I spent a week digging and studying and writing in order to give Susan the perfect eulogy. At the end of the week, I found myself in front of a sea of people fulfilling one of the hardest assignments I had ever been tasked to do. I started with the first prayer in Susan's prayer journal. To this day, I do not know who wrote it (neither did the internet when I checked) but there is much wisdom contained within this practical prayer:

> Dear Lord, so far today, God, I've done alright. I haven't gossiped, haven't lost my temper, haven't been greedy, grumpy, nasty, selfish or over-indulgent. I'm really glad about that. But, in a few minutes, God, I'm going to get out of bed, and from then on I'm probably going to need a lot more help. Thank you, in Jesus' name, Amen.[1]

We laughed, shed some tears, and as a family, bid our matriarch good bye. I finished the eulogy with a nod to the legacy Susan had left behind.

> Mom left us at 3:07 last Saturday morning to be with her Lord, and in doing that, she left behind a spiritual legacy and heritage that will last for many generations to come. Sitting in this room are many people who are a testament of her ministry and life. One of us had the pleasure of calling her wife, five had the joy of calling her Grammy, four of us had the honor of calling her Mom, but all of us had the privilege of calling her friend.[2]

As I've pondered the whole thing, from the night before my wedding to the wedding we catered hours after Susan passed away, I've learned about God's grace, God's love, and God's goodness. In the midst of the pain and dialysis, Susan was cheery and quick to pray. She knew who her most important relationship was with and she shared Him with everyone she knew—without apology. When Susan was at her worst, she often received a phone call from a friend or from one of the family asking for prayer. We knew she would pray, and we knew her prayers were powerful.

I learned that God grants us the power to do what needs to be done, with His help, in times when we could not nor should not be able to function. I also learned that laughter can heal a broken heart. It would take months for Amy to no longer be mad at God for taking Susan. Amy loved her mother and she knew she was loved by her mother. From the outside, their relationship looked strained. Sometimes it was. Most of the time it wasn't. When Susan passed, however, there were things Amy wished she had not waited to say. There were also many things she wished she had said repeatedly.

I watched Amy work through all the stages of grief. It was the first time

I had ever been close enough to someone to witness their intimate grief. It was a powerful and profound grief.

    I do have one regret. At the close of Susan's funeral, I was certain I heard God say I had less than ten years with Amy. As the message came to me, I immediately scolded myself. *That was not God. He said that at your wedding about Susan. Amy's young. Don't give in to fear.* If I could have done it over—the last nineteen years—I would have been all the more intentional with my words, my dreams, and my affections for my wife. I would have squabbled less and laughed more. I would have asked more questions about her dreams, about her goals for our boys, and about her bucket list. I would have been more intentional about many things. The Bible says, "people are destined to die once" (Hebrews 9:27, NIV). We only get once. So use your once for His glory. Bless those around you. Say the things you need/want to say without "waiting for the right moment." You won't regret it.

CHAPTER 7

# The Diagnosis

Amy planned a typical check-up with her primary care doctor. They ran the usual diabetes related blood tests which are drawn a few times a year. The results of the tests concerned her doctor. Amy was referred to a kidney specialist team at OHSU (the Oregon Health and Science University) here in Portland. I didn't want her to go alone. Every time she'd gone to a doctor alone—or at least without me—there was inevitable bad news. My presence there, I reasoned, would ensure the news was not bad news. I was wrong.

When we arrived at the kidney specialist's office, we were directed to the hospital's lab. They drew blood on a rush order. In an hour we'd meet with the specialist. In the meantime, we headed down to the cafeteria to get some lunch.

When Amy was hospitalized with her second pregnancy, she'd spent an entire month in this same hospital. Micah always wanted to get food in the cafeteria, especially pudding. We smiled at the memory as I put two cups of pudding on our tray.

Lunch was odd for us. Usually we both talked during meals. This lunch we were both quiet. Neither one of us wanted to deal with the reality of the need to be at the hospital.

When we arrived back at the specialist's office, the nurse invited us into a room, took Amy's vitals, asked a few standard questions, and then turned to leave. Just before she reached the door, the nurse turned back around and looked right at Amy.

"You know, I don't usually get personal with patients..." she paused. "It's kinda the policy around here. But I wanted you to know that things will be great. The doctors in this practice are nationally ranked. You're in good hands. I can tell you're nervous. You don't need to be. Someone..." At this point she cocked her head upward while pointing her right index finger. "Someone is watching over you."

We both exhaled the breath neither of us realized we were holding. Filled with a warm peace, I reached my hand around Amy.

"Yes, God is watching over us." We all three grinned, and then the nurse stepped out of the room.

Five minutes later the kidney specialist entered the room. He was very businesslike and clinical. The doctor logged onto the computer in the room and perused Amy's lab results. I was sure he'd already received them prior to entering; I got the feeling that he was stalling. Finally, he pushed the computer away from him and wheeled his doctor's stool over directly in front of us.

"I'm afraid the news I have to share is not good news." The kidney specialist was grim. His face was etched with worry lines. His mouth did not seem to have ever had the ability to smile.

We both sat expectant. I hugged Amy a little tighter. She squeezed my hand with all her might. A lone tear escaped her right eye.

"Our tests indicate that you have a kidney function of thirty-two percent." There was no sugarcoating to the news. "There are some people who live quite a long time with only thirty-two percent of their kidney function. What concerns me, however, is how fast you seem to have lost function in the kidneys."

Terror began crawling up my spine. It dug its talons into my heart and buried its fangs into the back of my brain. I began to see spots. My hearing was beginning to alternate from being turned on to off, to on and back off again. A cold shudder landed on me and fled down my body and into the floor beneath my feet, leaving me chilled. *God, I've got to hear this man. I've got to be strong for Amy. I've got to be present.* I felt like I was in a losing battle. Amy's grip seemed to tighten. She had a death grip on me, not intending to let me go. I felt like I was losing my grasp on the present. *God,* I tried again, *I've got to hear this! Please give me Peace.* That was all it took. In a nano-second, my volume dial was turned completely to maximum, and not a moment too soon.

"...understand your concern," he was saying. "Our goal is to stop the digression in the kidneys and help you live the best you can, for as long as you can, on the kidneys you have."

*Did I hear him correctly?* I shook the cobwebs out of my head.

"Are you saying that Amy's life is in danger?" *There, I said it.*

"The low kidney function is very concerning, and if we can't get the digression to hold, then yes, Amy's life is in danger." He spoke without inflection or warmth in his message. It was just as clinical as he looked.

"We have three boys at home!" My voice rose in pitch. "What am I going to tell them?"

"There are more tests that we need to run. Then we'll need to see Amy every month for a while to watch what's happening with her kidneys. I would suggest that you not tell little children anything at this point, but if your children are older, you might want to let them know. Do you have family in the area?"

"Yes, Amy's father and sister live close to us."

"Are they a good support for you and the children?"

"Yes."

"Then I suggest you start by telling them what I've explained to you. Tell the children when we have more concrete information, especially any younger ones."

The walk to the parking garage was drowned in silence. Screaming silence. My ears rang with each step. Neither of us could find words. I quietly walked hand in hand with my beautiful bride, hoping and praying that my grip was loving and consoling.

Amy and I had come to the hospital in separate cars since I came straight from work. Knowing we would both be driving home alone, with the weight of the news sitting on us, I hopped into the passenger seat of the van as Amy climbed into the driver's seat.

"Honey, are you okay?" I asked, almost apologetically. Amy winced.

"What makes you think I'm okay?" was her fearful retort.

I reached over for her hand. She didn't give it to me so I sat my hand on her thigh.

"Amy? What do you need right now?" I was having problems processing the news we'd just received. I couldn't imagine the state Amy was in; this was happening to her body. I waited for a beat.

"Honey…"

"We tell no one!" I reacted as if someone had slapped me, sprawling backward slightly.

"Wha…"

"No one!" she reiterated loudly. Then, as if she were from Stepford, her tone changed and she began again. "We've got to get home. Lisa has things to do. I promised her we would come home right after the appointment."

Again, I found myself shaking at the cobwebs in my brain.

"Well…let's get going." She wouldn't even look at me. Amy's eyes bore a hole through the concrete pillar in front of the van. Bowing my head, a bit in resignation, I backed out of the van and closed the door. Before I could get into my car, Amy had started the van and began backing out of the parking space. I tried to pick up speed, but I felt like I was trying to swim a 100-meter sprint in mud. By the time I was sitting in the driver's seat of my own car and backing out of the space, Amy had already exited the parking structure. I didn't even get to follow her home.

When I entered freeway traffic, tears were almost completely clouding my vision. Bluetooth in my ear, I called my father-in-law. There are very few times when I exercised the "God put me in charge" line in my marriage. Staring at this news, I knew we needed as much prayer as we could muster. I also knew Amy would be very angry when she found out I had called "half the world" as she would later claim. After calling Gary, I called my sister-in-law, and my best friend, Travis. Each call I tried to keep quick. Each call I tried to be factual. Each call I broke down a bit more. I'm not sure what Gary and Lisa thought after I got off the phone with them. I really didn't give them much time to process.

"I'm sorry, Thom," Travis said after I dumped all the news on him, with a heaping dose of tears I had been holding in since the doctor's office. "What happens now?"

We talked for the rest of my drive home.

"Jenny and I will be praying. Let me know if there's anything we can do."

I hung up when I pulled into my driveway and parked next to Amy's van. When I got inside, Lisa was putting on her coat.

"The boys did great. They've all had a snack. Gabriel might be asleep by now. He was really tired about an hour ago. I had him lay down, but he kept coming downstairs wondering if you were home yet. I just put him back up in bed about fifteen minutes ago."

From the moment he was born, Gabriel had a spiritual connection with his Creator at which I have marveled. He was always agitated when we were getting bad news, even if he wasn't with us.

I walked Lisa to her car.
"Did she tell you?" I asked.
"No. I tried to pry a little, but it was clear she didn't want to talk about it."
"I'm sorry. I didn't know what else to do but call and ask for prayer. She said she doesn't want *anyone* to know. I don't know how she thinks I can bear all that responsibility and weight myself. I'll let her know when it seems right that I've told the family."
"So…never?" Lisa asked with a wry half chuckle. I rolled my eyes.
"I'll tell her. I promise."
That was May 2013.

Months later, it was nearly time for school to begin again. I'd coaxed Amy to talk with both her dad and Lisa. I fessed up that I had told Lisa. Amy was angry. After talking for a couple hours, she began to see that I needed to work out my fears verbally so that I wasn't holding in all the pain and torturing myself. She also understood why I didn't feel like I could talk with her about the "what if…" pink elephant that seemed to be following us at that time.

By late August, Amy was more willing to talk with the family about the diagnosis, and I was "allowed"—that was her word, not mine—to continue talking with Travis. I never referred to Amy as "the boss." It always irritates me when men say things like, "Well, I have to ask the Boss," or "I'll have to get my allowance from the Boss." As I see it, the Bible is very clear on spiritual authority within the family. When I was in Bible College, my mentor made it clear that a marriage was a "partnership in which two people worked hard alongside each other as equals, and if anyone had to 'take the blame' or make a 'difficult decision'" that was the time God was calling the husband to stand for his family as the head. I took his advice at face value and that's how Amy and I worked in our marriage. I realized that Amy's life and faith were in a tailspin and she needed something she could control, so I let her "allow" me to talk with Travis. What she didn't realize was that I was praying she would drop the barrier and tell her other friends what was happening in her body, in her life.

During the last week of August, we headed into the specialist's office for a routine checkup. Things seemed to have plateaued. It was getting easier to go into the hospital. Amy and the nurse had become close over the months and Amy always looked forward to seeing her. The doctor was another story.

When the door opened for the doctor to enter that day, we were met with a different doctor. Our doctor had taken a leave of absence. The new doctor was a nationally ranked specialist the hospital brought on to fill in for the vacant specialist. After the normal pleasantries one expects in a new doctor's visit, the new specialist—much younger and more warm mannered than his predecessor—sat down on the stool in front of us.

"I'm afraid the news I have to share is not good news."

Déjà vu.

Amy grabbed my hand, again with a vice grip. She turned to look directly at me. This time more than one tear escaped and rolled down her right cheek. I was left looking at the doctor. After a mighty inhale/exhale, I looked from him to her and back.

"Amy," he tried talking directly to her, but Amy kept staring at me, "your kidney function is continuing to decline. We haven't been able to stop it. We were able to slow it down, but not stop it altogether."

I bit down hard on my teeth, trying to force my eyes and ears to stay present. Fear was already crawling up my back.

"We will continue to monitor things, but if Amy's kidney function gets below twenty percent, we'll have to begin talking about dialysis." Amy's eyes widened and immediately went bloodshot. Her vice grip turned into a trash compactor. I winced from the doctor's words and the new pain in my hand.

Dialysis was a *death sentence* to Amy. She'd told me as much the night before as we were talking about the impending doctor's appointment.

"It kept Mom alive for a few months," she'd said through tears, "but it didn't heal her. Dialysis doesn't heal anyone. It just extends their pain!" She knew in her heart what the doctor was going to say. She was terrified of the reality.

That night had been a difficult one, filled with much fear...for both of us. Amy finally fell asleep and I stayed awake until almost 3:00 a.m. fretting. Afraid.

All my life I had been subject to Fear. It has overwhelmed me constantly. My favorite movie as a teenager and early twenty-something was *Beaches*, with Bette Middler and Barbara Hershey. *Steel Magnolias*, with Sally Field and Julia Roberts, was a close second. In both movies, a main character dies—one of a heart problem, the other from complications with diabetes. Since Susan's funeral, I kept playing those two movie scripts over and over in my head, often feeling like I was living in them. I went through my weeks and months fretting about losing someone I loved. Each time the thought crossed my mind, I began playing the multiple scenarios in my head. Finding the body. Figuring out who to call first. Planning the funeral. Ad nauseum. Sometimes multiple times a day.

Looking back, I realize just how much Fear is a liar and a thief. I fed that fear with the "favorites" I acknowledged on the cinema screen and the smaller screen in my living room. Fear took from me the power of my faith; or rather, I gave it power over my faith. It would be many years before I finally understood what Romans 8:31-39 was talking about, even though my youth pastor spoke about it many times: "We are more than conquerors."

> "What, then, shall we say in response to these things? If God is for us, who can be against us? He who did not spare his own Son, but gave him up for us all—how will he not also, along with him, graciously give us all things? Who will bring any charge against those whom God has chosen? It is God who justifies. Who then is the one who condemns? No one. Christ Jesus who died—more than that, who was raised to life—is at the right hand of God and is also interceding for us. Who shall separate us from the love of Christ? Shall trouble or hardship or persecution or famine or nakedness or danger or sword? As it is written:
>
> 'For your sake we face death all day long; we are considered as sheep to be slaughtered.'
>
> "No, in all these things we are more than conquerors through him who loved us. For I am convinced that neither death nor life, neither angels nor demons, neither the present nor the future, nor any powers, neither height nor depth, nor anything else in all creation, will be able to separate us from the love of God that is in Christ Jesus our Lord." (NIV)

CHAPTER 8

# Holding onto Fear with a Death Grip

Micah was fourteen. Gabriel was ten. Isaiah was nine.

"Kids, we need to talk." It's an ominous statement to make to young children. It's a statement that causes children to shiver. *What did we do wrong?* usually pounds through their hearts and heads.

Amy was sitting in the front room of our home on the couch we normally used for guests. I was standing in the middle of the room. As our kids came down the stairs, the looks on their faces betrayed their nervousness.

"It's okay, boys," Amy started, "you're not in trouble." She stood up, motioned for the kids to sit down on the couch. We sat opposite them. Then Amy turned to me.

"Boys, there's something we need to share with you before you go to school in a couple days." They were seated with rapt attention. Micah, our rock, was in the middle of both his brothers. They were seated next to him without any space between them. Both boys look to him for strength. They always have.

"Mom and I have been gone a lot this summer, and we know you have questions."

"Is everything okay?" Micah asked, as if on cue.

"Mom's kidneys haven't been working right lately. We've been seeing the doctors and they are treating her, but things have not gotten better like we thought." I let that sit for a beat. "We've known since May, but we didn't want to burden you with the news until we knew more."

The air in the room was thick. I hadn't had to give my children news like this since their grandmother passed. I didn't know what to expect. While I spoke, the words came easily. Amy and I had prayed for peace and wisdom. I could tell God was in the room. I felt odd that I wasn't short of breath, that I wasn't overcome with fear, that I wasn't stammering. Usually, situations like this left me in a tailspin.

"Mom's kidneys are only working part of the time. The doctors have many different things to try. She and I will be going to the doctor's quite a bit over the next few months. As we learn what is happening to Mommy, we'll let you know. When you have questions, we will answer them." At that, Isaiah raised his hand as if he were in school.

"Is Mommy going to die?"

It was a question we knew would be asked. Gabriel's hands shot to his mouth. Alligator tears instantly welled in his eyes. Micah sat motionless.

"Right now, the doctors are doing everything they can. Could this get really bad and could it kill Mommy? Yes, *but* we are a long way from that. God is a big God. He is in control. It's our job right now to pray for Mommy and to trust God to do His work for His will. Mommy is going to be working to get a kidney transplant. If she gets a transplant, then she'll have perfect kidney function again."

"Ok..." Gabe began, rather loudly, "...so, Mommy might die?" I could hear the tremor in his voice, the high pitch of fear. Micah wrapped his arm around Gabriel to comfort him.

"Honey," Amy began, leaning over and touching his knee, "Mommy's here right now. God's not done with me here. I'm going to be here for..." she paused, looking over at me, "...for a long while." She ended with a smile. Gabriel lept from his perch and landed in her lap. His stifled sobs were buried in her shoulder.

I waited for a few moments, then turned to Isaiah.

"Isaiah, there's a boy in your class at school who is in a similar situation as you. His dad has had two kidney transplants. Sadly, though, his body is rejecting this last one. He might be a good friend for you, someone to talk to who understands what you're going through."

I worked at Isaiah's school, albeit in the Middle School, but I knew of the family and had permission to share the information.

"So, it'll be like someone's helping me carry my backpack?" Isaiah asked. Amy and I looked at each other. "You know, when something is too heavy to carry yourself, God sends someone along to help you carry the load," he added. I was officially speechless. Amy had no words. "Actually, while we talk, we could just let Jesus carry the backpack for us."

I fought to keep everything together. Tears were blurring my vision. My chin was quivering. Amy had rivers making their way down her face and into her lap. Isaiah was only nine years old. He was schooling us in the lessons of faith he'd been raised with...by us!

"Yes, Isaiah, it'll be like that. Jesus will carry that backpack for both of you."

Ten minutes later, the boys' questions had all been answered and faces had been wiped dry. They each headed out of the room for one reason or another. I turned to Amy.

"How about that?" I asked meekly.

"Out of the mouths of babes," Amy whispered.

I opened my mouth to speak, but the thought crashed in my head before getting out my mouth. I wanted to say, 'You can't leave me until Isaiah's graduated', but the reality of what we were facing pulled me up short. I had said it to Amy for years. It was our joke. No longer. The reality was too harsh and I knew I could never say it again. I leaned over and held Amy in my arms for nearly half an hour as we sat stunned, sometimes crying, sometimes not, pondering the scene of which we'd both just participated.

Shortly after we told the boys Amy's news, her kidneys completely plateaued. We coasted, allowing our hopes to build. Fear, although present, was no longer diverting all of my attention. The school year started. We joined a Family Life Group at the church that met every other weekend to "do life together." The schedule got very busy. Thanksgiving happened. Advent was racing by, and we found ourselves nearing the Family Christmas Eve service at church.

December 21, 2013, Amy was still adamant that "No one knows!" It was difficult for me to understand her reticence to share. Since meeting her mom and learning Spiritual Warfare from a master, I wanted to invite a group to the house and orchestrate a chorus of prayer.

"You can tell no one else! It's bad enough that we had to tell the kids and that you had to tell your coworkers. Who else have you told?"

*She's angry*, I thought. I backed out of the room a little stunned just shortly before that "discussion" became infamous.

*God*, my heart cried out, *what am I missing? Why doesn't she want prayer?*

The answer hit me hard.

*Ask her what she's afraid of,* came the response.

*That's easy,* my soul volleyed back to Heaven. *She's afraid of dying.*

*No, my son. Ask her what she's afraid of.* That was the end of the conversation.

Sometimes I doubt that I've heard God speak to me. Other times I try to believe that He didn't because I don't like the response. This time, the response was so outside of my expectations, I assumed it was God. I secretly argued with myself as I pulled on the courage to re-enter that conversation.

I took three, slow, long, deep breaths. Why three? Three is a perfect number. It's all over Scripture. I don't really know. Most likely because that's how long it took me to gain the courage I needed for the next part of this conversation. I shook my head slowly, almost in protest, as my feet carried me back into the room I had just left.

"Honey," I began, secretly hoping she hadn't heard me. "Can we talk?"

Amy turned to face me from her seat in the recliner. She raised her eyebrows and opened her arms, indicating the "floor was mine."

"Amy, what are you afraid of?"

"What?" came her slightly snarky reply.

"What are you afraid of right now? What's keeping you from telling people?" *There! I said it!*

"I don't want people to think I'm no longer capable. I don't want people to tell me I can't continue to minister in Children's Ministry. I don't want people to give me those looks of pity. I don't...I can't..." but she couldn't finish.

"I understand that, but what are you *afraid* of?" I took a slow deep breath to cover up wincing.

She looked at me, shook her head quickly, and then stood. I tried not to react, but I was terrified of what she was going to say. I hated making Amy cry and I was standing in dangerous territory.

"I'm afraid someone will give me their kidney but they'll die in the process and it will be my fault," she whispered. We both took one step toward each other. I caught Amy as her knees buckled and she began sobbing.

*That was not what I was expecting, God!* I looked toward the ceiling as if the look on my face were punctuating what my heart was yelling at my Creator.

God simply replied by saying, *That's why I told you to ask.*

Two days later, December 23, 2013, we arrived at the church, two hours before the "Christmas Eve" Candlelight Service. Beaverton Foursquare has a tradition of a Christmas Eve Candlelight service, but in order to get everyone through the service, we have to do it in two nights, over four services. Our boys were asked to sing in the choir. We walked in the door and they were whisked off to their designated spot. We headed for a quiet place to sit in the foyer.

God had a distinct plan for that moment. He arranged it all. As I look back, I am boggled by the overwhelming love and goodness of our Creator, that He would orchestrate a ten-minute conversation that would totally change the trajectory of our family.

"Amy!"

We both turned to see a wonderful friend headed our way.

"Kymra!" Amy replied. "It's been a long time since we've seen each other without kids! How are you doing?" Amy and Kymra had a very long history, which started at camp when Amy was in elementary school and Kymra was her camp counselor. Fast forward many years and the two had become very good friends. Our kids were the same age and we crossed paths often, usually coming and going to drop off or pick up our children from one event or another.

Kymra smiled a warm smile, but concern was clearly on the fringes.

"I've been praying for you lately. Is there something going on?"

I exhaled, expecting Amy to give the pat answer. I did not get what I expected.

"I've been diagnosed with kidney failure," Amy quickly replied, almost as if her heart was trying to get something past her head.

"I didn't know, Amy!" Kymra replied, catching a hold of Amy's left arm. "Whatever you need, I'm there. Have you been matched with a kidney transplant yet?"

Amy's eyes widened and I shook my head.

"You can have one of mine. As soon as your doctors are ready, I'll get typed to see if I'm a match."

In that short moment, everything changed. Amy stood a bit taller as the weight was lifted. My prayers, only two days old, were being answered in front of me. For the next three weeks, Amy began telling those close to her about her diagnosis and situation. Prayers started pouring into Heaven. Hope was returning to my bride.

It was short-lived, though not because of health.

Less than a week back into school from break, I was released from my contract at a Christian school where I had been teaching. It was a huge blow to both of us. We began to panic about money and insurance and health. So much worry poured into the house that it began to affect our children. As we fell to our knees, this time together, we began to earnestly seek God's will. We knew I wasn't supposed to have signed the contract for the 2013-14 school year. I had been at the Christian school for only three years. Money was tight. Jobs were few. We both knew God was moving us in a different direction, but fear kept us from talking to each other. I signed the contract and those four months were very difficult.

Fear quickly began flooding back into my days. I began substitute teaching in the public schools. I was good at that job and I kept being asked back to certain schools. God made sure our bills were met every month. Each month there was a different miracle or two that brought the needed money into the bank. We began to recognize God's provision and began teaching our children the power of obedience. We also began teaching them about tithing. We knew God was taking care of us because of our faith, even though we hadn't always listened to His direction.

Being a single father of three teenagers gives me pause here. I've always told my kids, "I love you, and nothing you do or say will ever change that." It wasn't until I became a father myself before I began to understand why the God of the universe would take the time to care about me. When my kids make decisions that win them negative consequences, my love for them doesn't change. They know that, and they've tested it. Sitting here right now, writing this chapter the way I thought it should go, I discover God landed the parallel in my lap, just like a Dad. My Dad. My Abba Father!

A few days after the school year ended, I took a long look at Amy and noticed that her coloring was distinctly wrong. She had a significant yellow hue. On our next visit with the doctors we were told that dialysis (peritoneal dialysis) was on the horizon. Amy's strength and hope instantly shriveled to a terrified mess.

I called Amy's best friend, Temple, and asked her to pray.

"Amy's 40th birthday is next week," she said, just before the call ended.

"I know. Are you going to be in town? Amy doesn't want a big party. In fact, she doesn't even want to be the center of anyone's attention right now, but I feel like we need to do something."

"I'm there."

Amy fought me about a birthday party, telling me that she didn't want even her family or our boys to celebrate. That triggered my memory. Last time we were deadlocked against each other like this, fear was winning and we were both losing. Setting aside the reality that Amy hated (and I don't use that word lightly) surprise parties, I made the calls: Gary and his new wife Mary, Lisa, Dale, and their kids, and Temple were all headed to the house. I knew it was the right thing to do, so I was willing to test the waters.

Thirty minutes before everyone was to show up, Amy realized the boys and I were being a "little weird." She had caught me. The argument was infamous. Finally, just five minutes before the doorbell rang, Amy relented. Lisa and her family were the first to arrive. Gary and Mary were close behind them. Amy began settling in to being around the family when the doorbell rang a third time. I was "busy" in the kitchen with one of the boys. The other two were upstairs with their cousins. Intentionally.

"Amy, can you get the door?"

She was not expecting Temple. Instantly she began to cry. Temple and Amy met in Sunday School when they were five. They were inseparable. Their lives were greatly intertwined. Just seeing her friend who, because of distance, Amy did not get to see often, warmed Amy's heart. She was no longer mad at me for breaking the "no surprise party" rule.

As the party wound down, Amy began opening presents. After opening a few, Temple knelt in front of her and presented her with a life-line gift. Three bracelets. Each with a different reminder: "choose joy," "blessed," and "peace." Amy wore them daily as a reminder that God was with her. It was a needed course correction.

The boys and I began seeing her smile again. She began playing worship music again on the piano every morning. She began cooking breakfast for the boys and me, even though her strength was leeching out of her system. As I saw God's joy and peace overcome Amy, I began seeking it for myself.

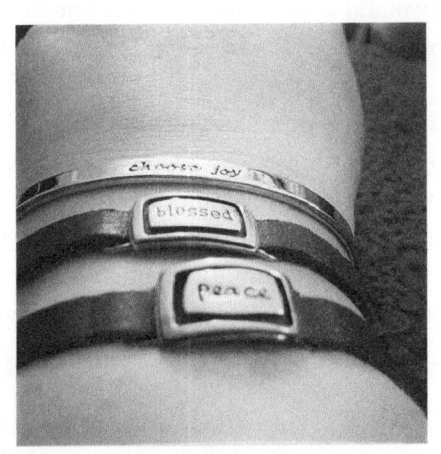

Amy's 40th Birthday Gift from Temple

God coaxed us through June and July, working on Amy's heart little by little. At the beginning of August 2014, Amy agreed to begin "at home" peritoneal dialysis. Susan had to go to a dialysis treatment center three to four times a week, for up to six hours at a time. Amy couldn't figure out how she could be a mom and miss so much of her boys' lives. When the doctors explained that she was a candidate for "at home" treatment, and that it didn't involve blood, she was sold.

The surgery to place the catheter in her abdomen was one and a half hours longer than anticipated. I waited in the surgical waiting area with heartburn and high anxiety. When the doctor was only five minutes late, I was pretty calm. But when the clock showed twenty minutes late, I began to panic. By the time the surgeon came to talk with me, I had convinced myself that something had gone terribly wrong and that I would be leaving the hospital…alone. Anxiety, the great Worry Monster, was riding on my back.

The anxiety and fretting was for naught. The surgeon came to talk with me, explained that the surgery prior to Amy's had gone overtime, thus causing Amy's surgery to be delayed a bit. Amy was doing fine and in recovery. There had been no complications.

As the summer quickly passed, I found myself praying for direction and a firm foundation. I wanted a job that would have good medical insurance. That's when God asked me to trust Him at a higher level. He handed me multiple long-term subbing positions that kept me working for each and every day of the school year.

I subbed for a month in the public schools.

Then I spent two and a half months at a Lutheran school where God taught me what comradery and compassion looked like from the receiving end. That school blessed us immensely. Just days after starting at the Lutheran school, Amy had to go back in for another port placement surgery. Her first port stopped working. I was a wreck, awaiting a text from Lisa, who had taken Amy this time. Everything went well. When the staff at the school found out, they began delivering meals in order to lighten my load at home. I fit in at that school; it almost felt like a family. The staff has kept in touch and continued to bless me and my family long after I moved on to another school.

In March 2015, I was teaching a fifth and sixth grade blended class at a different Christian school in the area. I started there in February. Everything seemed to be going very well. Amy had begun using a dialysis machine through the night. This method took even less time from her, allowing her to do more for her family. What I didn't realize was the stress Amy was putting on her body with the increased amount of activities.

Late one afternoon, I pulled into the driveway to find Amy lying on the ground in an awkward position just outside of the van. Her right foot was still in the van. She had gone to pick up the boys from school. When they returned, the boys went into the house for a snack. Amy often sat in the van until I arrived home (usually about twenty to thirty minutes). Her back had begun to cause her problems because of the extra weight of the dialysis solution in her body and the heated seats in the van helped immensely. The boys knew the drill. They were in the house obeying the house rules, none the wiser to their mother's situation.

I jumped out of my car and bounded to Amy in nearly one step. She was semi-conscious. I helped her to her feet, assessed her for obvious wounds, and helped her wobble inside. Micah was immediately repentant, feeling it was his fault his mother had been outside for nearly half an hour on the ground. It took me awhile to help him understand he wasn't to blame. Then I gave him orders to check on his mother every five to seven minutes in the future.

After being evaluated later that day by hospital staff, we realized Amy was terribly dehydrated. She was taking medicine at that time which required her to be out of the sun as much as possible. Who knew that sitting in a van, on a 70-degree day could cause dehydration and extreme fatigue?

My worry meter soared to heights beyond experience. It became difficult to stay on task at work during times my students were at music, P.E., or another place on campus without me. I started having "day-terrors," as I called them. I would be sitting in my classroom and would imagine seeing Amy contorted in grotesque ways, covered in active wounds, battling for air. Sometimes the day-terror was of her having just died, but it was clear that she had suffered greatly for quite a long period of time.

When I was at home, I hovered in an almost suffocating way. "Can I get you anything?" "Are you feeling okay?" "What was that noise?" When the school-year ended, I was relieved I could be with Amy nearly 24/7. My inner obsession to be her savior nearly ruined our relationship. When Amy realized what was wrong, why I was acting so erratically and irrationally, she requested I begin counseling. I met with a pastor at church a couple of times to appease her.

In the middle of May we were told we would have to move by July 1, 2015. The man who owned our home was battling stage four pancreatic cancer and needed to sell the house back to the bank. We searched and searched for a house to move into, but the housing situation in the Portland Metro area was bleak. Every time a house went on the market for rent, it was snatched up literally within minutes. It was a battle to try and get a house. Amy and Micah were already scheduled to work at the fourth and fifth grade summer camp for our church. Amy's job was Head of Hospitality and it wasn't something easily handed off to another. I told them to go, that I would be able to get us moved.

What I didn't expect was having to move into storage. We couldn't find a house. The day they arrived home was the last day we were supposed to be in the house. I had been packing, parenting, and panicking all week long. We had to move in with Amy's sister and her family. The boys slept in a tent in the back yard while Amy and I slept on a hide-a-bed sofa. We were there for three weeks. I felt like a failure as a father and as a husband. We were officially homeless and I didn't have a steady job for the coming school year. My self-esteem fell to an all-time low.

Lisa, Dale, and our nephews were incredible. They gave up nearly a third of their house for the five of us. We never once heard them complain. God, however, heard much complaining from me. I had never worked in an extremely lucrative business. Christian schools don't pay nearly as much as public schools, and subbing in the public schools was still significantly less than a livable wage for a family of five. With no options and a grim outlook of the future, I started having blackouts. None of them lasted for a significantly long period of time, but they were scary nonetheless. It was as if I were driving through a very long tunnel. My vision would begin to narrow, and everything would go dark. Just before all light winked out, I would lose hearing as well. Gabriel was with me once when it happened while I was behind the wheel. He reached over, put his hand on my knee, and shook me.

"Daddy!"

I heard something. It was very muffled. But I had heard a distinct sound. Slowly, my vision returned, as if I were driving out of a tunnel. The increase of light, however, did not come with an increase of clarity. Everything was blurry. I realized I had been hyperventilating and intentionally began to slow my breathing. I had a difficult time figuring out where I was. Then I heard the sound again.

"Daddy!" This time I could hear my son more clearly, as if he were talking through the bathroom door. I took a couple deep breaths, and my vision began to clear.

"Daddy!" The third time brought me completely out of the black-out. I could see and hear again. I looked at my son. He was sitting in the passenger seat, tears welling in his eyes.

"Gabriel?" I asked weakly.

"Daddy! The light turned green a long time ago! People keep honking. Can you go please?"

God had seen to it that the car was not moving at the time of the black-out. I quickly assessed where I was and then headed through the intersection as the now yellow light turned to red.

"Daddy," Gabe chided, "that was a red light. I'm going to tell Mommy."

On the way to my sister-in-law's house, I pulled into a donut shop and bribed my son. I think it was the only time in our family's history that Gabe kept a secret from his mother. She never found out about the traffic violation. Neither did anyone else. After some of my family reads this book, I might find myself in a heap of trouble.

That night I took stock of the situation. I found myself having difficulty sleeping. Instead of fretting, though, I turned my attention toward Heaven.

*God, I prayed, I don't know what's going on with me, but You do. Please help us find a house to move into and calm down my anxiety. I can't leave Amy in this condition.*

The very next day I called on a rental house I had found. There was an open house the next day, but there were many families who'd called and were interested. I made the appointment to go see the house with Amy and Isaiah. Gabe was having some alone time with his grandparents and Micah was a camp counselor at our church's junior high summer camp.

When we walked through the front door, I knew we'd found a home. Amy wasn't quite as sold. She had many questions. After the thirty-minute tour and grill session, we asked for an application.

"How late is the office open today to turn in the paper-work," Amy asked.

"It closes in fifteen minutes. We open tomorrow at 8:00 a.m."

"We'll be there at 7:45," Amy replied.

"How many other families looked at the house today? Would their applications be considered before ours?" I asked sheepishly.

"There were two families who were supposed to have taken a tour before you today, but they didn't show. I have two more scheduled after you leave. Whoever turns in their paperwork first, however, is the family with first consideration."

The next morning, we were at the rental company half-an-hour early. The parking lot was bare. Upon opening, we learned that no one showed up to the open house the day before except us. After a couple days for the rental company to check our credit and rental history, Amy and I were headed back to pick up the keys. Micah wouldn't get home from camp until the afternoon we were moving into the house. He did, however, bring a few of his counselor friends in tow to help. Many friends stepped up to help us haul everything we owned out of the three U-Haul rental storage units. By 8:00 that evening, we were the only ones in our house, surrounded by boxes and piles, but we were home. Once the beds were made and the dialysis machine was plugged in and working, my anxiety stopped.

Three weeks later, at 9:00 p.m., I received a tip from a friend about a partial year teaching position in Portland Public Schools. I applied for it immediately. By 10:30 that evening, I had an interview for 3:00 p.m. the next day. Two days later I was offered a contract for the last week of August through the end of December. I finally began to breathe peacefully. The blackouts had stopped that fateful day when Gabriel was in the car with me, and the chest pains—which felt like I was grabbing onto an electric fence every few hours—ceased as well.

Looking back, trying to assess all that was happening, I realized that during the time between being released from my job in January 2014 to gaining the teaching job in August 2015, I had been having a war with God in my heart. I began feeling like God was punishing me and my family because I wasn't the son He wanted me to be. I had stopped reading my Bible and praying during the last four months. I had stopped talking to my kids and Amy about God and His plan for us. I had come to believe He no longer had a plan for us.

Sitting in my new classroom for the first time, I realized that I had allowed worry, anxiety, and despair to come between God and me. I crawled back to my place of devotion, asking for forgiveness, sounding much like the Prodigal Son from Jesus' Parables (Luke 15:11ff). God, however, did not answer my meek request to pardon my family and bless them in spite of me. He rolled out blessing after blessing, *beginning* with me. Before my temporary contract ended, my principal told his colleagues in the district about me and I started getting calls for other long-term subbing positions. I didn't miss a day of school that year, except for the two snow days the entire district was closed.

God provided money we hadn't been expecting which helped us to keep all of the bills paid and food on the table. We were even beginning to get out of the considerable amount of debt we'd built up over our eighteen years of marriage.

Looking back now, I am amazed at my lack of faith and childish behaviors. Having experienced the miracles related to my battle with acromegaly, not to mention many other small wonders God supplied throughout the years, I should have known God would take care of us. Isn't it like us though? Westerners? Americans? We get so busy and wrapped up in the "here and now" that we forget God has us in the palm of His hand. We even get so busy focused on the "right and necessary" things of life that we lose track of what God is doing, sometimes forgetting to talk with Him at all. During that whole time, my attendance in church never wavered. When people asked, I replied "Fine" or "God is good" or whatever platitude would be considered socially appropriate.

It was near the end of that school year when God got my attention, *really* got my attention. Cracking my Bible for the first time in many months, I opened to a random page and just began reading. God's fingers had turned the pages, not mine. It is as clear to me today as it was then.

> Therefore I tell you, do not worry about your life, what you will eat or drink; or about your body, what you will wear. Is not life more than food, and the body more than clothes? Look at the birds of the air; they do not sow or reap or store away in barns, and yet your heavenly Father feeds them. Are you not much more valuable than they? Can any one of you by worrying add a single hour to your life?
>
> And why do you worry about clothes? See how the flowers of the field grow. They do not labor or spin. Yet I tell you that not even Solomon in all his splendor was dressed like one of these. If that is how God clothes the grass of the field, which is here today and tomorrow is thrown into the fire, will he not much more clothe you—you of little faith? So do not worry, saying, 'What shall we eat?' or 'What shall we drink?' or 'What shall we wear?' For the pagans run after all these things, and your heavenly Father knows that you need them. But seek first his kingdom and his righteousness, and all these things will be given to you as well. Therefore do not worry

about tomorrow, for tomorrow will worry about itself. Each day has enough trouble of its own. (Matthew 6:25-34, NIV)

Right there, God had my attention. It was as if we were standing in front of each other, eye to eye.

*Stop worrying, my son. Let me take this.*

I repented for being so distracted with anxiety and worry that I'd taken my eyes off my LORD and Savior.

*God, please help me to not worry. And please heal my beautiful bride.*

I didn't know what else to pray at that time. Sure, I had spent considerable amounts of time in prayer in the past. It wasn't that I didn't know *how* to pray; I simply didn't know *what* to pray.

Relief flooded over me and the burden weighing on my chest lessened. I was still terrified of losing Amy, and thus holding onto that fear with a death grip. I couldn't let go of it. Little did I know then that God was going to teach me about joy. True joy. His joy.

CHAPTER 9

# In Search of Joy

July 2016 held an incredible breakthrough for me, and in effect, for my family as well. All my life, I've been a worry wart. If there was something to worry about, it was at the top of my list. If I'd had a worry stone, it would have been rubbed into non-existence thousands of times over. Worry, I've come to realize however, is a learned behavior. Whether it is by seeing someone in authority over you worry—thus teaching you that it is necessary, acceptable, and expected—or by living through trauma that causes you to worry, it is still a learned behavior.

When we were a year married, Amy bought me my first cell phone as an anniversary gift. I was thrilled. I did not know then that the device would become the catalyst for much of my worrying throughout the years. I remember when our boys were little and I called the house to talk with Amy. She didn't answer. I called her cell phone. She didn't answer. A switch flipped in the back of my head. Panic. *What's wrong? Is she okay? Is she in danger? Has something happened?* I began furiously dialing back and forth between the two phone numbers until she finally answered one of the phones.

"Hello," she answered.

"What's the matter?" My voice was panicked and rising in volume. "I've been trying to call you for the last ten minutes and you didn't answer the phone. I've called the house and then your cell and then the house until you finally answered. Is everything okay? Are the boys okay?"

"Thom...everything's fine. The neighbor came over. I was standing on the front porch talking with her. When I heard the phone ringing, I figured it would just go to the machine. When it kept ringing, I excused myself and came inside to answer it. Everything's fine."

"Are you sure? There's no one there holding you hostage? You couldn't tell me that if they were. If someone is there and you are in danger, just say 'get some milk on the way home.'"

There was a long silence.

"Amy..."

Then I heard the giggles.

"Thom, are you okay?"

"You didn't answer the phone!"

It was then that I realized that my worrying had gone to an all-time, out-of-this-world orbit, one from which it would be difficult to extricate myself. Think I'm being a bit too melodramatic? Well, here's how I look at it. That day was not the worst day of my worrying. It intensified exponentially from there. People used to tell me that I would get a heart condition if I didn't stop. I was also told that "Worry was man's way of replacing God with self." This only made me more concerned that my relationship with God was dying.

It's like the snowball in the Goofy cartoons when we were kids. It starts out small, at the top of the mountain, then it picks up more snow, speed, and anything else in its path. By the time May 2013 rolled around, I had already had more panic attacks than I could count because I'd tried to get ahold of Amy and she didn't pick up within three rings. Each time, my head would begin the loop: *She's in trouble. Something's happened. I wonder if I need to call the hospital...or the police.* Each new elongated ring brought with it a heightened heart rate, a hyper-active imagination, and hyperventilation.

When Amy's diagnosis of kidney failure came in May of 2013, my worry orbit was no longer chartable. I was in a constant state of panic. I tried to not let it show on the outside...*much*. But, since I am more of an open book than most, I know that my meager efforts were wasted. People were always asking me "What's wrong?" Since Amy didn't want me to tell anyone other than her family, I found myself spinning out of control. I finally rationalized that my best friends were closer than family and I made a few calls. Simply talking about Amy's diagnosis helped my panic levels to recede enough that

I wasn't hyperventilating, (it was honestly that bad). But, each time my cell phone rang, I stopped breathing as my head sped through the check off list.

*If something's wrong, I'll get a sub immediately and go home.*
*But maybe I have to go to the hospital, or the morgue.*
*Who do I call to take care of the boys?*
*What am I going to say to Amy's dad or her sister?*
*I know she wants to be cremated, but do I need to give the mortuary an outfit for cremation?*
*How am I going to pay for it all?*
*How am I going to raise these boys without a mother? They get all of their good traits from her! I will mess them up royally!*

All of this ran through my head in the blink of an eye. My heart rate would soar, my blood pressure was palpable, and my sweat glands created rivers…which brings us to July, 2016.

Our Children's Pastor and friend (Todd) had asked me to join the team for our fourth and fifth grade summer camp. I had formerly worked two camps, and Amy and Micah had worked the last four in a row. Amy was head of hospitality at camp and the director's right hand. If he needed something done, she was usually either already in motion doing it, or had a fix in seconds. Hospitality meant taking care of the food needs of the entire camp and coordinating with the camp chef on all the allergies, gluten-free, dairy-free, and other nutritional needs of staff and campers. It also meant that she got to take care of kids who were invited to camp on scholarship and who might show up to camp without some clothing necessity that most of us take for granted. One year a girl came to camp with the outfit she was wearing and a pair of shorts in a brown paper sack. Since she was wearing only flip flops, and had no shoes, Amy had a field day shopping. She didn't usually get to shop for girls. That little girl returned to the nearby shelter she called home after camp with what amounted to her as a whole new wardrobe. It was only socks, underwear, shoes, a pair of pants, a pair of shorts and three new shirts, but for that little girl it was a Cinderella moment. She knew she was loved when she left camp. That's what Amy did. She took care of people, often without concern for herself, and never complaining about the sickness she was fighting.

When I was asked to join camp staff, I told the director that it would be difficult to do since there wasn't really a spot for Gabriel to go with the four of us at camp. God had a fix for that. Gabe became a part-time staffer working in the dining room, and it worked incredibly. With all of us at camp, I was free to focus on my role there. Little did I know that God had a much different, much bigger purpose for me being at that specific camp.

The theme of camp that summer was *Champions for Christ,* and it centered around the Olympics (since it was an Olympic year). The camp verse drove God's message for the week:

> Therefore, since we are surrounded by such a huge cloud of witnesses to the life of faith, let us strip off every weight that slows us down, especially the sin that so easily trips us up. And let us run with endurance the race God has set before us. We do this by keeping our eyes on Jesus, the champion who initiates and perfects our faith. Because of the joy awaiting him, he endured the cross, disregarding its shame. Now he is seated in the place of honor beside God's throne. (Hebrews 12:1-2, NLT)

The NIV version calls Jesus the "author and perfecter of our faith." It also says, "for the *joy* set before Him He endured the cross." I had read this verse hundreds of times in my life and many more times leading up to that camp, but I'd never truly understood it.

This point was driven home during the week through the different dramas each night (focused on the life of Paul and Barnabus) and the special speaker's message each morning. Smack in the middle of camp, God nailed me in the forehead with the simplest phrase of tremendous weight: "for the *joy* set before Him He *endured* the cross" (emphasis mine). I was stunned. Joy was not something I knew. I had been a Christian for over two decades, yet I knew not joy. When it hit me that Jesus *chose* to go to the Cross, to *endure* it, *and* that He counted it as *joy,* I stood weeping in the back of the chapel. The revelation was that Jesus counted ME as *joy!* I was the *joy* for which He *endured* the cross.

The special speaker was a woman whom I knew; I had taught her two boys in middle school. Ironically, her name is Joy. Her ministry's focus is to spread joy and to teach people what God's joy looks like in real time. She stood teaching fourth and fifth graders talking about a race she once ran and the turmoil she endured while running it. I don't know what was going through her mind as I stood in the back weeping. She probably didn't even see me, but each time she scanned the room, I felt like her gaze was purposely staying on me, even for the slightest second, in order for God to get my attention. And get it He did.

Amy had been on dialysis for both of the previous two camps. She was already in the groove of dealing with the machine and accoutrements. In the camp scene, I was a little out of my element. During the second full day at camp, Amy came down with a migraine and spent nineteen hours straight in bed. It was unlike her to not be in motion at camp. She didn't know how to handle her frailty. I stepped in when I could to help her teammate in hospitality do what needed to be done. While walking around camp that night, God told me, "Thom, this will be Amy's last camp." I heard it audibly. I was walking alone from having checked on her, returning to one of the evening dramas, when God's voice stopped me. I stood in the middle of the walkway, feet covered in proverbial concrete, lifted my head toward Heaven and replied, "You've got to tell her, God, because I can't. I can't be the one to take this ministry from her. If you make me, I'll do it, but God, please, don't make me." When I was sure God said, "I won't," I resumed my trip. Sitting in bed that night, looking over at my still sleeping wife, I knew why I wouldn't have to be the one to tell Amy she could no longer participate in this ministry she loved and fought to have the energy to continue. "God, please help me!" I pleaded, knowing that Amy's days were numbered.

When she woke up the next morning, she called her dad, who was already planning to come to camp and pick up Gabriel, as his job at camp was complete. She asked to borrow his scooter. When it arrived, Amy was mobile once again. She had figured out how she could have the energy to keep up with being the right hand of the camp director. When her strength began to wane, it was clear that she was pushing through it. Nothing was going to prevent her from completing the task she was at camp to do.

While I stood in the back of that chapel on those mornings, listening to the different stories and lessons on joy, God invaded my heart, intent on some industrial strength cleaning. On the last morning, I stood there and silently prayed, "God, she's all yours. I'm going to let you worry about her. I'm just going to love her." I felt an extreme weight lifted.

When I returned home, God led me to a devotional on joy. I began to devour it.

> What is joy after all? Is there a one-word definition that can begin to describe the intensity of this simple, miraculous word? I think not... but perhaps there is an infinite number of meanings found in the Word of God for this powerful word that makes all of the difference in a Christian's life!

Joy is the peace that passes understanding.
Joy is the crowd of witnesses that is cheering wildly for you!
Joy is the knowledge that nothing can separate you from the love of God.
Joy is walking on water! Just ask Peter!
Joy is turning water into wine and feeding thousands with the sack lunch of one generous little boy.
Joy is angels on a hillside over Bethlehem one starry night.
Joy is about the size of a mustard seed.[3]

It was with that mustard seed of faith I decided to accept God's joy. Amy saw a difference immediately. My boys, one by one, over the next three weeks stopped me and asked, in their own way, "Is everything okay, Dad? You're acting very different." I waited a month to tell any of my family what God had done in me in that hot, stuffy chapel, though I never told them about the conversation God and I had about it being Amy's last camp. I started with Amy. She was astounded; it had been such a long time since she had seen me full of joy. I only told the boys as they continued to point out, "You're different, Dad. What's happened?"

My favorite family picture
Taken from a time when life was joyful.
Picture courtesy of Leah O'Connor, LC Photography LLC

Almost three weeks after camp, Amy and I found ourselves in the surgeon's office. Her peritoneal dialysis port had stopped working. Upon further examination, it was deemed un-fixable. The port would have to be pulled, and a new one on the opposite side of the belly would have to be placed during the same procedure. While waiting for the new port to "heal," Amy would have to undergo hemodialysis. Very few times in our life together had I ever seen Amy so terrified. At one point, she was truly hysterical. Susan, her mother, had undergone hemodialysis, and for her, the treatment was "until death"—which happened a mere nine months later.

"What if they can't get me off the machine?"

*It will only be for two weeks, Amy. Your body will heal. I promise*, the surgeon said.

"I can't do this machine!"

*You can do all things through Christ who gives you strength*, I whispered into her ear later as I held her in my arms, lying next to her in the dark of our room.

"What happens if I can't be home for the boys when they really need me?"

*It's only for two weeks. I don't return to school for four weeks.*

"What happens...if..."

There were many more "What happens if..." questions. There were many late night "I can't do this" conversations. There were many opportunities for me to test God's gift. Each time we entered into one of Amy's terrified moments, I stood with her, at peace, silently praying for her, and holding onto the hand of my Savior. The joy never left me. Each time the terror screamed LOUDLY, I could still find the calm of peace and joy underneath it all.

One of my favorite Christian songs of all time— "Jesus Is," by the group Point of Grace –begins profoundly:

> *Speak a little softer*
> *So I can hear you*
> *Above the noise*
> *The noise*
> *The noise in this world*[4]

During each of Amy's floods of terror, I stood next to her, or held her hand, or wrapped my arms around her, and listened. Each time I reminded her that "God is bigger than this. He knows the outcome. He will walk through this with us." Although that might sound a little trite, it wasn't taken as trite. Each time, Amy would return to a peaceful state, breathing easier. "I love you," I would say, "and I'm not going anywhere." She would respond with, "I know. Thank you. I'm sorry this is so hard."

When the day came for the surgery, it was an odd one. We'd been through so many surgeries and hospital visits that it seemed like we were going through the motions. I prayed with Amy and sat with her until they took her into the operating room. She was more unsettled about this surgery than any prior surgery. There was a lot of listening, talking, and praying taking place centered around fear—Amy's fear.

The surgery took two and a half hours longer than what was expected. I kept fielding phone calls, texts, and e-mails from friends and loved ones, fraught with concern over the delayed results. When the surgeon paged me to discuss the results, my heart leapt while my breath stopped; the anticipation of the results was heavy. To make a long story short, Amy would have to begin hemodialysis in the hospital and wouldn't be released from the hospital until an "open chair" could be found at an insurance approved provider. She would end up staying five days in that hospital. Her frustration and fear were more palpable than anything else in the room. She had gone in for a day surgery, only to be kept for five.

"I don't want the boys to see me in here."

"I understand, honey, but it's been two days since they've seen you. Gabe's having a very difficult time, Micah's worried, and Isaiah's stayed in his room the entire time you've been gone."

Amy tried to put on a strong face, filled with peace and joy, while they visited, but she couldn't. The nurse came in while the boys were there to inform her that she would be staying through the weekend (the rest of the five days). Tears, hot, angry tears flew down her cheeks. I ushered the boys out of the room, prayed with her, and told her I'd be back after I took the boys home.

"No, don't come back. That will freak the boys out more," she finally said. "Besides, Lisa's coming to stay with me."

Lisa, Amy's sister, is an incredible woman. She practically raised Amy for the first nine years since their mother had to work outside the home. She stayed with Amy for a couple nights. On one of those nights, Amy told Lisa of four songs that she had been listening to lately, four songs that God put in front of her with which to wrestle. The conversation happened almost out of the blue. They were playing cards. When Lisa recounted the conversation to me later, it was clear to me that Amy knew her days were numbered. She knew she didn't have long for this earth.

At first glance, they are good songs, solid songs, three of which many churches sing during their Sunday morning worship. Upon further study however, there is a thread that runs through them, a thread that until it was pointed out to me much later, I did not see. The songs?

> "I Am Not Alone" by Kari Jobe
> "No Longer Slaves" by Bethel Music
> "10,000 Reasons (Bless the Lord)" by Matt Redman
> "Thy Will" by Hillary Scott

The Thread? No fear; God is mighty and in control. The second thread? God is with us. We do not need to go looking for him; He is with us.

Kari Jobe's "I Am Not Alone" begins with a powerful image:

> *When I walk through deep waters*
> *I know that You will be with me*
> *When I'm standing in the fire*
> *I will not be overcome*
> *Through the valley of the shadow*
> *I will not fear*
> *I am not alone...*
> *You will never leave me*[5]

This short excerpt from the song references three very significant stories from the Bible which not only show God's power, but also encourages believers to be without fear.

When Moses stood on the bank of the Red Sea, the Israelites all around him were clambering, showing their fear. With the sea before them, Pharaoh and his army were closing in on them from the other three sides and they had no place to flee. Quieting his spirit, Moses listened to the prompting of God. God said, "Do not be afraid. Stand firm and you will see the deliverance the LORD will bring you today...The LORD will fight for you; you need only to be still" (Exodus 14:13a & 14, NIV). A short time later, the entire nation of

Israel was walking "through deep waters" on dry land, exiting Egypt's grip altogether and entering God's deliverance.

Many, many years later, three Hebrew young men would defy the ruler of Neo-Babylon, Nebuchadnezzar. When "the sound of the horn, flute, zither, lyre, harp, pipe and all kinds of music" (Daniel 3:5, NIV) rang out, Shadrach, Meshach, and Abednego stood, unwavering in their faith. They stood resolute, knowing who they were and *Whose* they were. In answer to Nebuchadnezzar's questioning, they simply said, "If we are thrown into the blazing furnace, the God we serve is able to deliver us from it, and he will deliver us from Your Majesty's hand. But even if he does not, we want you to know, Your Majesty, that we will not serve your gods or worship the image of gold you have set up" (Daniel 3:17-18, NIV). When Nebuchadnezzar looked into the fiery furnace (which had been stoked seven times hotter than usual) and witnessed four young men walking about, he exclaimed, "Look! I see four men walking around in the fire, unbound and unharmed, and the fourth looks like a son of the gods" (Daniel 3:25, NIV).

During one of the darkest times of his life, King David wrote, "Even though I walk through the valley of the shadow of death, I will fear no evil, for you are with me; your rod and your staff, they comfort me" (Psalm 23:4, ESV).

Each of these three sections of Scripture teaches believers that God is able…no matter what, He is able! Our job is to take a solidarity stand in our faith and not hold onto fear. From Psalm 23, one can infer that God removes fear from the life of the believer *if we let Him*. We are simply supposed to "be still" and allow God to do the rest.

The song "No Longer Slaves" states simply the power God has to bring us peace and conquer fear.

> *You unravel me with a melody*
> *You surround me with a song*
> *Of deliverance from my enemies*
> *'Til all my fears are gone*[6]

Later in the song, the lyrics harken back to a familiar story.

> *You split the sea so I could walk right through it*
> *My fears are drowned in perfect love*
> *You rescued me so I could stand and sing*
> *I am a child of God*[7]

Once again, the image of deliverance through the Red Sea is used to show believers that God is Able!

I believe the other two songs, although tying into God's message to Amy, were meant to help carry and guide me through some pretty dark times. Redman's "10,000 Reasons (Bless the Lord)" calls the believer to focus on worship: Worship God for "His holy name," worship God for "the new day dawning," and worship God for "whatever may pass, and whatever lies before me."[8] The lyrics do not focus on only worshiping God for the good things in life; it purposely challenges us to worship God for everything that happens in the day. It goes so far as to claim that "when the evening comes," there will be breath and reason to sing—and not just to sing, but to "sing like never before." The song speaks of God's character—"You're rich in love and You're slow to anger; Your name is great, and Your heart is kind"—further encouraging the worshiper to see God for Who He is. Too often believers and un-believers alike blame God for the difficult, the uncomfortable, and the sorrow in their lives. God didn't invite evil into our world; in fact, He created a world without it. Man invited evil into the world. When we focus on Who God is, *truly is*, then it is so much easier to "be singing when the evening comes," even on days fraught with difficulty, awkwardness, and sorrow. Oddly enough, the final verse (or maybe it's called the bridge) speaks of death: "And on that day when my strength is failing, the end draws near and my time has come, still my soul will sing Your praise unending, ten thousand years and then forevermore."[9] It's a song of worship. It's a song of hope. And it's a song of joy. Fear cannot dwell amidst worship, hope, and joy. It just can't. Fear does not come from on High. Fear comes from the depths of Tartarus, the deepest pit in the bottom of Hell.

These three songs were encouraging Amy to let loose of fear and to embrace God. They were also sent to remind me to choose joy over worry, to choose faith over fear, and to choose worship over wallowing.

Not long before Amy's last hospitalization, I came home and it was clear Amy wanted to talk. "I have a song I'd like you to hear" was the gist of the conversation. I sat at the kitchen table as she played "Thy Will" by Hillary Scott. The story behind the song is one of heartbreak from the loss of a pregnancy, and Scott's performance is both haunting and timeless, especially since the song is crafted in a way to apply to severe pain of the heart of many kinds, not just the loss of a pregnancy. The song begins with an acknowledgement of a relationship with God and recounts a conversation in which "I heard you loud and clear," but the end is not what was expected in the slightest. Just seconds into the song, my breath stopped and tears began to fall off the end of my nose and chin. Scott had written about my pain. It was almost as if Hillary Scott had been reading my correspondence to the Throne of Heaven.

> *I don't wanna think*
> *I may never understand*
> *That my broken heart is a part of your plan*
> *When I try to pray*
> *All I got is hurt and these four words*
>
> *Thy will be done*
>
> *I know you're good*
> *But this don't feel good right now*[10]

It was on that day, after summer camp, amongst the search for joy, that I found myself praying the words of my Savior: "Not my will, [God,] but yours be done" (Luke 22:42b ESV).

When Amy was finally allowed to leave the hospital, she had to go to a dialysis facility every other day at 2:00 a.m. for her 7-hour treatment. She was nervous at first, but after the third day, she had more energy than she'd had in the entire year prior. Instead of Amy sitting in the recliner with the television going while she faded in and out of sleep, she was on her feet, cooking meals, going out of the house, and playing games with the boys and me. Amy was laughing, and dreaming, and talking about the future again.

In June we had to make the difficult decision to move our youngest out of the Christian school he attended and place him in public school. We did our homework and found an option school that would be perfect for our little genius. He had been testing at post high school levels in all subjects while in the fourth grade, and he now needed to be challenged in many more than the Christian school could provide. A week before school was to start, Amy received the phone call that Isaiah's name was chosen out of the lottery system to take the final seat in the seventh grade class. Amy was thrilled. We celebrated by splurging on Isaiah's favorite foods for dinner that night, complete with ice cream, chocolate sauce, and spray whipped cream for dessert.

During her dialysis center stint, I received a phone call asking if I was available for a one-month subbing job at the beginning of school. The previous year I taught four months at the school, covering a family leave. I fell in love with the school. I jumped at the chance. On Labor Day, one week into my school year, I received a text from the teacher for whom I was subbing. She had just arrived home after her second stroke and she would need me to sub at least until Christmas. Sad for my friend, but excited that I would be receiving contract pay instead of substitute pay, I called my wife while in transit home. We made plans to meet at a bowling alley and then to get ice cream on the way home to celebrate God's provision. Amy was so very excited. Her prayers—her huge, big, only-God-can-answer prayers— were answered: 1) she was able to have fun with her boys the way she used to, 2) Isaiah had been accepted into a school that would challenge him academically, and 3) I had a teaching contract. On top of that, Amy had received a call three days prior which ended with her being officially placed on the transplant list for a kidney. We were truly experiencing joy.

Halfway through the first game of bowling, Amy began to get dizzy and nauseous. She encouraged the boys and I to finish the game. She laid down on the bench and cheered for us. She was asleep two frames into the second game (which had already been paid for and she didn't want to waste). We quickly finished the game, I borrowed an office chair on wheels from the establishment, and I wheeled her out to the van. We did not stop for ice cream on the way home. When we arrived home, Amy made it into the front room and curled up on the sofa. Two hours later, my oldest and I helped her up the stairs to bed. We had witnessed many nights like this since Amy's diagnosis. It was par for the course. I tucked her in bed, asked if she needed anything, and kissed her good night. Then I went downstairs to spend the evening with my boys. Every two hours after helping Amy up the stairs, I went in to check on her and to see if she needed anything. It was the pattern that we had learned worked through these nights of illness. And since my getting in and out of the bed would jostle the bed and cause Amy to be even more nauseous, I often slept on the couch or in the recliner downstairs. When I woke to my alarm at 1:00 a.m. to check on Amy, she was soundly sleeping. I walked over to her side of the bed and removed the wet wash cloth I had given her earlier in the night. The motion woke her.

"Do you need anything, honey?"

"No. I think I'm past the nausea now," she haltingly whispered.

"Did you remember to pay the rent?"

"Yes, I paid it this morning," she murmured dreamily.

"I love you. Do you want me to wake you in the morning before I go to work?"

"No, the boys will wake me when they get up."

"Okay." I bent down and kissed her on the forehead. "I love you, honey."

"I love you, too," she slurred, and then she was back asleep. I returned downstairs to catch a few more winks before I had to start my second week of teaching.

CHAPTER 10

# The Darkness

There's that moment when everything around you is more real than anything has ever been real. It's that moment when your ears pick up the slightest brushing noise from the fibers of the carpet across which you walk. It's that moment when your eyes see six or seven different hues of red and purple and yellow, all at the same time. It's that moment when the stillness is so palpable you'd swear you were swimming through silence… and drowning.

It was 5:46 a.m. The alarm on my phone had been going off for over a minute. It was the first day of the second week of school—a Tuesday, the day after Labor Day. I was a bit disoriented, having slept in the recliner downstairs. I'd struggled to find the obnoxious chirping emanating from the misplaced smart phone, which took about a minute. I'd left the phone on the kitchen table. Connecting with it, I flipped it over, ended the silence-murdering noise, and placed the phone where it should have been…on the counter, next to the charging station.

I stood up straight.

That's when the moment hit me. I was awake, more than awake. My heart tuned in to the beckoning of the Holy Spirit, shutting off my typical intellectual "run through the day."

Looking back, I recognize the whisper. On that morning, I'm not quite sure my heart heard the words that now echo in my soul: "I'm with you, Son." A prickle fled down my spine and stole away into the floor. It was an electrifying message. Immediately I knew what I would find when I crested the stairs and entered my bedroom.

I took the stairs at a run. Bursting into the room, my heart skipped a beat. The bed was empty. My beautiful bride was not asleep in it. I slowly turned toward the master bathroom. Door ajar. Silence screaming. I pushed the door gently, knowing what I would find. Body slumped, sandwiched in the space between the commode and the wall. Fingers dark blue to purple. Eyes closed. Face at peace. Head tilted and resting on the wall.

For a second, which felt like an eternity, I stood, trying to let my eyes notify my brain of what my soul had already informed my heart.

The world stopped. "'Til death do us part" had come much sooner than my life plans allowed.

Without warning, silence, louder than a racetrack, slammed against me, waking me from a stupor. It was so eerily loud.

"Amy!" I reached for her left hand with mine. "Amy!" Grabbing her shoulder with my right hand, I shook her. No response. Letting go, I bolted from the room and plummeted through the door of my oldest son's bedroom. Frantic. Trying to find his phone.

"Micah! I NEED YOUR PHONE!"

"Whaaah...," slurred my sleeping giant.

"I NEED your phone! NOW!"

He shot to a seated position. "Here," he mumbled, reaching for the phone, plugged in next to his pillow.

"I need your help. Get up!" I dashed out of his room, dialing 911 in the 3 or 4 bounds it took to reach my wife's final resting place.

"911...What's your emergency?"

That's a job I don't think I could ever handle. I realize that a significant amount of training and counseling happen with those fearless men and women who answer that phone, not knowing what they will encounter screaming at them.

"My wife's dead!" I shouted into the receiver. "She's dead!"

"Sir, is she in a bed?"

"No, she's stuck in the space between the toilet and the wall." (Forgive me, Amy. I know that you wouldn't have wanted the world to know this, but it's important that people understand what happened, especially since your passing so mirrored your mom's.)

"Can you get her to the floor so that you can perform CPR?"

"Not by myself. But I can get my son! Just a minute..." and I dashed back out of the room and down the hall, colliding with Micah's door. His room was still dark. He'd settled back down on the pillow.

"Dad," he mumbled, "is everything alright?"

There was another moment that settled on me. My fleshly panic, my husbandly concern, stopped. I swallowed slowly. My "Dad brain" engaged. *How can I prepare my oldest son for what I need him to do?* I silently prayed. Micah must have realized the brain stutter. He sat back up in bed, swung his legs out of the covers, and abruptly stood.

"Micah, I need your help. Mom needs CPR. She needs to be on the floor and I can't move her myself." I turned and fled.

Lights flooded his eyes and Micah was a breath behind me. I pulled to a full stop just before entering the master bath. I know it may sound like I was wasting time, but I knew she was already gone, and I couldn't let my son enter the room without a bit more warning.

"Honey," I turned, peering into his terror filled eyes, "Mom's fallen between the toilet and the wall. We need to move her to the floor so I can do CPR. Your phone's on the counter and the 911 operator is going to walk me through what I need to do. After we move Mom, I need you to go find my phone—it's downstairs on the counter—and call your aunt. Okay?" He nodded. I could tell my rushed and slightly loud directions hadn't completely dawned on my son.

I turned back to the door and entered the room, not stopping. I reached under Amy's left shoulder while Micah reached under her right. Within seconds my bride was lying on the floor, Micah was fleeing down the staircase, and I was alone with the operator's voice on speaker. I'd taken countless CPR/First Aid classes over the years, but I was relying on the faceless voice in charge.

"You don't need to breathe for your wife. The paramedics are less than two minutes from you. I only need you to perform the chest compressions. I'm going to count. Each time I say a number, you need to press down firmly and quickly. You will be acting as your wife's heart. Can you do this?"

Oddly, this is when my brain stopped. I was a machine. I remember compressions and breaking ribs. I remember yelling down for Micah to unlock the front door. I remember the speakerphone droning through numbers. And then there were many EMT's flooding up the stairs.

I stood and stepped out of the way.

"Her fingers were purple when I found her," I stammered. The EMT just nodded. "Can I go to my son?" He nodded again. My feet wouldn't carry me as fast as my father's heart wanted. I stumbled twice down the stairs. My Dad's heart was pulling me down the stairs; my vows were pulling me back to the top. I had left a piece of me on the floor in that room.

Micah had fled to the kitchen and was just ending the phone call with his aunt. I barely heard the EMT's announce the time of death over my left shoulder.

"She's getting Dale and getting dressed. She'll be here as soon as she can," Micah said. His voice was quavering. He knew what I was about to tell him.

I just looked at him. There isn't a training manual for telling your son that his mother is dead.

"Dad?" It was both a question and a plea. "Dad?" this time with a tremor.

"I'm sorry, honey. She's gone."

He started bouncing on the balls of his feet. His breath flew inward and halted behind his teeth. His head wagged back and forth, quickly at first, but slowing with each swing.

I stepped the last foot between us and caught him in my arms.

"No!" He was my little boy again, holding onto me through the pain. His voice seemed much younger than his full seventeen years.

"I'm sorry." I didn't know what else to say. I was sorry that his mother was no longer with us. I was sorry that I needed his help. I was sorry that he had to see his mom in the state she was in, trapped between the toilet and the wall, dressed for bed, not for kids. I was sorry that he was stuck with me as a single parent. I was sorry for a lot of things.

There was a flurry of activity in and out of my house. One gentleman approached the two of us after a spell.

"Sir, I'm a chaplain for the Beaverton City Police Department. Can I talk with you for a moment?" I followed him to the living room. "I'm not sure of your belief system, but chaplains often go out with the police in situations like this to help the family." I nodded.

"I know," I managed. And then, after a pregnant pause, "I'm a licensed pastor myself. I'm not pastoring right now, but I know how it all works."

"I don't want to offend; I'm here to help however I can. Usually I stay with the family and pray with them if they wish and help them understand what the police and EMT's are doing. Would it be okay if I stayed to help?"

"We attend Beaverton Foursquare Church. I need to call my pastor."

"Would you like me to call him for you?" I shook my head. "I don't want to be in the way. I'll be here until your pastor arrives. Is that okay?" I nodded. "Do you know his number?" I nodded and then retired to the kitchen to retrieve my phone.

After a few rings, "Hello." He didn't sound asleep, but neither did he sound completely awake.

"Todd, it's Thom. I'm sorry to call, but..." The words stumbled in my mouth. I couldn't breathe. This was real.

"Thom, is everything okay?"

"Todd...Amy's...dead. I...found her...this morning. Can you come over?" In that moment, I felt guilty for asking for help. I had probably just awoken our Children's Pastor, starting his day on a horrible note, and I was daring to ask him to come to the house before 7:00 a.m. Who was I? He's a busy man! What was I doing?

"What?" There was a pause on the phone. "Thom..."

"Todd, the EMT's and police are here. Amy's dead. Can you please come over?"

And just like that, Todd was fully awake. "I'm on my way, Thom. I'll be right there."

"My pastor's coming," I managed to tell the chaplain after I hung up the phone.

There is a flurry of memories, of which I know not the order, that flood into recollection. Sometime before Todd arrived, I completed a number of tasks.

> I ascended the stairs, asked for a minute with my wife, and covered her with a clean, new, tan waffle-weave blanket. I knelt down next to her and whispered, "I love you and I'm glad you're no longer in pain...you're no longer sick. I don't know how I'm going to finish

raising these three boys without you, but I'll try not to let you down."

I called my mother-in-law, Amy's step-mom, to ask her to give my father-in-law the news. I couldn't bring myself to tell him.

I called my sister-in-law to see if she was on her way and we both broke down sobbing on the phone.

I talked with Micah again and encouraged him to go up and "say goodbye."

I talked with the head EMT and then the chaplain (at least twice) and then the lead officer, overwhelmed that the police were at my house and all the cars were choking our tiny, narrow, neighborhood street.

I'm not sure when my family arrived. Nor do I remember who came first. But all of a sudden, there I was, in my living room, standing next to my sister-in-law and her husband, with my father-in-law seated in a stuffed chair, his wife standing next to him, my oldest son standing behind me, and Todd.

I remember vividly looking directly at Todd and uttering the most ridiculous request: "Todd, can you stay here with my boys? I've got to go to work and set up for a substitute." My emergency sub-folder was due at the end of the second week of school. I had intended to complete the folder later that afternoon since I couldn't get it completed during the whirlwind of a first week. "My classroom is set up to do a project that a sub can't step in to do and I'm going to need a few hours to figure out what to have a sub do."

Todd simply looked at me and calmly replied, "No. You're not leaving. Your boys are going to need you here. Do you have your principal's phone number?" It was only around 7:30 a.m.

"It's in my cell, but he'll be driving to work. He has a long commute."

"Let me call your principal. What's his name?"

"Kevin," I stammered. Then looking at Micah I added, "My phone's on the counter in the kitchen." Todd took my phone outside and called Kevin. When Todd returned, with our senior pastor who'd just arrived, he said, "Kevin wants you to call him in a couple of days. He said not to worry. He's got it covered."

But I was very worried. I was worried about losing the temporary assignment I'd just been given at the school. I was worried about money, which Amy usually handled. The epiphany that I now was in charge of paying the bills landed on me, crushing my ability to think (although, it was quite apparent that I was already impeded and unable to think rationally at that point).

Then I realized Randy, my senior pastor, was standing in front of me. I was dumbstruck. Again, I felt guilty. When you attend a church the size of Beaverton Foursquare Church—of which my wife had attended for thirty-seven years (since she was five years old) and had been a part of the volunteer team in children's ministry for thirty-two years—you don't expect the senior pastor to make house calls. Don't get me wrong…we've had a personal relationship with our senior pastor for quite a while. He was my oldest son's basketball coach in middle school for three years. Amy had known him from when she was a kid at camp and he was part of the camp staff. Randy and his family had eaten dinner at our house. We knew him. But that still didn't stifle the feeling of guilt. Who were we to take up his time? There were so many things on his plate.

Randy asked some questions and began to shepherd us through this dark day. The feeling of imposing on this man of God's time left—or rather, it wasn't as strong as it had been initially. I simply remember my ears finally turning back on and Randy was saying something to the family…to me as well. I shook my head and came back to reality.

"Can I get you anything?" I remember asking. It's what Amy would have done. God had given her the gift of hospitality like none other. Had she been catering the wedding feast in Cana, Jesus' first miracle wouldn't have been turning water into wine because the wedding hosts had planned poorly and had run out of wine. Amy took care of everything, usually before people realized it was needed. That hallmark of our ministry together now rested on my shoulders. "I have water and milk. I could make tea or coffee." No one took me up on the offer.

Many things were said. Decisions were made regarding a mortuary. Lisa, Dale, and Amy's dad had all gone up the stairs to say goodbye. The police and EMT's filed out of the house to un-clog the street so our neighbors could take their children to school.

I found myself standing there in another moment of silence. I could see the lips of those I loved moving, but again I heard nothing. I kept slipping in and out of the tangible silence; the silence was cold and howling—as if I were standing on a mountain top in a gale.

In the center of the silence, I heard, *I'm still here, Son.* The cold began to ebb. For a brief eternity, I felt almost as if I were being held.

*Daddy,* a term that I've used for Abba Father before, *I don't know how to do this alone.*

*You won't be alone. You can't be alone. I haven't left.*

My confession was about raising three boys alone, but somehow I understood that God was giving me an answer to so much more than my terrified confession. He was reminding me of his covenant with Abraham, Isaac, Jacob, David, and many more who have gone before me. The conversation was very short. I heard it just as if I was standing face to face with my Maker in conversation. No one else was privy to that short conversation.

In an instant, the noise in the room flooded back in, my father's heart switched on, and I said, "How do we tell the little boys?" Gabriel and Isaiah were still asleep—aided, I'm sure by the Holy Spirit and a few soundproofing angles—but I knew they'd be up any minute. The eight of us stood there and made a plan. I talked with the mortician, who'd arrived by this time, and informed him of our desires. Then, everyone who my boys wouldn't know disappeared, either by going outside or stepping into the master bedroom, behind closed doors.

Within a few minutes, my youngest two boys sleepily descended the stairs. I was sitting in the middle of the living room couch and I beckoned the boys to sit on either side of me. I put my arms around them and pulled them closer. They were nervous, looking around at the family members and pastors surrounding them.

"Boys," I began, just above a whisper, "I have some bad news." My face scrunched up, trying to contain the tears behind the dam and keep the sobs from climbing my throat. I took a deep breath. "Mama went to be with Jesus last night while we slept." Gabriel shook his head slowly back and forth trying to understand what I was saying. (Sometimes I forget that autism doesn't understand figurative language.) Isaiah burst into tears.

"She's dead?" he blurted, burying his head into my chest. And then a little quieter and muffled, "Mom died?"

"Yes, honey." Realization struck my middle son, and there I was, the middle of a tumultuous sandwich of emotion, as both boys squeezed and sobbed and cried.

Then, without warning, Gabriel sat up and said, in a slightly quivering voice, "Well, we were five. Now we're four...until Dad remarries." That broke the tension in the room. There are times when I am completely confounded by the way Gabe's mind works. There were a few giggles. I was mortified, looking between my father-in-law and Amy's sister. Then it hit me.

"Gus," my nickname for Gabriel, "Daddy's not going to remarry," I managed through a grin. A few years after Gabe's grandmother had died, Gary remarried. It took us a few years to help Gabriel understand just what role Mary would play in our family. "I can't call her Grammy, because she's not Grammy," he'd said one morning over breakfast. "She's not replacing Grammy," we had told him. "God's just given Papa a new wife to love and to be with him. Papa doesn't have to be lonely anymore." Gabe started calling his new grandmother Grandma Mary so that there wasn't any confusion in his mind. To him, he'd recognized a pattern and knew what the next step in that pattern was. It was a black and white issue. (Oh how I wish things could be as simple as he sometimes understands them to be.)

After a few minutes, Pastor Randy took charge. "Boys, they're going to bring your mama downstairs in a minute so that you can say goodbye. I thought it would be appropriate to read some scripture and sing a worship song or two, like your mom loved to do. Did she have a favorite verse or worship song?"

When the men from the mortuary had finished bringing Amy down the stairs on the rolling gurney, she was covered with a quilt atop the waffle-weave blanket she had been wrapped in earlier. Randy read scripture. We sang two songs. And then we prayed. At that moment, I didn't know that I could feel any greater pain. More, yes, but not greater.

As each family member leaned over to say goodbye, some touching Amy's cheek, others a shoulder, Gabriel nearly climbed on top of his mom, supporting himself with only one toe, wailing. I had never before experienced wailing. Yelling, yes. Screaming, yes. But I had never experienced a broken soul wailing, crying out because there are no words to explain the pain, loss, anger, and loneliness. A simple, yet wholly profound realization reintroduced itself to me: Amy was Gabe's world. I used to joke that I didn't make his top ten list of favorite people. Gabe and I had just come through a hard couple of years as Gabriel understood what it meant to become a young man, still under his parent's roof. At one time he had decided that he was the Alpha Male; it was his duty to take care of his mother. In that moment, I was no longer necessary. He'd said as much. Fear crept into my peripheral vision. 'I will never be his favorite person,' I thought. The room began to slowly spin, picking up speed as Gabriel punctuated each inarticulate wail.

I looked to Todd, Gabe's childhood pastor, one of Gabe's favorite people. He was praying silently, heart breaking. I was looking for comfort and help, but Todd was not looking at me. That's when I realized, it wasn't about me. The next few days, weeks, months and years would be about my boys and how they would walk on in their faith and service, without their mom. It no longer mattered to me that I wasn't in Gabe's top ten; there could no longer be a divide between him and me. I stepped closer to him, put my hand in the middle of his back, and stood with him while he wailed. Standing there, allowing a boy to grieve over the loss of his mother in the way he needed to grieve was more painful than any experience I have ever had. There would be two more of those painful moments when my other two sons hit the proverbial wall and grieved—rather wailed—for the same loss. Unfortunately, it was not in that corporate setting and it took a little time for one, a few months for the other.

Gabriel finally stopped wailing, kissed his mommy one last time on the forehead, and then turned and clung to me, tears streaming onto my shoulder. Moments later, the gurney was removed and the silence roared once again.

# CHAPTER 11

# The Telling

"Temple," my voice was quaking, "Temple...do you have a minute to talk?" Temple had been Amy's best friend since they were five years old, growing up in church together. I was trembling, trying to hold the phone steady.

"Yes, Thom. What's up?"

"Are you sitting down?"

"Just a sec, I'm just getting out of a meeting and walking into my office. Is everything okay?"

I heard the door close to Temple's office.

"Temple...," I started shaking. Tears started rolling. "Temple...Amy's not sick anymore...she's in Heaven."

The line was quiet for a mini-eternity.

"What?"

"When I woke up this morning, Temple, I found Amy. She's dead."

The sobs were quick, loud, yet somewhat stifled. The conversation ensued. I explained what had happened, filled her in about the status of each of my boys, apologized, and then disconnected the line. I looked at the list. I had many people I needed to call personally before the news broke on Facebook. It was a race I would end up losing.

I knew my best friend was at work, and since he worked in a somewhat technical job, I didn't want to bother him. Selfishly, I wanted to be able to talk with him for as long as I needed, not just a five minute "guess what" conversation. I made a note to call him after work hours.

I called my grandmother and then my aunt. Both of those calls were difficult. My grandmother had lost her only daughter (who was more of a sister to me than an aunt) just six years prior, and the wounds had just begun to heal.

I called one of my closest friends from college with whom Amy and I had recently had the luxury of spending an afternoon. The conversation was similar to that with Temple. Over and over, call after call, the news was received with shock. There was always a pause of unbelief, and then tears. I was able to make only about ten calls before I was exhausted and the news was already trending on social media. One friend of ours, who'd known Amy since long before I was in the picture, is a fellow teacher. I had wanted to make sure I called her and was the one to give her the news myself, but, because I waited until school was out, I was not the harbinger of bad news. Rather, I was the receiver of blessing, kindness, and grief.

Natalene (Nate to her friends) knew immediately why I was calling. She answered the phone and began to ask me what she and her group of friends could do. "I don't know," was all I could answer. I was being truthful. I really didn't know what help I would need, what things needed done, or really how to move through the next few hours, days, weeks, and months. Each minute seemed like an ETERNITY. That day and night was the longest twenty-four hours I have ever endured. I didn't live through it. Living requires feeling. Living requires relationship. Living requires many things. After Amy left the house on the gurney, I was numb. Completely numb. I lost track of time, I lost track of what needed to be done, and I lost track of my kids…literally.

Not long after Todd and Randy left my house, two youth pastors showed up to minister to my boys. The senior high youth pastor took Micah to lunch. The junior high youth pastor brought his assistant with him. Both of these men have an incredible connection to my younger two boys. Both of them understand autism better than I realized. Both of them cared for Gabriel and Isaiah in the ways they needed. They took my younger boys so I could go to the mortuary and make decisions I had talked with Amy about fifteen years prior. Decisions I didn't know had to be made. Decisions about Amy's earthly husk which was with us, while she was in Heaven, healthy, happy, and whole.

Just before leaving the house to meet my father-in-law and his wife at the mortuary, I was alone in the house with Amy's sister and brother-in-law.

Still numb, I made a snap decision that at the time surprised both me and my in-laws. I opened the cabinet above the fridge (the one that is almost never opened) and retrieved the bottles of wine and spirits we'd been given over the years as house warming presents or thank you gifts. I put them in a bag and handed them to Dale and Lisa.

Amy and I didn't really drink much (one glass of champagne each New Years and maybe another drink once every two years). Both sides of my family have significant alcoholism and I've never wanted to know what it was like to be an alcoholic. But in that moment, I had a bit of clarity. The fog lifted briefly.

"Please take these out of the house with you, and don't bring them back."

"Why?"

"I don't want my boys to know that alcohol can numb the pain, and I don't want to fall into that trap either." Conversation finished. No debate. Dale understood completely and the bag went immediately out the door to his car. Then the fog resettled. The silence loudly invaded my thoughts. Numb was my only feeling. By this time, I'd stopped crying, partly because I was in shock, partly because my tear ducts were spent, partly because I knew Amy was just upstairs in bed, asleep, and she'd be down in a little bit, just like every other day. Then I would remember that she left on a gurney and wouldn't be returning. Looking back, I am astounded the lengths our brains can go to help us deal with a traumatic event, even to the point of letting us live in denial if even for a brief moment.

After returning from the mortuary, I was alone in the house. Totally alone. It was then that I made the phone calls I've already written about at the beginning of this chapter. I sat atop the stairs in full view of the front door, just outside the closed master bedroom door, calling family and friends to give them news that they were not expecting. Just four days earlier, Amy had completed all the requirements to be on the national kidney donor list. She had an appointment the day after she passed away with the head nurse who coordinated the kidney transplant team at the university hospital here in Portland. That was not a fun call to make either. I was very happy I'd reached the nurse's voicemail. One less person to talk to. One less set of questions to answer. One less painful moment of awkward what-do-I-say-to-Thom silences.

My boys returned home late that afternoon, weary, but not distraught. Just before they came through the door, I received a text from another one of our pastors who is also a very close, personal friend. He and his wonderful wife knew that although I am a decent cook, food was the last thing on my mind. He was on his way with pizza and soda. As it was, I had eaten very little for breakfast and even less for lunch. My brain was no longer connected to the pangs of hunger; the numbness had severed the connection.

Shortly before my friend arrived with food, one of Micah's best friends showed up at the door, politely asking if he could "abduct Micah" (his words, not mine). Micah and his friends had already made plans the prior week to get together on this, the last night before school started. Without Micah's input, the friend group decided they still needed to get together, but for an altogether different reason. They whisked him away to the parking lot of our church where they stood talking, listening and ministering to my gentle giant, the one who is usually trying to take care of everyone else. Food showed up at this event, although I don't remember how, and at one point the boys played some form of game in the parking lot. Micah was returned many hours later, exhausted, wrung out as if he'd cried his last tear, seemingly at peace.

I didn't realize how hungry I was until my pastor friend, Jeremy, arrived. We ate. The younger two boys played with the Wii. My friend and I sat at the dinner table for what could have been twenty minutes or two hours, I can't recall. We talked some. We sat in silence. We even cried together. When I realized that it was now late enough for my best friend to have arrived home from work, I excused myself, alighted the stairs, and took up my perch at the top, steeling myself for a brutal phone call. Jeremy stayed with my boys, talking, playing, hugging, whatever they needed, while I made the call.

"Travis..." I couldn't say anything else. I remember trying to speak more, but the only thing escaping my mouth was silence. Travis's and my schedules were so packed (both of us have three kids) that I often got his voice mail and we'd play phone tag for a day or two. This call, however, did not go that way. Travis had actually picked up the line.

"Hi, Thom..." I couldn't answer. "What's wrong?"

It was at that moment, that precise moment, when the numb wore off and all of the feeling I should have endured through the day came at me as if I were drinking from a fire hose.

"Thom...?"

There was another pause. Then I finally managed, "Travis...Amy's dead..."

There was silence on the phone.

"I...I...found her...this morning when I woke up..."

More silence.

Then something in me snapped. The numb returned like a heavy woolen blanket that is meant to choke out the cold during the dead of winter.

"I'm sorry I didn't call earlier." Even I could hear the *pleasantry* voice that people give when answering 'How are you doing?' in passing, after church, creeping into this conversation. "I didn't want to bother you at work."

Now, there have been a few odd phone conversations between Travis and I over the years, usually because I was a dolt and needed to ask forgiveness for something stupid I had done or said. Mind you, they weren't often, but when they did happen, I usually needed to be reminded God was in charge, I was loved, and Travis wasn't going to run away screaming because of me. God handpicked Travis and me, out of two very different worlds, with a few odd likenesses (but mostly differences) and birthed a friendship that has stood the test of time.

When I began writing this chapter, thinking about this phone conversation specifically, I wondered, *What was I thinking? Why was I apologizing?* Then it hit me. The simple realization that I've spent the majority of my life trying to make people happy thumped me in the middle of my forehead. There I was, trying to be pleasant, trying to not offend, trying to not intrude in Travis's busy life, in order to not push away my best friend! (Trust me, people, God has had to do MAJOR work on this redeemed sinner. I'm thankful He never gave up on me and I'm very thankful Travis hasn't either.)

I don't remember exactly what Travis said in response to my apology at that precise moment, but whatever it was it ripped the woolen blanket of numb off me for the rest of the conversation.

"What do you need? I can be on the next plane."

"Travis, I don't want you to drop everything and come up right now. You and Jenny have three kids. You have a demanding job. Right now, I just need to know that I can call you when I need to talk, and I need you to come up for the funeral."

"I'll be there. You know that. Whatever you need…"

We talked for over half an hour. I cried. He cried. Then I remembered my kids downstairs with Jeremy.

"I gotta go and try to be a dad," I remember saying weakly.

"I'm praying for you. Call me whenever. I mean it."

The rest of that evening is a blur. That is until I found myself sitting in front of my computer, staring at Facebook, contemplating what to say. The news had already broken; a very good friend named Tracey simply said she would miss Amy. Since that post, my phone had been ringing off the hook. I didn't answer many of those calls. The guilt was getting to me so I sat in front of the blue and white screen that begged me for an update.

It took me only a few moments to find my favorite recent picture of my beautiful bride, taken at a friend's birthday party a few months before the signs of kidney failure began yellowing her delicate skin.

I posted the picture with the simple statement, "Goodbye, my sweet." Then I turned off the computer and went to bed. Little did I know that God was using that little goodbye as the catalyst for healing and ministry that lasted nearly three years. When I woke in the morning, there were many comments to my post.

> It's unimaginable what you are all going through right now. Such a tremendous loss. I cannot find the words. Really, no words are enough, but please know we are here if you or the boys should need anything. We adore your family and will continue praying for peace and guidance. Please don't hesitate to reach out…Your sweet wife touched so many lives. She will be missed.[11]

> Thom, I am so, so devastated to hear about Amy. She was wise and godly and witty and a feisty force to be reckoned with. We love you and your boys and hurt with you. Praying His perfect peace and comfort.[12]

I've cried more in the last year than I thought humanly possible. I've also laughed, loved, and pondered much. At one point, I even told God He had "some 'splaining to do!" (That must have been hilarious from His perspective, as if I were a precocious 3-year-old telling Daddy "how things will work from here on out.")

Through this entire process, I have begun to understand parenting at an altogether deeper level. Our Heavenly Father wanted the best for us. He worked hard to give us His very best. We allowed sin to rob us of immortality and relationship with God in the Garden. We allowed sin to destroy our families. We allowed sin to bring sickness and death into a perfect world. Many people get angry at God for letting "bad things happen to good people," but I don't think it's that simple at all. My children have broken my heart over the years. Did I ever stop loving them? No. Did I ever run from them in horror? No. Did I impugn the love they professed after my heart was smashed? No. I came to them—or sometimes they came running to me—and I picked them up, told them the same thing that I've said for years: "I love you, and nothing you say or do in this life will change that. I will ALWAYS love you." God is no different as a Father, albeit, He's much better at it than I. He picks us up when we break His heart or when our hearts are broken. He holds us tightly and lets us cry on his shoulder. He plays with our hair while we sit in His lap. Why? Because He's Abba. Abba in the Hebrew tongue means *daddy*. Genesis 1 says we were created in His image. He authored the love a parent feels into our hearts, modeling it after His own. There are times when I have been furious with Abba. He gently (and sometimes not so gently) lets me know what He's doing, accepts my apology, and then says, "Nothing you say or do will ever stop Me from loving you."

CHAPTER 12

# The Numb

30 hours as a single dad and widower. 30 hours—mostly numb. We are doing okay, some minutes better than expected, others about as worse as one could imagine. Thank you to all who've left messages on my, Amy's and Micah's walls. We may not have responded to them all—he and I—but we've tried to at least "like" them. Those we haven't yet read, we promise we will read them. There just comes a point when the eyes water over so much that it's impossible to see and the heart is so overwhelmed with the kindness, generosity, and memories that it's nearly impossible to find words. Thank you all for your prayers while we find a new normal in the Johnson home.[13]

Trying to figure out how to navigate a world I had once "mastered" was unreal. Many days I sat, robed in numbness, vision and voice vacant. The Army of Help (as one of our pastor's wives had called the *servant hearts* at our church) had been given their marching orders. The moment this pastor's wife heard about Amy's death, she started a "Meal Train" account[14] for my boys and me. Less than a year before, her mother had passed away suddenly and she *knew* what we would need, even though I didn't know. Food began coming every other night. Someone else was taking Amy's and my place of servanthood at our church. It was awkward at first to be receiving when I was so used to be the one serving.

I was so glad that food only came every other day. Most people brought enough food to feed us for two or sometimes three meals. Some even came with snacks, baked goodies, and treats unique to each of us. Many asked for pardon as they were "not a baker like Amy" or "not as good of a cook as Amy." No pardon was needed. The food filled a need and it was delicious.

Sadly, I am allergic to many foods, so cooking for my family was not an easy endeavor. I can't have citrus of any kind, nor seafood, nor tomatoes. There are others, but these are the ones that make it challenging...very challenging to cook for us. The Army of servants from our church did not bat an eye. There were a few meals that I could not eat, but in three months, a few is nearly a miracle. Sometimes food would show up labeled "For Thom only." I would open it to find a meal that I could eat while my boys ate spaghetti, lasagna, pizza, lemon chicken, or something else that was off limits for my allergies. The food kept coming. By the end of the three and a half months, I had almost forgotten how to cook or plan a meal.

Besides food, people showed up with other kinds of help that blessed us tremendously. When my car broke down and the van had a flat tire (on the same day only a week after Amy had passed), God sent two different angels in disguise to help. One took the car to get fixed, while the other helped to fix the flat tire. When both returned, there were faith bolstering stories as God had met them while at the car repair places. The car came back with over $500 of repairs, of which I only had to pay half, and the van came back with a new tire free of charge since the one that went flat was under warranty. One friend sent over her house cleaner to give me time to focus on the details before the memorial service. My house hadn't been that clean since before Amy's sickness. I can't even begin to make a dent in relating all the help we received. It was overwhelming...appreciated greatly, but overwhelming in that I've-got-you-in-the-center-of-my-hand kind of way that only God can orchestrate.

Wednesday evening, only one day after Amy had passed, a few of Isaiah's very close friends from his former school met us at a nearby Red Robin restaurant. One of the moms helped call the other parents. He needed some time away from the house and the pain. Micah was out with a few friends and

Gabriel was with his aunt and uncle. The parents of his friends sat at a table with me while Isaiah and his friends sat together at a booth in the corner. I had called the restaurant in advance to inform the manager of the reason for our impending visit. We were given an incredible waitress who waited on us with great care. Isaiah's friends asked questions, listened, and spent time with him. When he was done talking, they made jokes with each other and enjoyed the rest of the evening. It was nice to hear Isaiah laugh with his friends.

After arriving home, I came to the realization there were some people I hadn't yet talked with whom I could no longer avoid: my life group, especially my leaders who had become so much an integral part of Amy's and my life, as well as our boys' lives, over the past three years. I knew they would all come around us to bolster our faith, listen to our rent hearts, and hold us while we wept.

When I texted our life group leaders, asking for an "hour coffee date" Thursday evening because I needed a favor. The reply was immediate. We planned for me to go to Bob and Susie's home—the meeting place of our life group—mostly because a public restaurant would be too public, and my boys were at my house and they needed to be shielded from their father completely losing his wits. Don't get me wrong, my boys have seen me cry, many times, and they will continue to see me cry as life progresses. But on that day, just two and a half days after Amy had passed, I was going to grieve in ways they would not, nor could not understand. The weight of that was something I could not put upon them. I would also be faced with questions they didn't have the wherewithal to endure, not yet.

When I arrived Thursday night, Bob met me at the door, Susie was in the dining room ready for whatever came out of my mouth. On the table, in front of the only woman I know whose gift of hospitality matched Amy's, lay a Bible, a notepad and pen, a box of tissue, a plate of treats, and a full coffee service. There was an eerie quiet in the house. I sat down in the chair offered to me—the one with the empty coffee cup, waiting for an occupant.

"I'm...um...I'm sorry," I began in a halting, tears-threatening-to-spill voice, "for not calling sooner." Bob placed a hand on my shoulder. Susie reached across the table and took my hands.

"There's nothing to apologize for, Thom," Bob assured me. "You've been dealing with a lot. We knew there were many things you needed to take care of."

"We knew that many people would be surrounding you, so we wanted to wait until you came to us. And we knew you'd call, otherwise, we wouldn't have waited," Susie added.

We spent the next hour in conversation, mostly me recounting the nightmare that I had been living. They listened, raptly. Every once in a while Bob would say, "Thom, I can't imagine…" or Susie would ask about the work to be done in the coming days, after asking about the boys. It was the first time I had unburdened my soul, face to face, with people I trusted more than words could deem appropriate. When I had spoken with my best friend on the phone each night prior to this one, there was release, yes, but he was a state away. Bob and Susie were next to and across the table from me. The human element changes things.

After I recounted the events I'd lived through since Monday morning, the day before Amy passed, I came up short of words. Amy and I were used to asking how we could help those around us who needed help, who needed to be ministered to, who needed a shoulder on which to cry. It was an odd place in which to find myself: I needed to ask for help. I knew I could count on Bob and Susie to help with anything I asked of them within those weeks. I also knew that the request I came to ask was a very big request.

Steeling myself, I took in a deep breath, held it longer than a typical breath, then exhaled.

"Susie, there is no one I've ever met whom God has blessed with the gift of hospitality like Amy's except you. I was hoping…" The tears began to fall, slowly at first, and then the dam broke. I'll save you the painful dialog; just know, these next few words were halting, full of pregnant and longing pauses. "…I mean, would you consider, well pray about organizing the reception?"

"I don't need to pray about it. It's done. I'll take care of it."

"Are you sure? It's a lot and your plate is really full right now." Classic Thom. Ask for help and then convince the helpers that they may have made a bad choice.

"I got this, Thom. I had an inkling that you might ask." Susie smiled.

The details were easy to relay from my meeting with the church regarding the service and the reception. Susie took notes like a stenographer. She is definitely efficient and well-versed in knowing what is needed in situations like these, especially when the person asking doesn't quite know what might be needed. Susie knows how to plan. She knows how to organize. And she knows how to get things done in a manner that is as if God Himself had commissioned the event. I was relieved.

After a final cup of coffee, another brownie, and a few hugs, we prayed.

There is one gift that God has given me in this married pair that is far more valuable to me than hospitality, baked goods, and a listening ear over a cup of coffee. Both Bob and Susie have been blessed with an uncanny wisdom and knack for prayer. They know how to listen to the Spirit of God and then pray as if everything depended on the prayer they were crafting. The blanket of prayer, the wash of peace, and the spark of hope that was brought through those precious ten minutes of prayer were used many times over during that season to remind me that, although I only saw one set of footprints marking the journey of my faith at that moment, God is, was, and has been carrying me. I went home that night and slept a total of six hours, two hours more than each of the previous two nights.

The Friday after Amy passed, just three days and a lifetime removed, all three of my boys headed off to school for the first time that school year. Amy passed away the morning before each of my boys was to begin school. I knew that they could not, nor should not, attend school on those first few days. I also knew that if I didn't intentionally force them into a routine, they would be reticent to leave the world of grief and it could take months or even years for them to possibly rejoin the "normal" world. When I had my wits about me the day Amy passed away, I called each school to inform them of the tragedy and my intent to have the boys enter later in the week. All three schools agreed to e-mail the boys' teachers and offered to help in any way they could.

On that Friday, I drove Isaiah to school. The car ride was a little quiet. I didn't want to taint Isaiah's first day of school with talk of his mother.

When we arrived at Isaiah's new school, I walked him into the building. It was an ominous day. He'd been accepted to an option school, meaning we had applied to the district for entry into a certain specialized school that would challenge him greatly. But there was only one spot and the choosing was a random lottery. Amy received the phone call just a week before she passed away letting us know that he'd been accepted into the program. It was a time for joyous celebration. But on that first day for Isaiah, we stood in an unfamiliar building, surrounded by strangers, waiting for the office staff to be able to help us. Once it was clear who we were, Isaiah was whisked off down the hall by a staff person. When I picked him up from school, it was with joyous news. Three of the kids from his youth group attended the same school; he was not without friends.

I returned home to pick up Gabriel and see Micah off to school. Micah also attended an option school, albeit a different one, which focused on the arts. Mama Mindee, as my boys have come to fondly call her, told Micah that when he was ready to go to school, she was taking him and picking him up, at least for the first couple of days. Mindee pulled down the street behind me. Micah lept into her van and off they went. When Micah returned home that evening, he too came filled with joyous news. Mindee had packed him a lunch (far larger than he ever could have eaten) which he was able to share with an acquaintance of his from the previous school year who had forgotten to pack his own. Mindee had also intentionally picked upbeat worship music to play on the ride, music that did not allow one to just listen. Micah was singing along at the top of his lungs, filled with joy, and ready for his first day. That was the first time anyone had seen a hint of his "Tigger" spirit returning.

I drove Gabriel to school and walked him into his classroom. Gabe was attending a second year in the Academic Learning Center with the same incredible teacher with whom he'd spent the previous year. He adored her, and I was so grateful he would have a familiar face to navigate his final year of middle school. He too came home with wondrous news. His class had written him cards and presented them to him at school. They also gave him hugs throughout the day when he needed them.

I had been at home through the day, taking care of a pile of issues, with a twinge of fear. I expected a phone call from one or more of the boys begging to come home. *I've got them*, God kept telling me through the day. When they all three arrived home with their great news, I wept. This time, however, I was weeping tears of relief and joy. God had come through on His promise. "Even though [you] walk through the Valley of the Shadow of Death, [you will] fear no evil, for [I am] with [you]" (Psalm 23:4a, ESV). We were definitely in the valley of the shadow of death, but, it was evidently clear, God was with us.

Two days later, the boys and I arrived at church. We had been told to "take the weekend off" from our normal ministry opportunities (maybe even a few weekends). However, I knew that just like with school, we needed to get back into the House of God. I desperately needed my boys to encounter God through the valley of the shadow of death. Since our church has three Sunday morning services, and since the middle school youth group and the senior high youth group meet at different services, we would be at church for multiple services. Micah agreed to sit in the back of the junior high service, just in case either brother needed him.

When I pulled up to the youth building to lead my boys into service, we were seen by many people getting out of their cars. Amy and my boys were very well known at our church, and people began to migrate our direction. With a firm grasp on each boy's hand, I walked quickly through the parking lot without stopping, nearly dragging my boys along with me. The youth pastors knew we were coming and had made a plan. My boys would not be pestered by well-intentioned, grieving parishioners, searching for their own understanding amongst this tragedy.

Amy was a fixture in our church, usually volunteering in the kitchen or in Children's Ministries. Our music pastor, who is also a close friend, caught me off guard when he said, "Thom, anybody who's been at the church for more than a month has been blessed by meeting your wife. She has been the first face that many people have seen, the first person they have talked to upon arriving at the church. And if they've been back, they've been the recipient of her hospitality, graciousness, and love. She catered so many weddings, funerals, and other events that she's probably single handedly fed nearly three quarters of the church multiple times. She also worked with so many of the kids. Amy's death will impact the church as a whole. We can't even begin to realize the impact Amy's death will have on the church." I had been blown away by this epiphany. And because of that conversation, I knew that my kids would become unintentional targets for people who didn't know how to handle their own grief or people who, though not close to us, wanted to give their condolences…even if it were part of a tsunami of unbearable attention. We Christians do not often realize the impact our well-intended actions in situations like this can have.

I walked past two groups of people without saying a word, without even glancing their way. One man whose name eluded me at the time in my grief, peeled off and followed.

"I'm sorry, Thom. Is there anything I can do?" I kept up the brisk pace.

"Thank you. I'm in a bit of a rush. The Youth Pastors are expecting me."

"I understand. Let me know if there's anything I can do. Amy was such an incredible woman. We're praying for you." By the time he finished these words, I was already three paces in front of him.

"Thank you. I will," I called back over my shoulder and kept soldiering on. I knew if I stopped to have that conversation, my son with autism would never make it to youth group. He would melt down right there in the parking lot. I, and probably his younger brother as well, would not let him cry alone.

Once inside the youth building, I breathed a sigh of relief. Waiting just inside the doors was a team of my boys' friends surrounding the youth pastors in prayer...for us. When they realized we'd entered, my boys were whisked away by warrior friends intent to listen and just be. The youth pastors had prepped them well.

I left the youth building and headed for the main building with a sense of dread. I didn't want to leave my boys, but I knew I needed to be in service. I knew I needed to be an example to my boys—when things go wrong, go to God. I knew I needed to hear our pastor's message. I entered the building and the tsunami started.

"Why are you here?" was asked of me multiple times. I'm still confounded by that question today.

"Why wouldn't I be here?" I asked back as kindly as possible. "I know there's healing to be found at church. I also know that my boys need to be here." I felt like a broken record before service even started.

Having been previously warned by my pastor that he was going to announce Amy's passing to the church during the beginning of the service, I purposely hung out in the foyer, not wanting to be in the sanctuary when the announcement was made. I was also looking for any one of about five faces whom I knew I could sit with in service—faces of friends, fierce friends, who would allow me to just sit and listen to the sermon and who would fight off the expected barrage of well-meaning people.

Unable to find any of the people I was looking for, I headed to the family room for a cup of coffee. Worship had started, and the announcement would follow worship. I needed to waste at least fifteen minutes. I wasted twenty. When I approached the doors into the sanctuary, my pastor was talking about one of the ministry opportunities available in the church. I assumed the announcement had passed. I sighed, collected a bulletin, and headed for the far entry doors.

"Thom..." The voice was behind me. I turned in relief. One of the five faces I had been looking for was now looking at me. "Do you want to sit with me?"

We went into the sanctuary and found seats together. I had no sooner sat down when the projectors changed from the mission focus picture to a giant picture of my wife. I was immediately pulled into a side hug as I sat listening to the murmuring and gasps around the room. My friend Brent had been right. Amy's ministry was more far-reaching than I had realized. As people looked around, I tried not to connect eyes with them, not wanting to lose my steel, not wanting to morph into a puddle. When the offering bags were passed moments later, I was approached by one of those of whom I spoke earlier—someone trying to make sense of their own grief, but not aware that the time or place was not right. I had the hushed conversation I had been dreading, hoping it would be the only one. Then I found myself being hugged by this person, again, someone I barely knew, while she blubbered on my shoulder. My friend was able to help extract me from the grip and the grieving parishioner returned to her seat. Later I would find out that this same person hunted down my kids, trying to get to them, to talk to them, trying to figure out how we were doing.

Please know that I believe this person had good intentions. In fact, I know she did. However, the situation needs to be addressed here. Hopefully this book will reach people who want to know how to reach out to those in grief. Hopefully this book will help people, even if it's only one person, understand that although grief is a shared experience—especially when the person who has died was so well known, liked, and loved as Amy was—sometimes it must also be a private experience as well. Sometimes we, as well-intentioned Christians, need to assess our actions before we commit them so that we are not needing to ask for forgiveness later.

When Jesus learned of his cousin's death, John the Baptist, He withdrew from people to weep (Matthew 14). The mob pursued him, even in His grief. He ministered to them, healed their sick, and even fed them (all 5,000 men, not counting women and children). What did He do right after? Jesus got right back in the boat to seclude himself again. He was tired, He was weary, and He was still grieving.

Granted, I was in church trying to seclude myself, but I still think there's a principal to learn here. People come to church for many reasons. Chief among them is healing, whether physically, spiritually, or emotionally. We need to be ready to minister to those around us who are hurting. However, we also need to be cognizant of those who need to be at church to heal without intrusion. I know why many pastors leave the church weary, broken, and angry. They were never allowed to heal. They were never allowed to put down the act of ministry in order for others to minister to them. There were about fifteen people that day who came to me in complete grief, most of them sobbing themselves, or having signs of recent tears, seeking to get comfort from me or my children. Do I regret going to church that day? NO! Having worked in the ministry, I knew people would seek to find. I also knew that those closest to me would be there at arm's reach to help and minister to me and my boys in the ways we needed. That's why I was intentional about going to church. That's why I had arranged with the Youth Pastors to never let my kids be alone. That's why when I picked up my boys from youth group one of the youth pastors went ahead of us, deflecting the charging onslaught (almost like we were the running back, charging down the field with the ball).

## CHAPTER 13

# Where's the Dress?

It was Monday, six days later. I was taking my youngest to school when the giggles finally broke into our world.

> This morning I took Isaiah to school. He picked up my phone and said, "How come you have so many messages, Daddy?"
> "Because your Mom didn't just belong to us."
> Without skipping a beat, he broke out into singing the song "Popular" from *Wicked*. Amy would have been so proud.[15]

It was a relief to finally laugh. I posted about it when I arrived back at home so I could spread the joy to those who were also mourning Amy.

I was thrilled that the boys went to school without any hesitation. I worried for about an hour but then thanked God none of them were falling apart in school. I sat down with the mail for the first time in nearly a week; the mailbox was so full it only contained a key to the "package mail box." I opened the larger box and nearly 50 envelopes and flyers were piled there. It was going to be a long day figuring out bills. Since Amy had handled the finances (although we talked once every month or two) I had a lot of bills to catch up on and make sure got paid.

## GOOD GRIEF

The day started out slowly. I began opening envelopes, mak[ing a pile] of bills, a pile of sympathy cards, and a pile of ads. It was a grueling [day.] Luckily, or rather as God would have it, one of the times I checked on Amy during her last night on earth, I had asked, "Honey, did the rent get paid this month?" Her reply had been "Yes," before she slipped back to sleep.

As the day pushed on into the early afternoon, I set aside my work, jumped into the car and headed to pick Isaiah up at school. On the way, I called my grandmother to check in as I usually do. As we were talking, the topic of my aunt's death came up in the conversation.

Carrie was two years older than me. We grew up together, even attending high school together. We were more like siblings than aunt and nephew. Five and a half years prior to Amy's death Carrie had passed away from a blood clot in the lungs, three days after a routine minor surgery. We were all devastated. It had been so sudden and unexpected. My grandparents had asked me if I would perform the service on the farm where Carrie had grown up and lived for most of her life. I was honored but also very overwhelmed. I had to learn how to set aside my own grief and minister to my grandparents and many other people who would attend the service.

Carrie's service was one of the most difficult things I had ever done. There were well over seventy-five people packed into the tiny farmhouse that was so familiar to us all. It was the first time I had ever seen my grandfather cry. Having grown up in a single parent home, my grandparents and I were really close. They stepped in and filled many rolls in my life as a child. Honestly, my grandparents had helped raise me; if it hadn't been for them, I would not have had decent clothes when school started. From the time I was ten until I graduated high school, Carrie and I were on the back of the hay truck every summer, bringing in the bales of hay one truck load at a time. Grandpa taught me how to work hard and how to be honest, even when it would have been easier to lie or cheat. Grandma taught me how to laugh, how to get along with the more difficult people in my life, and how to ask difficult questions in difficult situations. I wouldn't be the man I am today without their influence in my life.

During that phone call on my way to pick up Isaiah, Grandma started talking about how difficult it had been to "get rid of Carrie's stuff."

"Thom, I just started cleaning out Carrie's closet a few months ago. I just couldn't do it before that. It was one of the last pieces of her that I had left."

I listened intently, knowing that Grandma was trying to help me navigate my own grief, telling me it would take a while, maybe even years, before I could begin to move on and clean out things.

"While I was cleaning one day, it hit me, Thom...I couldn't find Carrie's wedding dress." Grandma and I talked for almost five more minutes after that comment, but I couldn't tell you what those five minutes contained. I had stumbled upon another time warp. But this time warp seemed to come with a ticking bomb. Just as I pulled into Isaiah's school I ended the conversation with Grandma and promised that I would call and check in soon. I know that's how the call ended because that's how all my calls with Grandma end. Isaiah came toward the car. I robotically pushed the button to open the sliding passenger door. He dumped his backpack into the middle seat, closed the sliding passenger door, and climbed into the front seat of the van. I know all this because of what happened when we got home. Unfortunately, I do not remember him getting into the car.

I do remember two things from the drive home. The first was stopping at Dairy Queen to buy us drinks and stall so that I could hear about Isaiah's day. I don't remember anything Isaiah told me about his second day of school past, "I went to the counselor's office during lunch because I was having a hard time." The second thing I do remember happened right before I pulled into the driveway.

"Daddy, are you okay?" I heard the question. I can still hear him ask the question; however, his voice was so very far away from me. The silence was ringing so loud in my ears I could barely hear him. "Daddy," he started again, "we're home. Are you going to come in?" His voice was still muffled, almost as if he were trying to talk through a solid oak door. Numbness was slowly consuming my whole body. The air grew stale and cold. I looked at Isaiah. His mouth was moving, but I couldn't hear a word he was saying. Knowing I would freak him out if I didn't answer, I remember willing myself to say something. What? I don't remember. The next thing I knew, I was flying up the stairs in the house, bound for the bedroom.

*Where is Amy's dress?* Since we had moved a little over a year before, my brain was folding in on itself. I remembered seeing the dress in the closet—in Amy's walk-in closet—as I crested the stairs. I took in a bit of a breath and went into our bedroom. When I went to the closet, I found myself in *our* walk-in closet, not *Amy's walk-in closet*! (In our previous house, we both had separate walk in closets.) As you may be able to tell, I was over half-way into a panic attack, the kind that has no rhyme or reason, the kind that grows in leaps and bounds no matter who might be around to watch, the kind that is not silent, not even in the least bit quiet. That's when the mumbling, or what I thought was mumbling, started. I would find out later that what my ears barely perceived, my youngest son could clearly hear from downstairs in the farthest room from the staircase. What he heard scared him. It scarred him, too.

I remember standing in the walk-in-closet when the realization hit me that Amy's dress couldn't fit in this closet like it did in our former house. That's when the panic destroyed my threshold. I couldn't even begin to picture the hermetically sealed box that housed Amy's dress. I tore down the stairs and dove into the garage. I searched frantically, high and low, moving everything I could quickly move to find the dress. No luck. After what felt like an eternity, I raced back up the stairs and found myself standing in the closet again. This time, I'd forgotten to close the bedroom door completely.

There was no wedding dress box in the closet. *You've already checked here, Thom! It's not here!* Shaking my head, I backed out of the closet, muttering, crying, trying to process. I stood next to my side of the bed and glanced across the room. Piled next to Amy's side of the bed and filling the window seat was Amy's dialysis prescription. There were about twenty boxes of dialysis solution, each with three solution bags and tubing per box; boxes of needles, three different sizes and gauges; a case of paper tape containing ten boxes filled with two dozen rolls each (because Amy was allergic to the adhesive in other medical tape brands); a blood pressure cuff; an overnight, peritoneal dialysis machine sitting on its own rollaway table; and a vast assortment of other necessities. The overwhelming feeling of that moment, of knowing that the last 2.5 years of dialysis was just to extend her life this far, but not get her to a transplant, landed on top of my already hysterical panic. I began sobbing and, as my son would tell me later, screaming at the dialysis supplies, at the ceiling, and at God.

The weight was too much.

I collapsed.

I began rocking back and forth on the floor, all the while curling into a fetal position. By this time, I could literally hear nothing, just the void, not even the silence screaming. At some point, I opened my eyes—*When did I close my eyes?* —and caught a glimpse of a pearlescent, off white box under the bed. With newfound vigor, I began pulling everything out from under the bed—mostly shoes, holiday décor, a couple suitcases, and some other where-do-we-put-this stuff—and hurled it out of the way.

Somewhere in the mania, my youngest son had slipped into the room and was standing next to me, shaking my shoulder, trying to get my attention.

"...has to stop, Dad!" Then he said something else that I couldn't hear. I looked up into his face and I registered that he was frightened, but my parenting hat had become lost somewhere in the wake of the tornado ripping through my room, my life. "...can...hear me..." His words weren't broken. He wasn't whispering. I just couldn't hear most of what he was saying. The silence and the mania were too loud.

I dove back under the bed, stretching my right arm to reach the box. As I did, Isaiah fell to his knees beside me and began to pull on my left arm. When I backpedaled, I was clutching the corner of the box, and as if someone turned on a television set at maximum sound, I could instantly hear.

"Dad!" He was yelling, and crying. "Dad, you've got to stop. Whatever's wrong, it's got to stop! Let me help you! You're not okay."

Trying out my voice, as if I hadn't made a sound for days, I croaked, "I just had to find her dress. I found it. I just needed to know where it was."

From downstairs we could hear the doorbell ring. Isaiah shot to his feet and made a dash for the door. I couldn't hear his conversation with the person at the door. I couldn't even remember that I had been expecting the person standing at the door. Moments later, my bedroom door opened, and a very close friend, and godmother to my second son, stepped into full view. I can't even fathom what was going through her head as her eyes fell on the remains of the tornado. She walked over to me and took my elbow and hand into hers.

"I just couldn't find her dress," I managed through sobs. "I needed to find her wedding dress."

Chris had seen Amy and me through some terrifying times in our life together, mainly the pre-mature birth of Gabriel (twelve and a half weeks early) and the closing of the first school I had ever taught in—the same school where Amy and I had met Chris, many years earlier. She'd seen me cry. She'd seen me sad. She'd even seen me angry. I don't know if she was prepared to see me in the state she did that night.

I hadn't been sleeping in my room since Amy had passed away. I couldn't bring myself to go in there for more than minutes at a time. It was the last place I saw her alive. It was the place I found her dead. It was the place I helped her with dialysis treatments. It was the place I heard the individual breaking of her ribs as I numbly followed through with CPR while waiting for the ambulance. All of it seemed to come flooding back to my memory each time I dared enter the room.

I had spoken with Chris a couple days before this. She knew I couldn't sleep in the room. She knew about the hoard of medical supplies that I could no longer bear to see day in and day out. She knew I had tried to dispose of them with the dialysis company and a few charities in town. She knew I didn't want to just throw the mountain of supplies away as I had been instructed by the dialysis company. These supplies had kept Amy alive for two and a half years! Knowing there were many people dying around the world whose lives could be saved if they only had access to what "little" was sitting in my home, I couldn't just send these supplies to the dump.

I was overwhelmed by the constant "no" in response to my desire to dispose of the medical paraphernalia in a responsible fashion. Chris saw a problem to solve and agreed to come help me. What is imperative to know about Chris is she is tough, she is crafty, and she can do just about anything—and I do mean ANYTHING. Need a problem solved at work? Chris will come and help you figure out how to fix it. What's more, the solution will be very intuitive to you and the way you process at work. Need to raise thousands of dollars to keep a Christian school's doors open and functioning? Chris can find money in the cushions of life or in the pockets of people who don't know what to do with their excess and stretch it beyond expectations. Need a creative way to say thank you? Chris is the person who can help you create a beautifully perfect offering of gratitude. I don't know of a problem, puzzle, or perterbance she hasn't been able to finesse.

Chris was in my house to help me fix my problem with the medical supplies.

That realization was all it took. Suddenly, I was back. The gale winds had ceased. The silence was no longer screaming. The wedding dress was lying at my feet and I had come to my senses.

"Um…Is Isaiah okay?" I sheepishly asked.

"I'm going to go talk with him. Are you okay for a couple of minutes?"

"Um…yeah. I'm okay. I just needed to find the dress."

"I know. It's okay. You've found it. I'll be right back, okay?" I nodded and Chris made for the first floor.

While alone in the room, I looked around at the disaster. Embarrassment began to wash over me. I moved to the master bathroom to take a peek at the mess that was me. I stepped inside and closed the door. I looked toward the mirror and caught sight of Amy's curling iron. Then her toothbrush and her blow-dryer. I began to struggle to breathe again. The pit of thick mud I had found myself swallowed by many times in the past six days had slowly begun to swallow me again. Seconds...minutes...an eternity in a blink passed and there was a knock at the door.

"Thom, are you okay in there?"

I reached for the door and opened it. When Chris saw me, I was shaking my head.

"Is he okay?" I asked.

"He's just worried." She waited for a beat. "If you want to just show me what you need me to do, I can get the boys to help me. You can go downstairs, get something to drink or eat, and we'll take care of it."

I managed a very weak smile.

"I'm okay, Chris. I just needed to find Amy's wedding dress. I'm sorry you had to see that." She just smiled.

In a flurry of activity, and less than an hour later, the last vestiges of Amy had been removed from the bathroom along with all of the medical supplies from the bedroom. Every scrap had been boxed or bagged and packed into Chris's compact SUV, sans the dialysis machine which had been tucked away neatly in its case, prepared for shipping and set by the front door. On one of her trips into the house, Chris had brought a loaf of home-baked, chocolate banana bread along with a few other snacks and set them on the counter in order to make room for the supplies that now sat in her passenger seat. There wasn't an ounce of space for anything else in Chris's car.

"Do you know what you're going to do with all of it?" I asked.

"Don't worry. I have some ideas. It won't go into the dumpster. I promise." Chris hugged the boys and then I walked her to the door.

"Thank you, Chris. I couldn't have done this without you. I'm sorry..."

"You don't need to be sorry, Thom. That's what I'm here for. Let me know what else you need help with. I mean it. You're not in this alone."

"Thank you." I saw a tear well up in Chris's eye. She gave me a hug. "I know," I finished. Seconds later I watched as Chris's car turned off of my short street and proceeded out of sight.

I slowly climbed the stairs. When I opened my bedroom door, dread wasn't waiting for me on the other side. The room was no longer dreary and dark. The bathroom had been cleaned, figuratively and literally. New sheets adorned the mattress and the bed no longer looked like someone had neglected to make it in weeks. Standing in the bathroom, I saw myself smile in the mirror. I took in a deep breath and opted for a shower.

Looking back on that evening, I've learned much about pain, about grief, and about the strength God gave the human spirit.

There are many times I wish that I could go back and "tone down" the events of that frenzied search. Many "would have," "should have," "could have" statements have haunted me as I've assessed the damage I inadvertently exacted on my youngest son. As the shame and guilt piled up to an almost unbearable state, I began walking on eggshells around Isaiah, trying to not let him see me grieve. I was terrified that if he saw me lose it again, he would be irreparably wounded...again. Moments of sudden grief that hit me found me running to hide from Isaiah.

A month after Amy's death, I was sitting in a counseling office with Isaiah. I knew my boys would need grief counseling, and I knew I wasn't equipped to help them through it all. (It's ironic to me now that I could make decisions to help my children grow and heal while making decisions that forced me to try and put my own grief and healing on hold.) Halfway through the session, I recounted the dress debacle and aired my fears related to Isaiah's involvement in that scene.

"Thom, your boys need to see you grieve. They need to see you struggle with this loss. If they don't, they won't see you heal, and they won't be able to heal. Was your grief extreme? Yes. Was it too extreme? Did you hurt someone in the process? Did you intend for your child to be injured? No, no, and no. A marriage of almost twenty years is going to be difficult to mourn. Give yourself grace to heal. Did you scare Isaiah? Yes. Will he get through this and heal from it? Yes. Let yourself be human."

It's funny how much I have healed by attending each of my sons' therapy sessions. Going every other week for each of them, while Gabe was also seeing a behaviorist and a nurse practitioner for his anxiety, autism, and ADHD medications, I was attending nine counseling-related appointments a month. I found a lot of healing in those appointments, listening and learning from the counseling staff...and from my children.

I learned a very difficult lesson in those first few months. In order for my boys to heal, they had to see me heal, which meant they had to see me hurt, to see me wrestle with God, to see me completely lose my ability to function apart from my LORD and Savior. By watching me heal, by witnessing my walk of Faith, by observing my struggles, my boys got to see me stand firm in my faith and continue to listen for the will of God in our family. They did not witness me crawl into a cave and swear off the rest of the world and my faith in God. I've told them about questions I've asked God, questions like "Why now, God?" or "Are you sure I can do this alone?" to name a few.

As I was doing devotions one night, many months after Amy's passing, I stumbled upon a passage I had not completely understood. After re-reading it a couple of times, I realized that my boys had witnessed me "work out [my] salvation with fear and trembling" (Philippians 2:12b, NIV).

As a parent, there are many times I know I have failed my kids or have failed God's directives in raising kids. When my oldest was really young, I had issues from my childhood for which I was just beginning to seek out help. I was very angry. When my youngest was born, I was very jealous of his attachment to Amy, especially since he wanted nothing to do with me. I know that many parents, maybe all parents, second guess themselves and cringe over their mistakes. I also know, however, that the goal of a godly parent is to point your children toward the Creator of the Universe in order for them to understand God's plan for their individual lives and for them to accept Jesus Christ as their own personal LORD and Savior.

There was another epiphany made from that night's devotional: Jesus knew, He truly knew what the pain my boys and I were dealing with felt like. Philippians 2:5-13 reminded me that Jesus "made himself nothing by taking the very nature of a servant, being made in human likeness" (Philippians 2:7, NIV). It also said that "He humbled himself by becoming obedient to death—even death on a cross!" (Philippians 2:8b, NIV). Having read the story of Lazarus's death a few days before, I was astounded with the weight of Jesus' burden while here on earth. I had not previously understood it fully. I'm not sure I fully understand it now, but I understand it better. There were two other lessons the Apostle Paul was trying to teach his readers in Philippians: 1) "In your relationships with one another, have the same mindset as Christ Jesus" (Philippians 2:5, NIV), and 2) "it is God who works in you to will and to act in order to fulfill His good purpose" (Philippians 2:13, NIV).

Those lessons are weighty, but I've come to realize that God is at work, whether or not I see His hand in motion, and He is working in and through me to bring His good purpose to fruition. If my children see me encounter these truths while in my care, then they witness my strengths, weaknesses, wins, and failures as just what they are. The rest is God's work.

## CHAPTER 14

# Doing Life with Others

"Thank you for coming," I said weakly, trying to smile. It wasn't my home, but we were all gathered because of me.

For three years, every other weekend we met with six other families. We met to teach our children and each other about the incredible God we served. We ate dinner. We played. We sang. After the lesson, the kids would go outside for thirty to forty-five minutes while the adults traded prayer requests. We spent three years "doing life" with these people. I felt guilty. I hadn't spoken to most of the people in the room since before Amy passed away.

The children were all outside playing in the industrial sized bounce house. Since there were ages varying from seventeen to six, we adults knew the kids would be safe. The oldest four were incredible babysitters. This night, all four of them knew the importance of the meeting in the house. It was nice to be bathed in the laughter from outside while we talked inside.

I looked around, trying to find the courage to speak. Susie smiled and nodded. It was her house. She was the hostess and one of the group leaders. Tonight, she was giving me the floor. I swallowed, blinked a few times, and started again.

"I'm sorry I haven't spoken with most of you since before Amy passed away. I've...been a bit...busy." The terror and raw emotion was crawling up my throat. My breathing sped up and I started to shake a bit.

"Thom," one woman began, "we understand. We all know you've been through a lot." She and her significant other were raising their granddaughter, and had been since the girl was just a few weeks old. Her eyes were kind. They'd seen a bit more of life than mine had. They held understanding that mine did not. I bowed my head in thanks, inhaled deeply and sat down to talk to my friends.

The next hour was filled with many tears, a couple boxes of tissues, and a few hugs. It was the first time we had all been together in over a year. Each time we met, someone was absent. Not this night. Everyone was present. I looked around the room as I told the story of the last few weeks. When my eyes alighted on one specific friend, my voice hitched a bit. His wife had been battling some health issues for over a year. At times they were hopeless. I was terrified of what he might be thinking, of what he might be worried about, of what he was feeling at that moment.

When the announcement came through leadership channels at the church that we were going to adopt Rooted as an on-going ministry, I was very excited. Praying about it, I felt very strongly I was supposed to be a part of Rooted. Our life group had been asked to participate, and I was ready to dive into the material. Amy was not. She did not feel the same calling. She wasn't really wanting to add something to our schedule either. We talked about it quite a bit, and she agreed to attend for me, with me, because she loved me. I now know why she didn't feel called to this ministry.

*Rooted* is an eleven-week program that goes over the basics of Christian faith. It's designed to bolster those new to the faith as well as help those who have walked in the faith for quite a time return to the basics. Most groups in the Rooted program would be comprised of people who didn't really know each other, except maybe in passing. Our life group was asked to participate in order to see if knowing each other would be a benefit or hindrance to the curriculum and the program. In truth, God engineered a plan to envelop me and my boys in arms that loved us—arms we saw multiple times a week. When we thought of running away, those arms kept us rooted in our faith and each other.

We met as a Life Group that weekend so that the first Rooted meeting, the following Wednesday, wouldn't be so awkward, tainted. I was concerned that if I didn't answer questions before we got to that little meeting room, I wouldn't be able to answer them. I was also afraid that the group would be mad I hadn't spoken up sooner. They weren't.

When the boys and I left Bob and Susie's house that night, I was relieved. A bit of peace settled on me as I drove home. It didn't last long, but it lasted long enough. When I got home, I knew peace could be had. Sadly, home meant pain, stillness, emptiness. Each of us dispersed when we entered, going our separate ways.

On the first night of Rooted, my youngest two and I exited the car and headed for the doors of the church. A really good friend of mine, who once owned an incredible restaurant in which Amy and I spent our last anniversary dinner together, approached me in the parking lot. He stood directly in my path. I tried to go around him because I knew if I started to cry, I wouldn't stop, but Larry was determined. He wrapped his arms around me.

"We're here for you. You know that, right?" I nodded, but didn't speak. "I'm so sorry, Thom. We love you and are praying for you."

I thanked him rather awkwardly, trying not to breakdown, and made a beeline for the registration table.

Once inside the church, my boys were whisked away to help with the younger children (fifth grade and below) and I tried to hide at one of the twenty round tables in the church's quickly filling family room. As God designed, my group leaders were already at a table, ready and waiting for me. I joined them hoping not to be seen. But, as people began filing into the large room, they did see me (it's hard to hide a 6 foot 4 inch, 340 lb. man in a large group of people—I tend to stand out, even when I try not to). My friends deflected many people, knowing I needed time to just sit, breathe, and prepare for the Bible study. There were a few uncomfortable looks, looks of sadness, looks of worry, and looks of fear as people noticed me. Some nodded. Some just turned away quickly and then began whispered conversations to their neighbors who would then try to catch a glimpse of the grieving widower without being noticed. I noticed. I wanted to bolt, to find a corner where I could hide, to go grab my boys, head straight home, and hide there. Period.

*What was I thinking?*

As I pondered leaving, I realized I was *rooted* to my seat. I couldn't stand. It was as if all function from my hip bones down no longer worked. The realization stopped me cold. The tears threatening to fall, clung to my eye lids, welling up into large pools, but they didn't fall. I began a furtive conversation with God.

*I need to leave, now!* I demanded. (Yelling at God in my head is a bit comical to me now. Then, I was trying to make sure God heard my silent prayer…so the yelling continued in my head.)

*I've got you,* He said, calmly.

*My boys are going to have a meltdown. I need to leave!* More silent yelling.

*They are with Super-T; they are fine.* It irritated me that God was using family nicknames for our good friend and children's pastor. I was offended. *You need to be here.* I felt a hand alight on each of my shoulders. My life group leaders sat down on either side of me and each reached over with that calming, caring, comforting touch.

*I'm going to lose it! I can't cry in front of all these people. I just need to go!* I tried to wiggle my toes. Nothing was moving. I was not moving. Then I heard my pastor's voice.

"Don't be surprised if you find yourself healing while you walk this road with your Rooted group. God can do amazing things if we let Him."

I stopped fighting. I stopped yelling. I simply stopped.

When the large group was dismissed to go meet with their Rooted groups in designated areas around campus, I was able to walk with those people I had "done life with" for the previous three years.

Our first meeting as a "Rooted Group," not a "Life Group," was awkward to say the least. Sitting there, so raw, I found myself more vulnerable than I had ever before been with this group. There were four adults from our Life Group who were not able to join us. We had met every other weekend. Now we were meeting every Wednesday.

I looked around the table. At the opposite end sat our group leaders. Both had graduated Bible College and had formerly worked in church ministry. To my left sat my pastor friend Jeremy and his lovely wife, whom my wife had adored. To my right sat the older couple whom God had called to raise their granddaughter as their own child. Between them and me sat one of our friends whom I had also known for many years. I was surrounded by giants in the faith. Many, if not all of them, will read this and deny that title. I can hear them now: *I'm not a giant in the faith. I'm just as messed up as the next guy.* But truly, they are all giants in my eyes.

The order of a Rooted evening was supposed to begin with one person giving a five to seven-minute testimony of how they came to know Jesus, or some aspect of their faith journey. That first night, Susie started. She had an incredible story. I remember forcing myself to listen, while my leg bounced to the beat of a double-time drum. If I didn't listen, I would fall back into the silence. I would lose time. I would offend my friends (or so I thought.)

After the opening, there was time for discussing the lesson from the week, talking about different Scriptures and lessons we'd learned. Then the group closed each night in prayer.

"How can we pray for you this week?" Susie had asked each time we had met for the past three years. That night was no different. Prayer requests started to Susie's left. When it got to me I froze. I knew the minute I opened my mouth the dam would break. I also knew if I didn't open my mouth I wouldn't go back. These were the people we'd trusted for three years. We'd done life with them. We'd prayed over multiple Special Ed meetings at Gabriel's school, stressful work environments, family issues, and many more things, life-altering things. Not opening my mouth was not an option. I felt the silence double. It had probably been a second when it became my turn, but my head was realizing everything in slow motion.

"Thom?" Bob asked.

"Um...My boys need a lot of prayer." Understatement of the year! And then the tears came. "It's Micah's Senior year. I'm worried he'll spin out of control. Gabe's...well...Gabe. Amy spoke autism better than I ever did. She was his world. I don't make his top ten. He's not handling things well, and I'm not sure I'm helping. And Isaiah's stopped talking. He's pulling away from everyone. He keeps disappearing in public places. He says he's overwhelmed and just needs some space, but he keeps disappearing. He won't talk to me like he used to." As I said it aloud, the weight on my chest doubled. Saying my fears aloud made them real.

The amount of guilt I've dealt with since Amy's passing has been tremendous. Those weeks in Rooted helped me to heal. Yes, it was designed to help me return to my roots in the faith. It did that, but it also helped me heal. Halfway through, I was able to identify what the guilt I had been living with truly was. Each time I looked about and had a minute to myself, I became terrified that I was messing up my children. *I told her I couldn't do this without her!* When the lessons came around to the evil one, it was easy to recognize the source of the guilt. I learned how to identify the attacks directly from Satan. Once I identified the source of the attacks, it was easy to call on the name of Jesus and command the enemy to flee. Guilt can be so divisive. It can kill the work God is trying to do in you. Many people wrestle with guilt more than they wrestle with their faith. Often times they end up losing both matches.

Each week we met. Each week my youngest two played with younger kids, laughing, and working alongside Pastor Todd. Each week Micah had a night alone to get caught up on homework or catch some time with one of his friends (the life of a high school senior is busier than the C.E.O. of a major company). Some days I would worry that Micah wasn't healing or getting the time with me he needed, but then I'd come home and he'd ask to talk. We'd stay up all hours of the night talking, crying, laughing, and sometimes watching TV while eating ice-cream. Each week got easier to talk, easier to smile, easier to be.

At the end of Rooted, which took us right close to Thanksgiving, I looked back on the whole endeavor. I was stunned at what God had done in me. I reconnected with my *first love*. When I was cleaning out Amy's nightstand, I came across a 3x5 card that caught my attention. On it was her "list" for God. She had showed me once, what she was asking God for in a husband and marriage. On the top of that list was the requirement, "Jesus must be his first love and I his second."

It is interesting to me that our relationship with Jesus can look very much like a rollercoaster. One minute, we're on top of the world with Him. The next, we're spiraling down toward the ground, screaming for all we're worth. Sometimes we're even looking around wondering *Where'd He go? Did He fall out of the car?*

I've had many people ask me how I've been able to keep going after Amy's death. The answer lies in those eleven weeks. I'm certain there are things in the Rooted study meant to challenge me and to help me "refine my theology." But that's not what happened for me. Through it I was able to remember the passion, faith, and trust I once had for my Savior. Those memories lit a fire in me that has continued to burn. I'm not saying I walked away from God. No. I just became complacent. Every day I was "same as the first, a little bit louder, and a whole lot worse." Every day my prayer time and devotions were rushed just a bit more. Sometimes they were missed altogether. Going back through the basics of a life of faith helped me recognize the state of my heart—beyond the pain of losing Amy. I had become the child who went off into the world and called home when I needed something.

Growing up I thought I understood love. Looking back, I shudder. The house I grew up in was a dangerous one, full of anger, back hands, and screaming. My father's house was no better. But I was sure I understood love. My youth pastors were a great example of a loving relationship. They were surrogate parents to me. Later in college, when I fell head over heels for a girl, I thought I understood love. That ended with a broken heart, and I was angry. When love found me, and Amy and I got married, I was sure I finally understood love. But it wasn't until after I became a father that I truly understood love from God's perspective.

Each night when my boys went to bed, I would tell them the same thing. As they got to be teenagers, I still say it, just not every night. What is it? "I love you. I will always love you. And there's nothing you can do to change that love." That's what God is saying to us. We're His kids and He wants us to know that He loves us. It's plain and simple.

Now that I understand the emotions and love of a father, it's much easier to accept the love from my Father in Heaven. No longer do I feel I need to run away, hide in shame, or ask to be accepted back at a lower station in His house. He will always love me. Period. He's loved me since before I was born, and nothing I do will ever change that love. Period.

# CHAPTER 15

# "So It's Not My Fault?"

"Micah, why'd you skip so much of school already?" a boy in one of his classes asked him that day. They had known each other from the previous semester, but they weren't really friends. (Micah had transferred from a private school to an Arts-focused option public school in the middle of his junior year, and it had been rough. He'll talk more about it in chapter 22.)

"There was a family emergency," he replied, not wanting to get into an emotional loop that might send him home.

"Yeah, right!" the kid snarked.

"Um...right," Micah mumbled.

"You just didn't want to come that's all. Right? Be honest."

"I am being honest. There was a family emergency."

"Right!" came the sarcastic reply. "Who died?"

Micah left the room. He didn't respond to the boy's taunts. He was upset and he didn't think it was anybody's business that he was dealing with his mother's death.

It had been ten days. Ten days full of numb, full of tears, full of silence. My boys had been acting "fine," telling me a little bit about what was going on at school, but I knew there was something deeper, much deeper, happening within them. I just didn't know how I was going to get it out of them.

I began praying that their faith would strengthen through this nightmare, that they would not walk away from the truths with which they had been raised. I began praying they would have opportunities to honestly deal with their feelings and their pain. Then it dawned on me: *God, what's going on with the boys? What am I missing?* The answer didn't come in a whispered response like many had come in the past ten days. It came later that evening, almost twelve hours after I asked—at least, it came for Micah.

After his brothers were in bed, Micah and I often talked. It had been a whirlwind type of day. For him, it was the end of his first week of school. After five days of school, he was exhausted. He hadn't talked much to anyone about what had happened. His school guidance counselor knew. His teachers knew. Lexy, his only friend at the school, knew. That was all.

"What's bothering you," I asked Micah. We were both standing in the kitchen. It was after 10:00 p.m. His brothers had been in bed for over an hour, and we had gotten up from watching some mind-numbing television show to get something to eat. I kept forgetting to eat. Micah had missed dinner, having returned to work in addition to school.

His response to my question was just raised eyebrows and a cocked head. It was as if he was saying, 'What do you think is wrong with me!'

"You've been acting a bit off tonight. More off than usual for these past few days. Did something happen?"

That's when he told me about the boy in his class.

"Why didn't you put him in his place?"

"I just couldn't. I didn't want to make a scene."

"Why?" My tone was probably a little irritated from the boy's comment.

"Because I don't want everyone to look at me with pity and feel like they need to feel sorry for me."

"But, the way he talked to you..." I pressed.

"No, Dad, that's how last year was. We would harass each other in class. It's how it's done at this school."

"Do you want me to sic one of your friends on him?" I was only half kidding. Micah gave me a faint smile.

"No. If it comes up again, I'll take care of it."

We returned to the family room, Micah with a sandwich and I a bowl of cereal. We watched something else that was supposed to make us laugh, and then decided we should try to get some sleep. Walking to the kitchen with my dirty dishes, I still felt unsettled.

"Is that all that's bothering you?" There were immediate tears. *I wish I had pressed harder earlier*, I chastised myself.

"Um...I just...um..." and then there were more tears.

"Micah, it's okay to cry. Tell me what's going on."

"I just keep thinking...um...well..." He looked me in the eye. I could tell he felt guilty for something.

"It's okay, Micah. It's okay to feel. It's okay to be mad. It's okay. But it's not okay to hold onto things. You need to tell me or someone what's going on." I was trying to be as gentle as possible. I knew my boy was fragile. Who wouldn't be?

"I just keep thinking, what if I had checked in on her in the middle of the night?" He paused. "I mean I did get up to use the bathroom. I could have checked on her. I could have called 911. I could have saved her life." The gravity of that revelation hit me full on in the chest. My eyes watered.

"Micah," I took him by both hands and stared him straight in the eyes, "when I talked with Mom's specialist on the phone, he said, based on where your mom was and how she died, he's pretty sure it was a blood clot. There's no way to know for sure because there was no autopsy, but he's pretty sure." He started sobbing, heaving at the shoulders. He covered his face with both hands. I wrapped my arms around him.

"Then it's not my fault?" he whispered.

"No, this isn't your fault. There's nothing that could have been done. If it were a blood clot and she was in the hospital, she would have still died. The monitors don't usually scan for blood clots. It's not your fault."

Micah's legs ceased working. He began to crumple. Being over three inches taller than me, and a few pounds more, I was struggling to keep us both from falling onto the floor. I didn't let go. I flashed back fourteen years. Micah was three and he'd been injured pretty badly. I was holding him while he was sobbing. I picked him up and cradled him in my arms for a long time. Then I returned to the present. I couldn't pick him up off the floor. He was a full grown, extra-large, man sized boy with a broken heart.

"I can't hold us both up," I said finally, wishing I didn't have to even try.

It took a minute for Micah to regain his footing. But he didn't stop crying. We stood in the kitchen for a long time, me still holding my "little boy" in my arms.

"There's nothing any of us could have done," I whispered again. We stayed up talking for another half-an-hour. I wanted to make sure Micah had let go of the guilt. I knew it was too much for him to handle. He wasn't guilty.

After Micah went to bed, face a little damp, but the rivers having stopped, I began reflecting on what had just transpired. I completely understood Micah's feelings of guilt; I was struggling with my own. When I had talked with Amy's family on that fateful morning, I left one detail out of the story, and that detail was sitting on my chest causing panic to rise.

*What will they say when they find out?* I had asked myself.

*They won't forgive you!*

Lying in bed later that night, I really began to wrestle. I knew my family, Amy's family, loved me. I knew they knew I loved Amy and was doing the best I could to take care of her, that I always had.

I don't want to give undue credit to the devil, because I think he gets blamed for many things in which he has no part. Not that he minds, I'm sure. But sometimes I think Christians find the devil in the details of many things, even when he isn't there. This time, however, I'm pretty sure my boys and I were right in the middle of spiritual warfare.

One of the names for the devil is "accuser" (Revelation 12:10, NIV). He is also called "the father of lies" (John 8:44, NIV). I know that "the devil prowls around like a roaring lion looking for someone to devour" (I Peter 5:8 NIV). I also know that his lies are usually subtle, but deadly. If he could entice Micah to believe his mother's death was his fault, he could cause a lot more havoc and possibly pull Micah away from his faith. If he could get me to continue thinking Amy's death was my fault, I would end up a shallow, defeated man. My faith would be shaken and I would most likely begin pulling away from God and the church as well. I've seen it happen to others.

Upon realizing the battle my boy was fighting—that I was fighting—I decided to talk with my father-in-law right after I talked with Amy's sister. If Lisa forgave me, Gary probably would too, I reasoned.

It was an awkward conversation that Friday.

"Lisa, um…I need to tell you something." It sounded ominous as I heard myself say it. The two of us were going through photos for the slide show of Amy's life. Lisa stopped and looked at me. "I missed the last alarm on my phone to go check on Amy." I had set an alarm to check on Amy every two hours through the night, like any other night. She'd gone to bed with a migraine. "I wasn't there with her when she died. She was alone." I paused.

"Thom, it's not your fault."

"I was afraid you'd be mad. I haven't told Dad either. I don't want him to be angry." In truth, I didn't want him to blame me for his baby girl's death. Typing it brings revulsion. Gary took on the role of being *my* dad when I entered this family. He loved me like the son he never had. I didn't want to tell him, but sitting there, talking with Lisa, I realized that if I didn't tell him, I would hold onto the guilt. I would also be holding onto the assumed anger I expected Gary to have toward me.

When I finally talked with Gary and Mary, I could let go of the guilt crushing me. He was not angry with me.

"Dad, I thought she had a migraine. I slept in the recliner so I didn't disturb her while she slept. I checked on her every two hours, but I slept through the 3:00 a.m. alarm. She died alone." I paused to let the gravity of my words settle. "I'm sorry. I didn't tell you because I was afraid you'd be mad."

"Thom! It's not your fault. I know that. I know you loved her." Gary hugged me. I broke. The irony of him hugging me like I had with Micah is not lost on me.

Sadly, it would be many months before Gabriel and Isaiah had similar epiphanies. Here's what happened.

We'd spent most of the Thanksgiving weekend with family. It had been awkward. We all felt like someone was missing. We were still in the phase of ignoring the feeling, but holidays made it especially more difficult. Emotions around the house were high. Micah had been in a car accident the day after Thanksgiving. That added to the stress. It was a couple days into December when Isaiah hit the same wall of guilt, or rather, the wall hit him.

Isaiah had started grief counseling shortly after Amy's death, but it wasn't working. He wouldn't talk about anything of consequence for any length of time. Every time his counselor or I would bring up the topic of Amy's death, Isaiah got jumpy. He wouldn't sit still, sometimes purposely sliding off the couch onto the floor. He would try to change the subject, often to something "funny," whatever it took to not have to talk about Amy's death. Sometimes he said what he thought we wanted to hear, but it was clear by his actions he was just talking for our benefit. He has a tell, however, that makes him easy to read. When he's overwhelmed, Isaiah runs away...or rather, he hides. When he's hurting, he often lashes out at those close to him for very petty things.

That Sunday night in December, Isaiah could no longer keep everything bottled inside. It was after dinner. Isaiah and Micah had a loud verbal disagreement over something minor. I knew what was happening.

"Micah, just drop it. Isaiah's in a mood. He's just going to say hurtful things."

I was trying to get Micah to break away from the fight. I truly wanted him to get a cool head. It didn't work. Now he was just as mad as Isaiah had been. Micah felt slighted. He thought I was siding with his youngest brother. He didn't think I was being fair; he was clearly right. When I realized my attempt had failed, I switched tactics. I apologized to Micah and told him he was right.

"I'll take care of it," I reassured Micah. "Let me talk with him."

"You ALWAYS choose him over me! You ALWAYS take his side!" Isaiah retaliated. That's when I knew the wall was near—a crash was imminent.

"No, I don't," I stated quietly and calmly. "I'm not choosing sides. I'm saying Micah's right. Usually I defend you, but you're not right this time." I knew that by talking quietly, calmly, Isaiah would be pushed over the edge. He wouldn't calm down until he truly blew his top. Helping him reach that boiling point would lead me to the heart of the problem.

"It's not fair!" He was screaming. "Just leave me alone!" Isaiah was enraged. He stomped up the stairs, louder than he had ever done in the past. I climbed the stairs slowly after him, further pushing the boiling point. He stormed down the hallway and slammed his bedroom door behind him. I took almost twice as long to climb the stairs and make my way to Isaiah's door.

I knocked.

"Go away!"

"Isaiah, what's wrong?"

"I said, GO AWAY!"

I reached down and opened the door. Isaiah was laying prone on his bed. His face was buried in his pillow. When he realized I had entered, he screamed into the pillow.

I took my spot on the side of Isaiah's bed. I put my hand in the middle of his back.

"Isaiah," I began, just above a whisper, "what's wrong? I know this isn't about Micah. What's really wrong?"

"Just please go away," he said through the muffle of the pillow.

"I can't, Isaiah. I need to know what's wrong, and I'm not leaving until we get to the bottom of this."

I sat on that bed in near silence, hand upon my son's back, for nearly three hours. Every once in a while I would ask Isaiah "What's wrong?" He never answered. Midnight had come and gone. I was tired and I had to teach Monday morning. I needed sleep. I could have justified leaving and going to bed, but I knew the situation would multiply by the morning.

Isaiah and I are so very alike. I usually know what's going through his head in any given situation. It's the closest thing I have to telepathy (which I've asked God for many times). This time I knew he was angry about something related to his mom. There had been so much stress in the house. Everyone had cried buckets—that is, everyone but Isaiah. He'd cried…briefly. He witnessed my breakdown over Amy's "missing" wedding dress. He'd listened to conversations Micah and I had while he was supposed to be asleep. He knew Gabriel was an emotional mess. I added everything up and realized Isaiah had decided not to feel. He saw everything falling apart around him and decided he'd be the stable one of the family.

I finally broke the silence.

"Isaiah, you've got to talk to me. I'm not going to bed until this is settled."

He finally rolled his body a little to the right and looked up at me.

"What's going on in your head?" I asked rhetorically.

"It's my fault," he whispered.

"Are you talking about Micah, or something else?" Isaiah sat up in the bed.

"It's my fault," he repeated. "She didn't have to die," he whispered.

"Honey, it's not your fault," I said, still rubbing his back.

"I *should* have heard her. I *should* have woken up. I *could* have helped her." Each statement got a little louder.

"Isaiah, there was nothing you could have done."

"You mean I didn't do anything."

"No. You couldn't have done anything. When God calls someone Home, it's their time. We can't stop death."

"But…" he didn't finish.

"Isaiah, listen to me. The doctors believe Mom died of a blood clot. There wasn't anything that could have been done to prevent it. She would have died if I had been upstairs in the bed. She would have died if you or your brothers heard her and tried to help. There was nothing you could have done."

"Really?" he asked feebly.

"Really," I replied, arms outstretched. Isaiah fell into my arms and sobbed. I cried with him.

When I finally got to bed, four hours had passed since I followed Isaiah into his room. I managed a brief amount of sleep. Teaching the next day was easy, though; I was ecstatic Isaiah was no longer believing a lie, that he was free of guilt. It would be another month before Gabriel hit the wall.

Friday, January 13, 2017, I had been waiting for this day. The first season of *A Series of Unfortunate Events* had been released on Netflix. I had read the books a few years earlier and thought they were genius. I had tried to get my boys to read the books, but none of them took me up on the charge. I knew if they liked the show (which only covered the first four books) they might read the books. Everyone was going to be home and we were going to watch it as a family. It never dawned on me before we watched the first episode (spoiler alert) that the parents die in the first two or three pages of the first book. What happened that night was heart-rending, but I don't regret watching it with them. It was the first time my "little man of great faith" began to ask the questions that would lead him to healing.

When the second episode ended, Gabriel bolted for his bedroom. It was a little odd for Gabriel to act that way so I followed him.

"Why did she have to leave ME, Dad?" He was screaming. He had emphasized the word ME; I did not.

"Honey, it was time for Mommy to go to Heaven. She's not in pain anymore. She's not sick anymore." I was trying to be calm and reassuring. What followed was a cacophony of questions, sobs, tears, screams, and more questions.

After each question, Gabe sobbed while I tried to answer calmly and compassionately. I struggled with words. Amy was the Autism Whisperer. She always knew what to say. She always knew what Gabriel was trying to say, even when he was frustrated and his speech was coming out all jumbled in fits and starts. At first, I thought about trying to explain the "5 Stages of Grief" —a.k.a. D.A.B.D.A. Denial. Anger. Betrayal. Depression. Acceptance. After a quick thought, I realized I didn't know how to deliver that information filtered for autism. I was struggling with my answers.

"How was she sick?"

"Why did her sickness have to kill her?"

"Why did Jesus have to take her?"

"Why wouldn't she wake up when I saw her? I tried to wake her up! I tried! Didn't she want to talk to me?"

"I kissed her on the cheek. Isn't true love's kiss supposed to wake the princess?"

The last two were the hardest to answer. Gabriel's goodbye to his mother before the mortuary attendants took her was the most painful thing I had ever witnessed. He had kissed his mother on the forehead and on the cheek. Now I knew a little more. I thought he was just saying goodbye.

Unlike his brothers, Gabriel never blamed himself. He blamed Amy. She had been his world. He would have taken her place if it meant he would get to talk with her one more time. To him, Amy knew his orbit centered around her. How dare she leave him? How dare she?

I was struggling to calm down Gabriel. Each answer to his question brought more pain and more volume. Finally, Micah stepped in with a rescue.

"Gabriel, I got the new Hillary Scott CD for Christmas. It has mom's song on it, the one we played at the memorial service during the slideshow. Do you want me to get it so you can listen to it?" The album is titled *Love Remains*, and it deals with some difficult topics, always reminding the listener that "Love Remains"—that is, "God Remains."

Micah retrieved the CD and put it into Gabriel's boom box. I was sitting on the bed, holding a still sobbing little boy. He cued up "Thy Will," the song Amy had listened to at least once or twice a day just before she died. As the song played, Gabriel's sobbing began to calm. When the song ended, he was only sniffling.

"Can you play it again, Daddy?" he asked. Gabriel rarely called me Daddy anymore. I breathed a sigh of relief, thinking the term of endearment meant I had helped him understand, even just a little bit. I got off the bed, turned off the light, and re-started the song, this time pushing the "repeat" button. As the song continued to play, I stood there in his room by the bed, holding my little miracle's hand. I was taken back to the concert of prayer we had in our living room when we thought Amy's pregnancy was not going to end with a healthy baby boy. The emotion coursing through me was similar in both places. Through the first three times the song played, Gabriel cried a little bit less each time. After the fourth play, he asked, "Tomorrow, will you tell me Mom's whole story? Everything you know about her, I want to know. Would you please tell me?"

When he woke the next morning, Gabriel was happy, really happy. For the first time in months I saw true joy in him again. Later that day, I was driving the van and he was with me.

"I have five questions today. Would you answer my five questions, and then tomorrow answer five more?" I smiled and nodded. His five questions:

"What happened on your first date with Mommy?"

"Were you nervous the night before you married Mom?"

"What was it like being married to Mommy?"

"How was I born?" (He liked hearing the story of his birth and his mother's heroic battle with her body to keep the pregnancy.)

"Do you have any fun memories of Mommy?"

The whole car ride (nearly an hour) we talked and laughed. He was a different kid. It was nice having my "Gus Gus" back (as Micah had nicknamed him at birth). The fount of joy that is Gabriel was again flowing freely.

That night, I was reflecting on the previous forty-eight hours with Gabriel. I sat down to post on Facebook about it. A very wise counselor friend of mine helped put it into perspective:

> What a powerful reminder that the only way that we can get to JOY is by going through the pain. Your little man is no longer avoiding the pain and he was allowed to experience it while being held by you. You did it right dad. I'm proud of you…Like I told you, he will teach you about grief. He doesn't have enough filters up to know otherwise.[16]

I grinned at the comment, and then replied:

> "Thank you for your kind words and encouragement. I had to chuckle when you said, 'He doesn't have enough filters up to know otherwise.' That's so true. Sometimes I wish we could mimic him more in that arena. Just think what the Church would be like."[17]

Right around the time of Gabriel's incident, Micah grew incredibly anxious. One Sunday morning I was trying to get everyone up and out the door for church. I had minutes to get out the door when Micah came down the stairs.

"What's wrong?" I was able to ask in spite of the irritation I was feeling.

"I didn't get to sleep until around 4:00 a.m."

"How come?"

"When I close my eyes, I keep seeing Mom's body. Then I open my eyes and I can't fall asleep."

"How long has this been happening?"

"For a few months."

I was stunned. Immediately I felt guilty for not knowing, for being an unfit father, for not having expected this problem. Then a crushing realization hit me. I had caused this.

"I'm sorry I had to wake you up and ask you for help," I managed.

"It's not your fault, Dad." I could tell he believed what he was saying, but I couldn't bring myself to do so. We talked for a couple more minutes, then I hugged him and sent him back to bed.

At church, I reached out to Miss Michelle, asking for prayer. She's a counselor who specializes in working with fathers of daughters and people who have experienced trauma, but I knew she'd know how to pray. What I didn't know was that God had a plan to fully relieve me of my own self-imposed guilt.

Michelle texted me back to meet with her after the service ended. I filled her in on my conversation with Micah.

"It's funny, Thom," she began, "I was just in a class about the brain this week, and I learned something that I think was meant for this moment right here. Micah's unconscious is trying to deal with the trauma. While we sleep, our brains deal with the events of the day and file away each event for future recall. When trauma happens, it can prevent that process from happening correctly. Micah's brain is trying to file away the pictures of his mom, but as soon as he sees the pictures in his head, he wakes up and can't get back to sleep."

I listened raptly as she was talking, trying to take it all in, to not forget an iota of a step. The anxiety building in me, however, was threatening to take over my vision and hearing.

"There's a way you can help his sub-conscious file these pictures in his memory banks and move past this. Let me show you. While we talk, I'm going to tap on your knees. Keep talking. The action will help, I promise."

I was nervous, thinking, *This isn't going to work*. Michelle is a good friend, so I decided to at least hear her out and go with it.

"Close your eyes, Thom," she began. "I'm going to ask you to get a picture in your head, and then I'm going to begin tapping. Are you ready?"

I closed my eyes and nodded.

"Focus on the moment you first saw Amy the morning you found her dead." I fixed the picture in my mind, wincing a bit. "Tell me, what you see."

I explained the scene to Michelle, including all the details I could, including Amy's purple fingers.

"Now, how do you feel?"

I opened my eyes, startled.

"Close your eyes, fix on the picture again, and tell me how you feel." Michelle's tone wasn't demeaning or correcting. She was simply compassionate. I closed my eyes again, slowly, and brought up the picture.

"I feel guilty," I managed meekly.

"Why?"

"Because I wasn't there. She died alone." The words came out of my mouth before I really heard them. Then I fought to keep my eyes closed. My epiphany startled me greatly. I hadn't really known I was still holding onto this guilt.

Michelle prayed.

"Now tell me what you see, Thom," she directed.

I refocused on the picture in my head. It had changed drastically. Amy was no longer alone in the bathroom. Standing just behind her, with His hand on her shoulder, was a man in a white tunic. He was glowing slightly. I couldn't see Him clearly, but I knew immediately who He was.

I stumbled with my words, continuing to stare at the picture in my head. "Um...Jesus is standing behind Amy. She looks at peace. Her hands are still purple and she's still leaning up against the wall," I paused. "But she wasn't alone," I finished.

Time stopped. I couldn't hear the many people still milling about in the church sanctuary.

*I never left her side, Thom.*

Rivers began cascading down my face. A weight that I had not realized was crushing me lifted in that moment. I exhaled a breath I seemed to have been holding onto for nearly five months. Then I opened my eyes. Michelle had stopped patting my knees. She was grinning.

"Sounds like Abba wanted to heal you too," she said.

I stood up and hugged her. I was overwhelmed with joy and peace.

"It wasn't my fault," I managed quietly.

"No, Thom, it wasn't. And Jesus was with her the whole time."

That night, after the younger boys had gone to sleep, I sat Micah on the couch and walked him through the same process. He was as hesitant as I had been. I reminded him that Miss Michelle was a licensed professional counselor with a PhD in Psychology. I also reminded him that she loved us greatly and she loved God too. He finally agreed to the "odd therapy" (his words). That night, both Micah and I slept soundly. Relieved of guilt and night terrors.

It always astounds me when God uses the everyday, "non-holy" things in our life to move us from point A to point B. For each of my boys, what moved them from point to point through the battle with guilt was different, but each vehicle God used was specific to each boy's needs, personality, and maturity level. I don't think they've all "made it;" grief doesn't just vanish. The loss of loved ones stays with us for life. We miss them. We remember them with tears and with laughter. We wish we could talk to them, and sometimes we do as we go about our day, as if they were still right next to us. The pain doesn't go away. I don't think it lessens either. I think God teaches us how to grow from it, and live with it, without it destroying us completely.

## CHAPTER 16

# A Final Goodbye

It was three days before Amy's memorial service. I had helped my boys with their comments for the service and then put them to bed. I was texting a very dear friend. I had no energy for talking, but texting I could do. During that interchange, I stumbled upon an epiphany I was still reeling from over a year and a half later. I hadn't known the gravity of the statement until after I hit *send* and then re-read it: "I never dreamed that helping my three boys grieve would be so much more painful than the hole in me."

Did I crumble into a sobbing, blubbering mess? Yes. Did I get mad, then un-mad, then mad, then un-mad at the situation in which I found myself? Yes. Were there amazing people pressing in to meet the needs of a family of brainless, numb boys hoping to wake up from their nightmare? More than I could count. That's what Amy would have done: press into those who were in pain to help heal their hearts. Three days before Amy's service I was upright, holding my boys upright with me, because of some truly heroic people who had come alongside me, wrapped their arms around me, and cried with me.

"I'm so glad you're here," I said to Travis two days later as I pulled away from Portland International Airport. It was Friday and Amy's memorial service was the next day. I needed help with the kids after the service and I needed someone to talk to about some of the dark fears bubbling up inside of me.

After Starbucks and lunch, we met the boys at the house. Travis is Micah's godfather, but all three of my boys love him and look forward to spending time with him. Although it would not be a weekend full of laughter and silliness, I knew Travis would find a way to help us see joy. I also knew I could rely on him for whatever I needed.

There were many things to do that afternoon and evening in preparation for the service. The most important was watching the video of pictures from Amy's life that would play during the Memorial Service. Lisa and I had pulled pictures together, then she painstakingly put them in order and delivered them to the church for the tech team to put into a video with background music. After having dinner with my uncle and a few cousins that night, Travis and I herded the boys into the family room and pulled up the video. As Laura Story's "Blessings" came through the television's speakers, the stills of Amy's childhood began artfully crossing the screen. Gabriel was seated on the couch between his brothers. He immediately began to sob. Micah and Isaiah wrapped their arms around him and tried to comfort him. Travis and I were standing behind the couch. By the time the pictures showed Amy's teenage years, Hillary Scott was singing "Thy Will." When the pictures of the day I met Amy's parents moved into our season of dating, I was struggling to see through sheets of tears. I didn't want to upset the boys by distracting them with my own crying. I knew they needed to see the video before the actual service. They needed to be ready for it. When "For Good," from the Broadway Musical *Wicked* began playing, the pictures of our wedding and the beginning of our family began to show. With each one, my boys' sobs and sniffles grew louder. I felt terrible with each one, as if I were the cause of the pain. I was the one, after all, who was making them watch the video.

When it ended, there were hugs all around. Micah was surprised that Lisa and I had used his suggestion for the music. He and Amy had such a bond through music; I couldn't think of a better way to honor their relationship.

"Can we watch it again?" Gabriel asked through stifled sobs while he mopped his eyes and nose with his sleeves. Isaiah shook his head and pointed at Gabriel's back. He was afraid of an "Autism Meltdown."

Placing a hand on Isaiah's shoulder, I replied, "Yes, Gabe. We can watch it again."

The second time was a little harder than the first. Many of the pictures were so real to me. I could close my eyes and remember the day, the moment, even hear Amy's voice. Halfway through, I opened my eyes and looked at Travis. He turned toward me, tears streaming down his cheeks. Sobs stumbled past his lips.

"Every time I see the pictures of Amy and her dad, all I can think of is Maddie and me."

He didn't need to finish the thought. I understood. We sobbed together. We go through life thinking we're invulnerable, or worse yet, not realizing our mortality until something tragic happens. Those stolen moments between a parent and child, arrested for all time in the form of pictures, speak of bonds we never want broken.

While Travis and I finished watching the video with my boys, I was struck by a realization about fatherhood with which I had been struggling. I didn't really, truly understand what LOVE was until I became a dad. I thought I had figured it out when a beautiful blonde stole my heart, but there were aspects of LOVE which were still unknown to me. Once I became a dad, I really began to understand God in a different way. I began noticing things of this world through the eyes of a father.

That night was probably one of the hardest things I ever had to do as a dad. While we watched the video the second time, Micah and Isaiah laughed at the funny pictures and a few tears crawled down their cheeks at others. But Gabe screamed. He didn't just cry. He didn't just bawl. He SCREAMED through the entire video.

It was only the second time I'd heard true lamenting, both times happening less than two weeks apart, and both from the same individual.

Gabriel stood up from the couch, caught his breath, and bolted to my side. He clung to me as if afraid I might leave him suddenly. Then the wailing began again. I tried to calm him down, but I couldn't even understand his words. After nearly ten minutes, Micah stepped in and tried to calm him. In the past, when Amy wasn't able to calm Gabriel down, she would ask him if he wanted to call his aunt, and Lisa would be able to calm him. I tried Amy's advice, but it didn't work. We tried two other phone calls to people who could usually calm Gabriel. None worked. After the third failed phone call, Gabriel tore up the stairs and buried himself in my bed, where his mother used to sleep.

As I lay on the bed holding Gabriel, rocking him, I asked God how could I help heal my son's heart. Inviting God, the Spirit, to fall on the room with a Peace like no other, I asked Gabe to practice his speech for the memorial service. Then I asked him to sing "10,000 Reasons" with me. As we sang, his little heart began to fill with Hope, while dread and fear were removed. Finally, my little Gus was able to take in a couple deep breaths.

I slipped out of Gabriel's room after he fell asleep. I hugged my other two, calmed them a bit, and sent them to bed. After a wrap-up conversation with Travis about the evening and the plans for the next day, Travis headed upstairs to try and sleep. I sat down at the computer and penned one of the hardest posts:

> In about 12 hours, the service for my beautiful bride, my Amy-zing wife, my perfect counterpart, will be coming to a close. It's a bit surreal. After receiving the link for the video of Amy's life in pictures, we decided (Lisa, Gary and Mary, and I) that it would be best if we watched the video before the actual event so that we weren't caught off guard by anything...I was struck with a question that still has me up, two and a half hours later.
> Does God's heart rend when we scream?
> It didn't take long for me to stumble onto the next epiphany.
> As Jesus was flogged before his crucifixion, did the sound of his cries pierce God the Father so much that He wanted to "end it all," push reset, and then create a group who wouldn't usher pain, destruction, and death into their world?
> I don't think I've ever heard true lamenting before tonight....
> Gabe's asleep now, and I'm still pondering the immensity of pain and anguish God the Father endured while His Son lamented the torture of his body.[18]

Over three and a half years later, I'm still pondering the immensity of pain and anguish God the Father endured while His Son lamented the torture of his body.

It was a long night for all of us as we tossed and turned in bed, trying to get any amount of sleep. Alas, Sleep eluded me most of the night. In total, I only saw the backs of my eyelids for a mere four hours.

The next morning, I woke the boys and started everyone on the process of getting ready. I had already been up for nearly an hour. I conferred with Travis about the day's plans and then headed to the church. I wanted some family and friends to say goodbye, publically. There wouldn't have been a dry eye in the house; mine would have started the flow.

Seconds before I disappeared to await the start of the service, a great friend palmed me a cross of nails she had made the previous night. I was holding a symbol that had caused so much pain and brought with it forgiveness and joy. I later found out that she palmed one into each of my boys' hands too.

I decided that I'd better vanish before the growing crowd caught sight of me. I went to the prayer room behind the sanctuary to wait with the rest of the family. It was an odd feeling. Waiting. Waiting to say goodbye to my bride—publically. I wasn't getting up in front of anyone to speak, but my nerves hit high gear. Ten minutes after the service was supposed to start, one of the church's pastors came into the prayer room to let us know that the line of people coming into the service was still significant. They decided to pull the guest book (announcing that it would be put out after the service) and herded people into the pews.

As we entered the sanctuary and took our seats, my nerves were not as raw as I'd expected them to be. The boys and I sat in the front pew on one side of the center aisle. Amy's family sat opposite us in the front row on the other side of the aisle. I stole a glance at Lisa and took in a deep breath. I was very overwhelmed by the number of people in attendance. When we'd been asked earlier in the week how many people we expected to show at the service, we honestly had no clue. Amy had attended Beaverton Foursquare since she was five years old and she'd been a volunteer there in many different aspects of the church—mostly in children's ministry and hospitality—for thirty-two years. The Sanctuary was well over half full. We were later told there were more than 700 people in attendance.

In one last action of fathering, I hugged Gabriel and Isaiah close to me, while pulling Micah into the hug as best as I could, too. Then we all sat up straight in the pew and anticipated the one event we did not want to witness. Although Amy had been cremated, this service served as a finality for us. I am not going to say it was an easy service. Far from it. But, there were moments of laughter as well as tears all the way through to the end.

Amy left a great legacy on the church. I asked Pastor Vickey Thivierge (called "Miss Vickey" by her four and five-year-old charges) to open the service. Vickey was the first pastor Amy volunteered for at the church. I asked Pastor Todd Crist to close the service. He was the pastor for which Amy volunteered when her ministry came to a close.

time alone. I needed to grieve before and during the service because after the service I would not have the opportunity to grieve. From the reception at Susan's funeral, I knew there would be people seeking out me, my boys, and my in-laws. It would be a time of ministry from our family to the people who'd come to the service. Travis agreed to drive the boys to church in the van. They wouldn't arrive until a few minutes before the service was to start. The plan was for him to also remove the boys within thirty to forty minutes after the service ended. They would all need a break from the crowd and the grieving.

It was raining when I got to the church, as if God were crying with me.

When I finished setting up the table that would display some of Amy's precious things, I took a minute to just remember. On the table were camp t-shirts, her favorite scarf, a mini-Christmas tree with Starbucks ornaments on it, our engagement picture and her favorite candy, Circus Peanuts, among other things.

What gave me pause though was her Bible, sitting in front of the Willow Tree family set. I didn't have a plan. I just knew what I wanted to put on the table. The family and the Bible landed where they did simply by chance. Amy's Bible was worn, and the Willow Tree family looked so new, so full of life. I found it fitting that it seemed Amy's life, and our family were centered on the Bible.

I headed to the Family Room to make sure everything for the reception was in order. I was stunned by the beautiful display. The ladies of my life group, led by their fearless leader Susie, had created a beautiful, elegant space that honored Amy in a very profound way. On each of the tables were vases filled with Fire and Ice roses and green hydrangeas. That rose was Amy's favorite flower. The green of the hydrangea was one of Amy's favorite colors. They were beautiful. It was as if each and every small detail was handwoven together by God in a way Amy would have enjoyed.

A few minutes later I was standing amongst a small crowd of people who had arrived early. I found the son of a friend who had agreed to read Micah's and/or Isaiah's speech if either of them were too overwhelmed with emotion or otherwise unable to give it. I was so thankful he was willing to step into such an awkward position. At first, both Micah and Isaiah didn't want to speak. Within twenty-four hours, however, they'd changed their minds. I couldn't begin to think what it would take to stand in front of my

I won't bore you with a play-by-play, word-for-word script of the service. When I first outlined this book, that was my plan. However, as God has shaped the book in front of me, He gave me a different goal for this chapter. There were things spoken in that service that still ring in my ears, things so profound and appropriate I believe it fitting to pass them along, in the words of the ones whom God used to deliver them. It should help you understand the "grandeur and humble" that was Amy.

> On behalf of the Johnson and Stanley family, we welcome you to a God celebration of Amy Johnson's life. I met Amy when she…[and] her family joined our church…Instantly, I saw Amy's love for God and how far along she was in her journey of walking and living for our Lord.
>
> God…made Amy everything He wanted her to be: a people person; an encourager; a leader; a teacher; an administrator; a loving, caring and wise wife and mother; a wonderful and spunky daughter and sister; a gifted friend; and a wonderful and tremendous servant of God![19]

After the opening welcome and prayer, it was time to worship. Some might think it odd to sing at funerals, some may not. For Lisa and me, it was not an option. Amy's soul was infused with music. From an early age, she played the piano. She sang and led worship at the church. For a few years, she even helped oversee a teenage worship team who led the first and second graders each Sunday. I had asked one of Amy's favorite worship leaders if she could start the service off with worship. Miss Michelle agreed immediately.

> I imagine some of you don't feel like singing today. It's hard to sing, isn't it, when our hearts are heavy. And yet, we can look to the Psalms. Forty percent of them are lament Psalms. They put their grief into song, didn't they? David talked to himself. He said, "Bless the Lord, Oh my soul." His spirit had to tell his soul what to do to process grief. And today, I want to invite you to join as we're going to sing some of Amy's favorite songs Thom said they have been on her playlist the last six months. I noticed there's a theme through them about fear. As we sing them, I just invite you to sing from the depths of your heart cause today your spirit needs to tell your soul how to get grounded in the Truth of who God is, even in our pain.[20]

We sang "I am not Alone" and "No Longer Slaves." It was a truly freeing exercise. As we sang, I could feel the tension begin to unfurl down me. I was no longer struggling to breathe while fighting the pounding of my heart and the ever-looming rivers of tears. At that point, it didn't feel like the service would be as difficult as I had imagined.

After worship was over, it was time for Lisa to sing. When we first sat down to discuss the service, I had asked Lisa if she wanted to sing. She has a beautiful voice. She'd sung at our wedding and I had heard her sing many other times. Music is a part of her make-up.

"I'll have to sing before the video and before anyone starts talking or I won't make it through the song." Realizing that her song would be right after worship, Lisa considered not singing. As the conversation for the service continued, she and I both knew she would regret not singing. "I really want to sing 'My Heart, Your Home'," she said. I think it's really important for the service and it was special to Amy." It was a done deal.

As she mounted the stage to sing, I smiled, knowing Amy loved her sister's voice. As Lisa sang, her voice quavered with emotion, but the song was not hindered in any way. It was beautiful. I found myself singing along with Lisa, meaning each word.

> *Come and make my heart*
> *Come and make it Your home*
> *Come and be everything I am and all I know*
> *Search me through and through 'till my heart becomes a home for You*[21]

When Lisa finished, it was time for the eulogies. We all sat in anticipation of what Amy's friends and mentor would say. First to speak was a married couple who had a long history with Amy and later myself. Natalene (Nate to her friends) and Eric Aaberg took to the stage together. Nate spoke first.

> What did I love about Amy? Her passion for everything. She loved her friends, and that's evident today. She loved her family, and she loved God, most of all. She was committed fiercely to each of us. She was like a lioness with her cubs. If Amy said "Yes" to something, she was all in. This became most apparent when she had her boys. They brought her great joy...
>
> Amy was a protectress. She didn't accept impossible, but she envisioned God's promises and acted to see them happen.

Amy was an advocate for her boys. She was committed to praying for and seeking out the best for them. At school meetings, she was armed with paperwork, notes, and questions. She fortified herself with prayer. And…she brought baked goods to bring everyone together and make them smile. Who didn't love it when Amy baked?

Amy had an amazing gift for navigating the complexities of our school system. The whole time, she kept the heart of the meeting focused on creating a plan to support her sweet boy. If you have ever been in one of those meetings, you know how daunting that task can be, but that's what mom's do, and Amy was truly amazing at it.[22]

Eric spoke after his wife.

> She was fierce in her uncompromising love of Jesus…And she wasn't preachy. I'm a little rough around the edges and she wasn't preachy around me. She just loved me. She loved other people around her. And we had the best conversations.
> Ames, I'm going to miss you tremendously.[23]

After Nate and Eric took their seats, I began to pray. Amy's mentor and friend, Kim Tienken, was up next. She had been so nervous when I asked her to speak. She was honored, but had never stood in front of a group of people to speak. I asked God to give her peace.

> Every life tells a story. Amy told hers through her faith, marriage, family, home, and ministry…
> One of the things I grew to admire about Amy was her "jumping off spot." By that, I mean the place from which she began everything, and for her, it was God's Word. Always. It truly was a lamp to her feet and a light to her path. She was very careful what spoke into and over her life. As we prayed God's word together, no matter the request or the size of the need, she trusted God with unwavering confidence in His promises for her life. There were times through the years that Amy would want to process a situation with me. After listening, I would say, "Amy, what does Thom think?" And, as sure as the sun rises each morning, she would say that they were on the same page.

> Thom, you two were a unified team. What a gift that was and is to your boys.
>
> Amy considered being a wife and a mom her greatest accomplishments. She absolutely loved being a mom![24]

I wanted so much to get up in front of that Memorial Service and speak my own goodbye, but I knew I couldn't. Speaking at Susan's and Carrie's memorial services taught me that the closer I was to the person whose service I was giving, the more difficult it was to do well.

One of the things Amy and I shared a passion for was music. I wanted to grow up and make a living as a Broadway star. My voice, however, leaves a bit to be desired. Not Amy's though. She had a beautiful voice. A couple months before our wedding, I penned a song and asked a friend of mine to put it to music. One of my longtime mentor-become-friends sang it at our wedding. I had *no* idea that my love for Amy—which, compared to twenty years later, could only be considered infatuation—would deepen to extremes unknown at that time. My heart is still caught up in the message of the song I wrote. The song's title is "For a Lifetime." I will love and honor her 'til my dying breath.

Since I could not speak, I asked a friend to sing the song for me. It held in it so much more than I could try to say at that moment. As I sat quietly singing along, Isaiah laid his head on my shoulder and began to cry. I silently said a prayer for him, asking God to bolster him enough to be able to give his own speech, to say his own goodbye.

By the end of the song, the room was rent. We needed a little levity and a charge. Enter Kymra. Amy's one-time-camp-counselor-and-mentor-turned-friend.

> It's a privilege to watch one woman's life for thirty-plus years, and to reflect on the facets of her character that were there from the beginning and those that were forged by life circumstances. The personality that is Amy is a beautiful example of both....
>
> Amy became your friend if you needed one. Amy fed you if you were hungry. Amy welcomed those who had no other place. Amy lifted those who needed encouraging. Amy was a trusted caregiver for the youngest and the most vulnerable. Amy volunteered for the kinds of jobs that required gloves, hairnets and bleach. Amy led with both tenacity and grace from behind

the scenes. And Amy did all of this because she loves Jesus and she loves *us*....

There are times when I have glimpsed an extraordinary person in action and I have wondered if I really wanted to know (so to speak) 'how the sausage is made'? Every time I leaned in for a closer look at Amy's life, I witnessed a transparent and surrendered servant. She was both Mary AND Martha, running the logistics of hospitality *while* sitting at her Saviors' feet. Amy's order of priorities was obvious—God, Family and Others. And I feel lucky to be one of her others![25]

I was glad that the service was being recorded. Kymra's description of Amy—"She was both Mary AND Martha"—caught me off guard. I had often called Amy a "servant warrior," and she was; but Kymra had described Amy in such a more acute and accurate way. I smiled. I actually smiled... and then cried.

To all of Amy's family: I have experienced grief, and it is overwhelming. I think it's because our hearts and souls were created for forever. When you have sad thoughts and confusing feelings, remember to allow yourself to think the sad thought and to let yourself feel the confusing feeling (because that is the only way to move through grief). And then look around for someone in this room (because they love your Amy, they love Jesus, and they love you) and ask them for help! And I promise (we promise) to say "How can I help?" and we will do our best!...

I ran into Amy [at church] in August...She and I stopped for a few moments to quickly catch up....I suggested we get together over Pumpkin Spiced Lattes after 'Freedom Day.'

"Freedom Day?" Amy questioned.

"Yeah, you know, the Tuesday after Labor Day – 'Freedom Day,' because that's the day that most kids go back to school and us Moms get a bit of our freedom back."

"It's a date!" she said

I now understand that God who created and holds each one of our lives tenderly in His hands called Tuesday, September 6th, 'Freedom Day' too!

Amy, I can hardly wait until we can sit down, get that Pumpkin Spice Latte and catch up! I Love You.[26]

I sat stunned...again. "Freedom Day." I was grieving over the loss of my bride. She was in Heaven whole. No more pain. No more sickness. No more exhaustion. Whole. Freedom. I actually began to feel lighter. And then, it hit me. Isaiah was next. I looked over to my friend's son, looked down at Isaiah, and before I could look back across the aisle to motion for a substitution, Isaiah was on his feet and heading for the stage. Lisa followed. He had asked her if she would stand behind him as moral support. It was something he would have asked his mother to do if she had been there. He had never asked me. I think he knew I would not be able to stand. My heart lept. God had given my twelve-year-old the strength I did not have. I was stunned he was actually going to speak. Earlier in the week he was vacillating, asking even twelve hours earlier if I had contacted "the backup." My friend's son nodded as Isaiah stepped up to the mic.

> The first thing that I think you should know about my mom is that she changed me through her ministry to other people. Mom taught me many things and gave me many qualities of herself to continue on in her memory. She taught me to be creative and to try new things; she taught me how to cook; she taught me how to be nice to and serve others; and she gave me a passion to work with kids....
> The second thing I want you to know about my mom was that she loved everyone she met. I want to live up to her example. You may not know that there were many people who loved and trusted my mom with many different things. She loved everyone, and hardly ever said "No" to serving others, even us kids.
> I loved crawling into her lap—even just a few weeks ago—and she would hold me until I fell asleep in her arms. I may have surpassed her in height this summer, but I will have to strive to come close to her supernatural height and her model of faith.[27]

I had read Isaiah's speech a couple of times before the service, preparing myself. I made him practice a few times in front of the mirror and especially in front of me. I wanted to be the shining face in the front row encouraging him onward. I did not want to be hearing his words for the first time in the memorial service. Hearing him speak, I realized in that moment my youngest was going to be okay. The road ahead would be long and full of pain, but he would survive it. He would be pushed on by the memory and legacy of his mama.

When Isaiah finished, Micah bolted from his pew and caught his brother in a bear hug. I couldn't stand. I would hug him and hold him close when he sat down beside me. What he needed was that hug. Not just the one his aunt had given him, but the one only his big brother, whom he adores and looks up to, could give him.

I was floored. My children have always been given compliments for their behavior and their maturity in a vast many ways. But kids are kids. And having worked with teenagers for nearly three decades, I know that, although my children are exceptional by society's standards, they are still kids. Kids who can and will make mistakes. Kids who will grow and regress through life's ups and downs. I honestly expected my boys to fall apart and be unable to stand in front of over 700 people and talk about their mama. That's when I realized, *she taught them well!* Both Isaiah and Micah were tapping into the strength they had witnessed their mother tap into throughout their lives, especially since August 2013. I was simultaneously honored and humbled by my children.

Isaiah sat down next to me and his big brother took to the stage. Because of the unique design, what follows is Micah's entire speech honoring his mother. He has an uncanny ability to bring joy reverently to a very difficult moment in his life...in our lives.

> My freshman year I went to my school's graduation ceremony, and every single graduate had the opportunity to give mini-speeches and thank the people they love. Mom leaned over to me and said, "Twenty bucks says that you couldn't fit song titles into your speech." So, instead of a graduation speech, I decided that for the circumstances, maybe we could make it this speech instead? Besides, she owes me twenty bucks already. But I guess I should just "Let It Go."[28]
>
> From the time that she watched me do the "Single Ladies"[29] dance that I have regretted since, to her pummeling me with a stuffed shark because I couldn't understand the lyrics to "Hit Me with your Best Shot,"[30] to her trying (and succeeding) to make me crumple to the floor by tickling my earlobe, mom was always mom.

Over the last two weeks of her life, Mom persistently pestered me about college applications, particularly, an essay for one specific college. They wanted a paper on my Jesus story, and how I have grown in Him. And although I know there was "Something to Believe In,"[31] I struggled to find a way to write about my faith story. "How can I help you?" she kept asking me. I didn't know what help I needed, so I didn't answer my mother's question. I spent so much time upstairs in my room or with my friends to avoid her bugging me. Today, I wish I hadn't. For those of you wondering, I have not finished that essay, but I know who it will be about. Don't worry, mama. I'll make you "Proud of Your Boy."[32]

Two weeks ago, to this day, I was at work for an eight-hour, on my feet, being nice to people, shift. I was having a no-good, very bad day, and I called home. My supervisor was going to let me go on a meal break soon, and I felt like I just needed to come home. So I came home and had dinner with the family. It was a bit chaotic: I felt like a rushed mess, and they all had finished their food already. Mom made them wait at the dinner table for an extra forty-five minutes just for me, but it felt normal. I didn't even remember that mom was sick. "I Want the Good Times Back."[33] "That Would Be Enough."[34] We were laughing and playing games until I had to race back to work.

"How can I help you?"
Mom always asked that. To everyone.
I asked, "Are you okay?"

The day before her passing, we were having a great time. We went bowling to celebrate a final day of summer as a family of five. Little did we know, that was our last celebration as a family of five. About halfway through the game, Mom started feeling sick. We thought it was just another bad night. She has had so many over the last two years. When we got home, Dad and I helped her upstairs. I wish I remember the last thing she said to me. But I remember what I told her: "Are you gonna be okay, Mom?"

So many people had no idea how sick my mom was.

You see, she didn't want all the attention on her. She didn't want everyone to treat her differently. So, instead of complaining, she changed the topic. She chose to focus on her gifts, rather than her sickness. My mom served in ministry for thirty years. Knowing her state of health, it "Blows Us All Away"[35] how continually and unfailingly hospitable she was.

I'm wearing those bowling shoes now. We called the venue, and they let me borrow them to honor the last time Mom was Mom, focusing on celebrating with us. I kinda wish I could just click my heels and we would be together again. She taught me to laugh, she taught me to love. So much of me is made of what I learned from Mom. And it will stick with me "For Good."[36]

As Christians, we don't have to be eternally sad because we know that we will someday meet again in the Presence of the Lord. So, I get to say "Goodbye Until Tomorrow."[37] [38]

Amy would have laughed at that eulogy. She would have been very proud of him. From Beyoncé to Pat Benatar, from *Hamilton* to *Wicked*, from *The Last Five Years* to multiple Disney on Broadway shows, Micah referenced songs which held special memories with his mom. Whether it was seeing *Frozen* on opening weekend as a family, dancing in front of his entire student body at school (while mom used her phone to record it for posterity), or taking his mom to see her favorite musical, *Newsies*, just months before she passed away, each of the ten songs Micah referenced has a strong significance to the memory of his mother.

The slideshow of Amy's life, from birth through her last few weeks, played over the screen at the front of the sanctuary. I hugged Micah as he came to sit back down in the pew. Once again, the four of us watched what had been so very difficult the previous night. With my boys' speeches over, this was now the hardest part of the service. When the song "For Good" ended, my favorite picture of our family hung out on the screen for an extended moment. The picture is black and white, all of us holding hands, walking away from the camera. Our youngest was only three years old. Our whole future lay ahead of us. Nine years later, here we were, in the future, arm in arm, facing away from our family and friends, facing a future without Amy.

When the picture faded, Pastor Randy mounted the stairs. His message was for all who were grieving, but uniquely directed at my three boys. I'd never before heard a message like it at a memorial service. What caught me off guard was the message he was giving, was the same message God had been telling me about my own boys in the days leading up to the service.

> I felt like God gave me a verse to share with you guys, for everybody here, but primarily for you boys...The Scripture that came to my heart, came to me that morning when we were together in your home before they came to take your mom...
>
> In II Corinthians chapter 4, the Apostle Paul is talking about... how our lives are like containers. God took these average, kind of unimpressive containers and put something...he used the words to describe as a treasure that was all surpassing in its value in its greatness. That nothing can compare to it. He uses these words: "We have this treasure," and the treasure he's speaking of is the surpassing knowledge of who God is, the truth of who Jesus is, the glory of who God is, he says, "We have these treasures in jars of clay" (II Corinthians 4:7, NIV) in order that we might be able to show everything that happens in and through our life is from God and that it's not from us. So my wife and I, we went and got some jars that were made out of clay and we painted them last night...We put a little light in there and we've got one for each of you because I wanted to give you something that might be a little more tactile, [something] you could hold on to and remember this verse by....
>
> God took this form, this body, and He breathed into it and made it come alive in Him...So that what gets seen, and what is recognized isn't the pot but that which the pot contains...There's going to come moments when what is inside needs to be revealed and everybody's going to go, "What is happening in your life is more than you. There's something at work in you..."
>
> Paul says these four things. When "we are pressed on every side, [we are] not crushed" (II Corinthians 4:8, NIV). So I just want to encourage you guys, when you go forward you will feel sometimes the constraints of your circumstance, the reality of your new normal. These are uncharted waters, and sometimes it's going to feel like a lot of pressure. And this is what Paul says, "But because of who's in me, I'll never be crushed."...Then he says, "there's times where we're going to be perplexed." Do you know what that word means, perplexed? It means, "I've got questions I can't answer. I'm a little uncertain. I'm in the dark about what is going on." But he says

that "I'm not in despair" (II Corinthians 4:8, NIV). I might not be able to figure this out, but God is in control. And in those moments when I'm the most perplexed is when I'm going to be able to realize that God is going to be the most present and the most faithful with me....And then he says these words; At times we're "persecuted" (II Corinthians 4:9, NIV). Sometimes we feel the enemy's lies and the opposition of darkness. And he says, "But I'm not abandoned because of who's in me" (II Corinthians 4:9, NIV). I am protected by the one who is in me because greater is He who is in me than he that is in the world. The last thing he says, "I'm struck down, but I'm not destroyed" (II Corinthians 4:9, NIV). Sometimes humanly it looks like something's the end, but in God, because of the resurrection of Jesus Christ, and who He is in us and His resurrected life and in the resurrection that's going to come of our bodies, I'll never be destroyed....In times like this it's possible that there's something in you that can pour out so significantly that it will bring glory and it will be praise to God.

Do you know that your mom brought so much glory to God by the way she lived her life? That even in this moment, in her death, she's glorifying God because she fully, as the Scripture says, put her trust [in God]? She was persuaded and fully convinced that she was able to entrust into the hands of God those who are most precious to her. And I have a feeling that those most precious to her was you.

[Then Paul] says, "[So] we don't lose heart." and I'll finish with this, "Though outwardly we are wasting away, yet inwardly we are being renewed day by day. For our light and our momentary troubles are achieving for us an eternal glory that outweighs [everything else we've experienced here]. So we fix our eyes not on what is seen, but on what is unseen. Since what is seen is temporary, but what is unseen is eternal" (II Corinthians 4:16-18, NIV). So we put our eyes on Jesus....

Amy trusted in Jesus, and if she could come back in this moment, she would want to say one thing, "You don't want to miss what I see, what I know. Don't miss this moment. Put your faith and trust, not in your own goodness, not in your own sense of rightness, put your faith in Jesus' righteousness. The Scripture says, "Because He lives, we will live" (John 14:19b, paraphrased, NIV). And we can overcome death, we can overcome the grave, we can overcome fear because of the resurrection of Jesus....[39]

Pastor Randy finished with a prayer and it was time for a final worship song; it was time for Gabriel to honor the memory of his mother. As Gabriel stood to take the stage, I started to pray. Autism can always surprise me, and I don't always know what might come out of his mouth. I also didn't know if he was going to break down on the platform or not. The plan was for him to say a few words—which we'd typed up and practiced dozens of times—and then lead, with Miss Michelle, the final worship song for the service: "10,000 Reasons."

Miss Michelle stood behind Gabriel as he took a mic. He looked down at me, then his brothers, and finally his aunt. He inhaled deeply and began. It didn't take long before he went off script. Micah and I kept motioning to him to go back to the script he'd written with me. I started to worry that the message he really wanted to say, the one he told me the first time he said he wanted to be like his brothers and speak, and every day since, would get lost. Then I began to worry about what people in the audience would be thinking about Gabriel, or about *why* I let my son with autism speak at his mother's memorial. When I realized what I was worried about, I shook my head and grinned. To be honest, I really didn't care what anyone in that room thought. From the moment God named Gabriel, I knew he was being sent as a messenger of good news. He caught my gaze one last time, understood my gesture, finished his "off script" comment, and inhaled another deep breath.

> Amy was my mom, and I'm going to miss her so much...Her hugs made my heart really happy...I just wanted, for all of us, if we could just love on her and wrap around her heart. I am going to miss my mommy, but I am really excited she's stuck up in Heaven right now...[40]

They told us he would "be a vegetable" (those were the doctor's words). God, in His wisdom and glory, sent us an angel of Good News. Sometimes his words get a bit jumbled. Sometimes they are so overly simple. This time, they were so very apt, profound. He finished his speech with something not written on his sheet of paper.

It took me years to figure out why she was my mother. And then I got it. She loved Jesus very much. I hope you do too.[41]

Miss Michelle welcomed the audience to stand and sing the last song. And then they led. Gabriel wasn't standing next to a worship leader as a "door prize" for being the "special son." I didn't let him do this because I felt guilty. No. Gabriel, who was named after a great angel, stood there, joined his voice with Miss Michelle's in harmony, and they led worship together as they had done a few years prior in another service.

Michelle told me later, "I just remembered something from when Gabriel and I closed out the service singing side by side. I actually decided to pull back from the mic so he could lead as the more dominant voice. And at one point, he shouted out something like, 'sing it out!' and people did! Their voices got louder, and I had people afterwards tell me that they struggled to sing…but when Gabriel challenged them to sing out, they responded! He truly was a worship leader by leading them in worship in a powerful way that day!"[42]

I was so overcome with joy, peace, and pride for my boys. All three of them had the courage and the wherewithal to do what many could not, what I could not. They stood in front of a crowd of hundreds of people and proclaimed who their mother was and why she was the way she was.

> "I may have surpassed her in height this summer, but I will have to strive to come close to her supernatural height and her model of faith."[43]

> "She chose to focus on her gifts, rather than her sickness. My mom served in ministry for 30 years."[44]

> "She loved Jesus very much. I hope you do too."[45]

They each used their own words.

For a moment I stopped singing, thanked God for His grace and strength for my boys. Singing that last song reminded me that God was in control. I didn't have to try to be in control. I just needed to submit to His plan. I don't think I've sung that loud in worship since I was in high school. It was a very freeing moment. The pain was not gone, but Hope and Joy had taken root in my heart and they were not being evicted.

I breathed a sigh of relief. The service was near its end. Pastor Todd was headed for the platform to give the Benediction. We'd wept. We'd laughed. We'd reminisced together. It was now time to say one last goodbye. Todd's prayer would bring an end to two agonizing, numb-filled, silence-screaming weeks. I took another deep breath. When I looked up at Todd, he was placing a can of Diet Coke and a family sized bag of Mega Peanut M&M's on a little table next to the lectern. The tears were instant, but they had a smile a mile wide as their companion.

> If you wonder why there's a Diet Coke and a bag of Mega Peanut M&M's, you might not know that it is a reminder to me how special, how amazing Amy was. So Amy-zing. Right? Amy was amazing. I googled the word *amazing* and found this definition: "to overwhelm with great surprise." Now, I'm not sure if I can change Google's definition of *amazing*, but instead of the word surprise, Amy, in a very healthy way, overwhelmed us with great love.
> 
> At home, and within our faith community, she was a frontline servant. A warrior for Christ...She was patient and kind. She deflected praise to Jesus and to others. She was not easily angered. And she never kept records of wrong. She rejoiced in the Truth of Jesus Christ. She protected people. She was trustworthy. But, let's be real, even though I thought she was perfect at times, Amy wasn't perfect, but now lives with the one who is. Amen?...
> 
> Our camp this past summer was Champions for Christ, and Amy, like she has done for so many years, was in charge of hospitality. Our verse was Hebrews 12:1, which says,
> 
> "Therefore, since we are surrounded by such a huge crowd of witnesses to the life of faith, let us strip off every weight that slows us down, especially the sin that so easily trips us up, and let us run with endurance the race God set before us. We do this by keeping our eyes on Jesus, the Champion who initiates and perfects our faith." (Hebrews 12:1, NLT)
> 
> Amy epitomized that verse. She was a true Champion for Christ. I have never seen anybody love her family, love others, love kids, and love Jesus like Amy...She overwhelmed hearts with her God-given gifts of hospitality and service....
> 
> It's obvious that her love of Jesus and others is alive and ongoing with those four boys right there. Three boys and one man.

I know she is so proud of you. Keep running the race with eyes fixed on Jesus.

I'm grateful that I was able to know and love and serve with Amy, but more importantly, I'm grateful for the example of what it truly means to Know, Love, and to Serve Jesus.

I love you, Amy. Looking forward to seeing you again. And when I do, I'm sure you'll have a Diet Coke and some Peanut M&M's just waiting for me. Do they have those in Heaven?[46]

Todd asked the congregation to join him in prayer and then he closed out the service. Just like that, it was all over. We were escorted to the reception room. Before I could get half way into the deep room, there was already a line forming behind me. I looked to my best friend Travis.

"In thirty or forty minutes, just grab them and go," I said.

"No problem." I knew my sons' friends would be at the service. I knew they needed to talk with their friends and family. I also knew by the sheer number of people in attendance they couldn't stay at the church as long as I was needed to stay. The next hour was a blur. I hugged many people. Thanked them for coming. Listened to stories of "The last time I saw Amy" or "The last time I talked with Amy." The stories were incredible. They spoke of joy, of service, of hospitality.

I started to get dizzy.

"Thom, have you eaten anything? Do you need something to drink?" my friend Chris asked me. I hadn't realized she had been standing at my elbow.

"No…um…yes…I mean…"

"I got it." She'd brought one of the tall-standing barista tables to me to hold my plate, and me if necessary. It was easier than moving me and the line of people.

"Thank you," I said, a little puzzled. Amy and I were the ones who served at the church, catering weddings, events, and funerals. It was usually me who was taking care of someone else. God's message was clear to me right then: *I've got you.* I leaned on the table with my hand and kept talking and hugging people. For over an hour and a half every time I looked up, I couldn't see the end of the line. It would not be until much later that night while Lisa, Micah, and I read through the guest book, that I would realize how many more people were at the service than I even saw.

When I woke that morning, I was dreading this part of the day. I didn't think I had enough in me to minister to those people around me who were also grieving. But I knew that I was going to do the best I could. My expectations were not met; they were blown away. Each handshake, story, hug took some of the weight. For a space of about two and a half hours, I did not feel alone.

When the last of the line was gone and most of the food had been devoured, I looked around the room. It needed cleaning as rooms do after such a large party has ended. Susie, Chris, and a few other people were beginning to clean up the Family Room. I rolled up my sleeves, intent to help them.

"We've got this, Thom. You need to go to your boys. Where are they?"

"Travis took them to a restaurant for a real lunch," I told Susie.

"Good. I'm glad they weren't here the whole time. I'll help you pack your car. We got this. Go be Dad."

Susie and Chris had already packed up Amy's personal treasures, the condolence cards, some of the left-over food, and a bouquet of flowers. They helped me pack the car and saw me leave the premises. Travis and the boys were less than a mile away.

I didn't have time to process.

When I entered the restaurant, the entire table was filled with laughter. Amy's and my good friends from my home church had gone to lunch with them. My boys grew up calling them "Aunt" and "Uncle"; their daughters grew up with the same titles of endearment for Amy and me. They had been assistant youth leaders when Travis and I were in high school. As the years went on, they became very dear friends. I was relieved my boys were surrounded with such love and joy after such a draining day.

It wasn't long after I arrived that Uncle Spud, Aunt Julie, and their girls had to head home; they had a four-hour drive ahead of them. After hugs all around, everyone piled into vehicles and headed home. Gabriel wanted to come with me so I "wouldn't be alone." He chattered all the way home.

A few hours later, sitting at a large table at a family favorite restaurant, surrounded by my in-laws, my sister and her husband, my kids, and my best friend, the silence took over again. Everyone was involved in some conversation. We looked like a well-adjusted, happy family from an onlooker's perspective. Amy would have been right in the middle of the conversation and laughter. I looked around the table. I was so happy to be surrounded by family. But I had never felt more alone.

There was finality.

The service was finished. Friends and family had come to say goodbye and then had gone home as one does. Life was moving on, no matter how much I didn't want it to continue. I took in a deep breath. I set my jaw. My lips narrowed. Yes, I was alone, but I was also a dad and I had a big job ahead of me. I needed to take care of my boys.

## CHAPTER 17

# Returning to Life

The idea of going back to work after the memorial service was both welcome and terrifying. I had spent two weeks handling the affairs related to Amy's death, grieving, taking care of the boys, and trying to figure out how to balance a checkbook. It was exhausting. It was also very consuming. I looked forward to getting back into the classroom. It was a familiar space for me. I anticipated that getting back into a rhythm like I had forced the boys to already do would be a good thing for me.

Ten days after Amy's death had been "Back to School Night" at my school. When the year started, I was introduced as a substitute teacher. My students had been taught by a "sub-for-the-sub." I knew I needed to go show my face and try to give clarity to parents and students alike whose school year started off really rocky. My administrators told me I didn't have to come. They would cover. According to the teacher's contract, I didn't have to attend; I was on bereavement leave. I made my case, asking to come. My principal relented, willingly it seemed.

"We're here in case something happens and you can't do it. We understand," Kevin finished. "Everyone will understand."

On the morning of Back to School Night, it seemed I was in a flat tailspin and the speed of it kept increasing. I went outside with Isaiah to take him to school. That's when I found the flat tire on the van. I jumped into our second car, the one Micah would need to get to school, and raced Isaiah to school. On the way home, the check-engine-light-of-doom caught my eye. I called Mindee to see if she could pick up Micah and take him to school while I tried to deal with two downed vehicles.

When I arrived at the house, Mindee was picking up Micah.

"I'll bring him home after school, too," she yelled out the window as she pulled away from the house.

I headed for the mailbox before going into the house. The top envelope in the mailbox was a utility bill, attached to a shut off notice. I was losing my grip. I walked into the house and sat on the floor of the kitchen, having set the mail on the counter. Just after I began to cry, my phone rang.

"Thom, how are you doing today?" It was Todd. He'd been checking on me daily, sometimes multiple times a day, seeing what he and Julie could do to help. In a jumble of words, I filled him in on the tail-spin.

"Have you eaten yet?" he asked. The question caught me off guard.

"No, but I have some leftovers I was going to eat."

"Don't do anything but eat until I get there. We'll get it all settled. Okay?"

"Um...okay." I felt as if I were doomed to repeat the emotional meltdown I'd encountered when looking for Amy's dress.

When Todd arrived, I had just finished a glass of milk. I opened the door. He came into the kitchen with me and began creating order, much like Amy would have done. Within thirty minutes, I wrote three checks to pay three different bills, called AAA to come and change the tire on the van, and gave Todd the keys to the car.

"I'll take care of the car and get it back to you as soon as I can," he said.

"But, don't you have to work?" I asked, still in an emotional fog.

"Thom, I'm a pastor at the church. This is my work. But even if I weren't, I'd be here helping you. Don't worry about me. Are you going to be okay alone?" he asked.

"Yes. I have a couple of appointments who are coming to the house today. I won't be alone for long."

Todd gave me a bear hug.

"You're going to get through this, Thom," he said as he released me. "We love you, and we've got you. God's with you too."

"Thank you," I managed, "and I know." The last part was almost an afterthought, as if it were the correct thing to say in this situation.

As the day happened, a verse kept coming to my mind. "Be still and know that I am God" (Psalm 46:10a, NIV). By the end of the afternoon, both vehicles were working again, food was being delivered, and friends were on their way to sit with the boys while I attended Back to School night.

When I entered my school, two hours before the parents would arrive, I headed straight for Kevin's office.

"I'm here," I said, poking my head through the open doorway. Kevin turned to face me. "I've got some things to finish typing up and copying and I'll be ready."

"Do you need any help?"

"No. I have time to get it all done. Thanks though."

With that, I headed for my classroom. On the way, I crossed paths with a few different teachers with whom I'd become friends the previous school year.

"Do you need any help?" each one asked. I shook my head and smiled each time. "I'm here if you need anything," each one said as I turned to continue on my mission.

"Thanks," was all I could get out of my mouth. I was thankful none of them had asked any personal questions. I didn't have much in my emotional vat from which to pull.

Two hours had been just enough time. As parents began entering my classroom, I took in a deep breath and donned a professional persona. Many were surprised to actually see me. A letter had gone home to the parents explaining why I was suddenly absent from the classroom. I focused on being the ultimate professional. I thanked each of the parents for their well-wishes and got down to business. At the beginning of my last session of parents, I was losing steam. I'm sure it showed.

"I'm so glad my son has you this year," one parent said at the close of my ten-minute talk. "I'm amazed that you are here and standing, but I'm also excited for him to see what life looks like in action." I was a bit confused. She didn't say more. By the end of the school year, I received the rest of the pieces. The young man's father had abandoned the family when the student was a little boy. His mother was raising him attending church. He believed in God and had an evident relationship with Jesus, but he was struggling with the unknown. For him, he wished his father had died instead of abandoned the family. "Maybe it wouldn't hurt so much," he confided in me one afternoon. "Now, I just think it's my fault he left."

The morning I was to return to work after bereavement leave, this particular young man was one of the reasons making it easy to focus on school and not the pain. When I was in high school, my grandfather continually told me to "find something I loved doing and then figure out how to get paid for it." For me, teaching is the thing I love doing.

Getting into the groove of school didn't take long. There were a few panicked phone calls from my boys in the beginning. My two teaching partners in seventh grade Language Arts and Social Studies were ready to step into my class at a moment's notice if anything went wrong. And there were those times when I needed someone to step in and cover for me, either because one of the boys had called, or because the emotion caught up to me and I needed a few minutes to move past it. By the end of the first month, I was back into the rhythm of school.

Shortly after returning to work, I began the process of reconnecting my youngest two boys with their counselors. For many years prior to Amy's death, Gabriel had been seeing his counselor who specialized in autistic children and teens. We had started to wean him off the counseling and switch to a behaviorist who worked in concert with the counselor shortly before Amy died. Because of the regression that grief can cause, Gabriel and I started seeing the counselor every two weeks and the behaviorist on the alternate weeks. It was slow work, painful and difficult due to Gabe's communication challenges.

Isaiah had been seeing a counselor for nearly two years before Amy died. Growing up with an older brother who has autism became a very difficult issue for Isaiah when he was ten years old. He had trouble deciphering between willful meanness and autistic meltdowns. After Amy was diagnosed with kidney failure, the counselor then began working on Isaiah's fears as well.

When Isaiah became overwhelmed with emotion, no matter where he was, he would simply disappear. For this single parent in grief, it was almost the breaking point. He disappeared in a restaurant once, sitting against the door so no patrons could enter the bathroom. He disappeared in the mall a couple of times. He began disappearing in the house. And once he was so angry and hurt he left the house, wanting to disappear from the reminders of his pain. Although I began panicking each time I couldn't find him, God was faithful. After many sessions with the counselor, in which he would struggle to keep from talking about anything painful, we were finally able to set up some boundaries with him. From that point on, I would know where he was if he disappeared. Depending on where we were or what was happening, we'd carved out safe spaces for him to go.

The week Amy died, I posted a few things for my own benefit to mark the event and to spread the news about the upcoming memorial service. I received so many positive comments in the beginning that I kept posting. Isaiah's counselor asked him to journal during that first month, hoping that if he wouldn't talk about the painful things in her office, he would at least get them on paper. Her encouragement to him encouraged me as well. Not being afraid of Big Brother, I decided that I would continue to use social media to help myself heal, to encourage my son(s) to heal and to write, and to possibly help those literally around the globe who were affected by Amy's death heal as well. I became more methodical in my posts. Each time I would post, I would feel like a weight was taken off my back and thrown to the ground. It was extremely cathartic. Not everything I posted was painful and somber. There were some laughs to be had through the process, and I posted those as well. There were also praises to be made. As I said, the army of help we received was welcomed. I didn't always name names, but I did want people to know we were thankful. I wanted people to see us for who we were, not for what people might think about us if they looked from afar.

Right after going back to work and after the first appointment with Isaiah's counselor, my heart was full.

> Today was two weeks. It seems as if those two weeks have blown by AND crept by. It's been an adjustment, coordinating schedules, Back to School nights (I missed 2 of the 3—go Dad!), laundry, showers (1 of my kids realized that it's been a "few days..."), after school activities, Micah's work schedule and a myriad of other things. Although my heart is broken and numb, my God is not. He has been faithful through this entire ordeal. I see Him show up when I'm at my lowest. I see Him show up in my friends who've stepped in to help. I see Him in the faces of my three little boys who stand proud of their mama and tell the world that she was Amy-zing, no matter

how much they hurt themselves. I see Him in the actions of those same three little boys who are reaching out to minister to those around them dealing with the same—albeit different—loss. I see Him in the little things—the cookies delivered today that happened to be what I was craving. I see Him in the big things—the meals that are coming, the generous gifts, and the neighborhood we live in that is wrapping their arms around my three little boys. God has been very good to me and my boys. It's only because of His GRACE, PEACE, and JOY that allows me to see His hand in our lives. My wife is no longer in pain. She is no longer ill. She is standing in His PRESENCE. There is nothing more that I could ask for her. For us, there is still ache, there is still longing, there is still that void, but God is good! That's all that matters.[47]

I tried to be upbeat when I could be, for my boys and for those who were checking on us through Facebook. But I'd made a promise to myself, I would not post anything fake, anything "Christian for the sake of being Christian." Too often I've read things people have written or listened to what Christians were saying and their message was disingenuous. When our kids were born, the number one rule in our house became, "Do not lie." Because I was grieving in a public forum, I wanted to make sure my children would see genuineness, not a mask.

The first really difficult hurdle for me once we'd found our rhythm, our new normal, was my birthday. Amy was incredible at throwing parties. She knew I loved birthdays. For my 40th birthday, she'd thrown a party for me in one of our favorite restaurants, on a Sunday while they were closed. It was Superhero themed. When I was in Bible College a wise man once told me to "Never grow up, Thom. Christians who grow up on the inside get all crusty and grouchy. They tend to get stuck in their ways and definitely in God's way. Don't grow up and get in God's way." I lived by that advice as much as I could. Having enjoyed superheroes as a kid and then realizing their origins were in the world religions and mythologies I got to teach about as a Language Arts and Social Studies teacher, superheroes have claimed a large part of my entertainment and even classroom décor.

Amy had asked her step-brother's wife to make my 40th birthday cake. It was incredible, magazine worthy. Each layer represented a different superhero. People were encouraged to come dressed in the theme. When

I entered, not having known the theme, I was given a cape to wear. It was an incredible party. It had taken place seven months after Amy's diagnosis, when she still had some of energy.

Just two weeks after the memorial service, I turned forty-three. I didn't feel like celebrating. When you have a son with autism who is used to celebrating birthdays, not celebrating wasn't an option. Gabriel asked me one night what we were going to do for my birthday. "Nothing," I said. "We're skipping it this year." I meant it. My autism translator wasn't working that day. I didn't hear what he was trying to say. *We needed something to celebrate, Dad.* Micah, without my knowing, organized his brothers and sent out invitations to the family via text. My sister-in-law stepped up to the plate and upgraded the party to the Cheesecake Factory. She knew it would be difficult for the boys to get the house in order. She also knew we needed to get out of the house. Amy and I loved going to the Cheesecake Factory. We would order three or four dishes from their appetizer menu to split as a meal. Then we would get cheesecake. Sometimes we would split a piece. Sometimes we would have our own. But we always got cheesecake.

The night of the party came and I had been having a rough day fighting my emotions. I honestly wanted to never celebrate another birthday without her. When we walked into the restaurant and were seated, I was happy that the lighting on that night seemed quite a bit darker than usual. I don't remember the gifts I was given, but I remember being happy that my family had been very thoughtful with what they got me, trying very hard to bring some celebration into our dark days. When it was time to order Cheesecake, I chose the banana cream. Amy hated the smell of bananas; they made her gag or worse, so I had never ordered the banana cream. When it came, the wait staff, along with my family, gave a rousing "Happy Birthday." I remember forcing myself to smile. I didn't want anyone to see I was really struggling in pain; they had worked so hard to do this for me.

When I took a bite of the cheesecake, it was heavenly. I knew it would be. Banana Cream pie is one of my favorite types of pie, how could cheesecake not be even better? My next thought was one of guilt. *Instead of ordering what you usually ordered, you ordered something Amy wouldn't have been able to eat. Way to go!* I know the thought was irrational, but it was still there. Tears were immediate. I hid them well, noticing that only Micah saw them.

The night after my Cheesecake Factory birthday party, my life group met at the church for our weekly Rooted meeting. At the end of our study, my life group began singing "Happy Birthday." I was caught off guard. I shouldn't have been because we always celebrated birthdays in life group. As the treats were being passed out, my group handed me an envelope. They had all gone together to send the boys and I to the beach for a weekend away.

It was a great weekend. When I look back at our time in the hotel, our time on the windy beach, and our time shopping, I can see the joy that God was re-introducing in my heart. Being away from the house and all the reminders of our loss, I was able to set aside my grief, briefly. Both events taught me that God cares deeply about the little things. Amy loved celebrating birthdays (all but her own), and God made sure I noticed it was okay to continue on with some of the same traditions. Those traditions would help us remain tethered to Amy, even in her absence.

A little over a week after returning from the beach trip, the bottom dropped out from under me.

> I've spent much of my free time since Wednesday evening in tears, for one reason or another. It started when I realized that the one person who knew me the most, the one person who never judged me for the person I judged myself for, was gone. I so wanted to talk with her on Wednesday night. I wanted her to look at me like only she did and hold hands. I wanted just 5 more minutes…to say "I love you" one more time; to hear her laugh; to feel her hug.
>
> Then Thursday happened, and I was holding a very distraught young man who wanted to know why I would keep secrets from him about my marriage to his mama. (He wanted to know what our biggest embarrassing moment as a married couple was. I can't tell him that! I haven't even told my best friend that!) It took me a long while to realize (over 24 hours actually—sometimes I can be very slow) that he was just wanting to hear more stories about his mama. "I loved her, too, Daddy!" I didn't know what to say when he made that accusatory statement. I just held him as he cried. Those words still echo in my head this morning; my response: "I know, Gus, I know." There are times when I miss "the Autism Whisperer" who would have—in that very minute—been able to tell me what Gabriel was needing. I took him to dinner last night, just him and me. His bucket was full by the end of the night. He just needed my undivided attention.

Yesterday I spent some time with Isaiah. We [were reminded] we should be journaling daily about what we are feeling, especially regarding our Amy-zing loss. He's so much like her, wanting to stay strong for everyone around as they grieve. I never realized just how strong he is. It was nice to see him cloud up though, as I know he must release the tears too.

Micah's turning into an Amy-zing man of God whose legacy was started generations ago. His heart, his wisdom, and his insight have stopped me in my tracks. He changed his work schedule to have Mondays and Wednesdays off so that he could take care of his brothers while I had to work late or attend my Rooted Bible study. When his bosses accepted his request, but have since (3 times) scheduled him to work on those nights, he began looking for a new job so that he could honor my time. My time. Not his needs. He's also been working very hard to become his little brother's best friend. It's been awesome to watch.

I deserve much less than these boys have given me of late, but I am so honored that they are mine. My prayer is that I can honor Amy as I venture forward in this single parenting adventure (I'd use the term "nightmare" but I'm trying to be more positive—especially since I have 3 wonderful boys who love Jesus, serving, and their mama.)[48]

Figuring out how to balance my time between work, church, and each of my three boys, making sure their needs were met first, is not easy. But through the process of learning that aspect of single parenting, God has brought me closer to each of my boys. God is very good at healing broken people and weaving families together after tragedy.

At the end of October, Chris, Jen, and their two kids were coming over with dinner. It was "Chimi Night" as we'd come to call it. Jen makes the best chimichangas. We'd started a tradition the summer before Amy died. Jen makes chimichangas, we bring chips and a few other things, we watch a live musical on TV and enjoy the evening. That was the plan.

Minutes after Chris and Jen came in the door, my phone chimed. I looked at it with horror.

"Jen, Chris, I hate to do this to you, but...um...I gotta go."

"What's wrong?" Jen asked, "Is everything okay?"

"Um...Tracey's in the hospital on her way into surgery. Um..." Panic. The Worry Monster was back and Fear was climbing my throat. "Matt's at the hospital with her. I can't...I mean...He's alone at the hospital...Would you mind?"

"Go, Thom. We got this. The kids will be fine. We'll have some fun. Eat some food. Watch a musical. Go. We got this."

I fled to the van and raced to the hospital, fear choking me the entire way.

Tracey had posted on Facebook, asking for prayer. She was headed in for an emergency surgery. She'd been very sick and her health declined rapidly over night. When she was evaluated in the ER, the doctors found an infected gall bladder and gall stones to blame. The post was more than I could take. It was clear things were really bad. The grieving widower inside me prayed for healing, but was also too afraid to leave Matt alone in the waiting room at the hospital. I grabbed some coffee and headed to the surgical waiting room.

When I arrived, I handed Matt a Starbucks cup. He and I talked for almost two hours waiting for the surgery to end. Any time someone would enter the waiting area, he and I both paused to see if it was Tracey's surgeon with news. We were there past the time the surgeon had told Matt it would take. My anxiety was very high and I was fighting to not let it show. I truly wanted to be there to support Matt, not cause him more anguish.

Our conversation that night turned out to be very instrumental in helping us know each other more. We'd worked together on camp staff and in Children's Ministry many times, but we didn't really know a lot about each other's childhood, how we met our wives, or other hallmark stories of our past. The conversation not only helped us pass the time, but it also created stronger bonds of friendship.

Finally, the surgeon entered the room. Tracey had come through surgery nicely. I was relieved. I hugged Matt, let him go sit with his wife in recovery, and headed home. The entire drive home I was sobbing. I was angry I had let fear overwhelm me. It was that fear that drove me to the hospital. I didn't want Matt to be alone if the unthinkable happened to him like it had to me.

When I arrived at home, there was laughter and joy and the smell of wonderful food. Chris and Jen didn't stay for much longer, but it was clear they understood why I had to go. I filled them in, thanked them, and hugged them goodbye. When I put my boys to bed later that night, I hugged them a little tighter. I was happy God had intervened.

"Well, this year's going to be a Blue Christmas," Gabriel said from his seat in the van at the end of October. Not being an Elvis fan, I thought Gabe's comment was actually very funny. I had to hold in my laughter, though. He wouldn't have understood why I was laughing. I didn't want to hurt his feelings.

We were on our way home from Costco. The stark realization that Gabe would be entering his fourteenth year without Amy hit me like a ton of bricks. Mommy always made birthdays fun, special, and memorable. Gabe's birthday weekend needed to be fun, special, and memorable. Being the first birthday I was in charge of since Amy's death, I had to get it right.

My initial reaction was to try and cheer up my son.

"Gabriel, it's okay to miss Mommy, but just because she's with Jesus doesn't mean that the holiday is ruined. She loved Christmas; it was her favorite time of the year. Let's celebrate this Christmas like she would want us to celebrate it!" I didn't even get a response, just a *harrumph!* "What about we talk about your birthday?" I said, trying the ole bait-and-switch method of changing Gabriel's mood. It didn't work. He buried his face in his hands and began to sing "Blue Christmas" over and over as he cried.

Gabriel's birthday was in four days and here he was talking about Christmas and what a bummer it was going to be. "Dad, can we talk about my birthday yet?" is the usual question I get to answer on October 2nd. Every year I have to remind Gabriel that we can't talk about the plans for his birthday or what presents he might want until after my birthday, especially since his birthday (November 4th) is more than a month after mine. Otherwise, we'd hear about it every day of the year, beginning the day after his last birthday. Not this year. He didn't want to even broach the subject.

I remembered how I felt a month before when it was my birthday and I understood a little of what might be going through Gabe's head. After we arrived home and unloaded the car, I sat down with Gabriel on the couch. I hugged him as he wrestled with his feelings.

"Can I go to bed, now?" he asked. It was an odd request. Gabriel never asked to go to bed unless he was physically exhausted or sick. I helped him get ready for bed, tucked him in, and prayed with him like I had done every night since he came home from the hospital. When I left his room, I began going over the details of his party, wondering where I needed to improve the plan.

Since moving into fifth grade, Gabriel's parties traditionally were just family parties. We'd tried friend parties, but they were really difficult for him. Too much overstimulation. All of the family came over and we had fun. One of Gabriel's favorite things to do is play games. My brother-in-law, Dale, is a master board gamer and collector. He's been helping my boys find new and wonderful games to play. It was a great night. Gabriel's tank was overflowing at the end of the night. It wasn't a Blue Birthday. Helping him get through the next two months would be challenging. It would be challenging for all of us.

## CHAPTER 18

# Celebration and Thanksgiving?

Shortly before Gabriel's birthday, he started having trouble remembering to take his morning medications for help with anxiety and emotional control. The house was in turmoil. I tried everything: schedules, alarms on his phone, even bribery. Nothing worked. It was hard to identify if it had been a willful act or something related to grief. Throwing my hands in the air one night, I simply asked God for help. Amy had been so good at speaking a language that helped him understand the world around him. She could also identify what was usually causing whatever problem presenting itself. I didn't get an answer to my prayer that night, probably because I climbed into bed and passed out from exhaustion. Since going back to work, I was only averaging five to six hours of sleep a night.

The next morning was Sunday. I was scheduled to work on the soundboard in Children's Ministries. When I arrived to set up for the drama team, Auntie Jody, as she is known by all of the Children's Ministries Drama team at our church, sat down next to me to walk me through her lighting and sound cues.

"Are you okay?" she asked. Amy and Jody had been very good friends. Jody and I were as well. She could tell by looking at me that something was amiss.

"I'm not getting enough sleep lately," I said brushing off her question.

We proceeded with the morning's activities. When Micah showed up at the church with Gabriel and Isaiah in tow, I sighed. I could tell there was a storm brewing. Isaiah was red-faced. Micah's angry eyes were blazing. Gabriel was walking between them, seemingly oblivious. When they all three reached me, all three decided to talk at once. It took a while to calm down my oldest and youngest and get a straight story. Once I felt like I understood, I leveled my gaze at the child named after an angel who wasn't acting at all like an angel.

"Gabriel, did you take your meds this morning?" I asked.

"Um…" he giggled, "I forgot." Then he broke out in a string of giggles. His brothers left the room with the wave of my hand.

"That's three days in a row," I said. "This can't keep happening. When you don't have your medication, you end up pushing everyone's buttons around you."

"What does that mean?" he asked, still giggling.

"It means you're making everyone crazy around you."

"Well, I'll tell you what's making me crazy!" Gabriel's volume and tone climbed rapidly. "I'm tired of everyone treating me like a little kid! I'm almost fourteen. I should be treated like an adult."

I was stumped. I did not know the formula to untangle the information coming at me. I desperately needed a solution to the morning medication routine. I was usually leaving to take Isaiah to school when Gabriel and Micah were getting out of bed. Five of seven days, I couldn't make sure he had his meds.

Re-enter Auntie Jody.

Having watched what transpired between Gabriel and me, Jody, who was standing on the stage getting ready for the second service, called out, "Gabe! Can I get your help?"

"Are we done, Dad?!?" I put the added punctuation for you to understand what I was hearing. Truth be told, I couldn't tell if he was truly irritated at me or just in a hurry to go see Auntie Jody.

"Yes," I sighed. He left. Minutes later, I looked up from what I was doing and both were gone.

Todd walked into the back of the chapel at that moment and headed for me.

"You okay?"

"Did you hear what happened?" I asked, thinking he'd seen everything.

"Hear about what?"

"Gabriel just happened," I said. "He keeps forgetting to take his medication in the mornings and then he's nearly impossible to live with. I fear the other two might gang up against him." I tried to smile.

"Do you want me to talk with him?" he asked. Todd was one of Gabriel's favorite people in the entire world. It didn't matter what Todd said, Gabriel would listen and usually follow through with whatever was asked of him.

"I would love that."

I was not expecting Todd's response when he returned from tracking Gabriel down to have a chat.

"Sounds like Jody's already helped him figure it all out," he announced. "Guess I'm not needed." He finished with a wry smile.

At the end of the third service, Jody came to fill me in on the new plan. She'd worked out a point system with Gabriel. She was going to take him shopping to get special stickers and a special pen. My job was to make a three-month calendar. Gabe's job was to make sure that one of his brothers or I saw him take his pills in the morning so that he could receive a sticker. Each time Gabriel collected thirty stickers in a row without missing a day, Jody would take him out for some special time with her.

"Okay," I said hesitantly. I had already tried bribery. I didn't expect Jody's plan to work. But it did. His first "date" with Auntie Jody happened just after his birthday. She took him out for a treat and for some art supplies: crayons and a couple new coloring books. He was thrilled. It wasn't until after the second date, shortly after December started, that I realized the reason why Jody was successful and I wasn't. Gabriel needed "Mom time." Jody identified it right away. It took me over two months to realize what the problem was. These events happened about the time the Mom Mafia was born. (I'll explain the Mom Mafia more in chapter 23.)

As November flew by, I started getting a bit antsy. The Friday four days before my wedding anniversary, was one of those I-can't-breathe-and-my-chest-hurts-so-bad-it's-nearly-numb kind of broken moments. When I convinced myself to get out of bed, twenty minutes late, I trudged into the bathroom for my morning routine. Everything in me wanted to climb back in bed and live that day in a vacuum void of emotion. A few weeks prior I had begun playing worship music through my Spotify account on my phone while I took a shower. It usually perked me up and helped me face the day with peace. Without thinking, my hands turned on the worship play-list and I stepped into the shower. I just stood under the cascade of water.

When the first song ended, I realized I should get moving or I would be really late to work. Halfway through washing my face the song "Just Be Held," by Casting Crowns began to play. By the time the chorus played I broke.

> *Your world's not falling apart, it's falling into place*
> *I'm on the throne, stop holding on and just be held*[49]

When I realized that I had been singing along, I stopped. *God, I don't see my world falling into place. All I can see is the broken.* I sat down on the seat in the shower and began sobbing. By the end of the second verse, I was very angry with God. *This hurts too much! I can't do it anymore! They deserve better!* "They" referred to both my kids and my students. I felt like a failure as a father and as a teacher that morning. Just before the bridge of the song played, a calm washed over me. I stood. As the bridge played, I felt as if God was speaking directly to me through the words of the song.

> *Lift your hands, lift your eyes*
> *In the storm is where you'll find Me*
> *And where you are, I'll hold your heart...*
> *Come to Me, find your rest*
> *In the arms of the God who won't let go*[50]

"You've taught me before," I started praying aloud, "that You are always with me in the eye of the storm. I'm going to just crawl into your lap and let you hold me through this storm because I can't do it without You."

In the late 80's, I attended a Brian Duncan concert and was introduced to an image of God that's stayed with me. The opening act was a new band named Allies. I didn't know them well, but I was excited to see one of my favorite Christian artists at the time. Ironically, I don't remember Bryan Duncan at all. What I do remember was what lead singer Bob Carlisle said in the middle of Allies' set.

"My wife told me once when we were dating that when she is having a difficult time, she closes her eyes, and envisions herself crawling into God the Father's lap, and she calls him *Daddy*. While she tells *Daddy* her problems, she envisions God the Father is playing with her hair." That picture continues to surface in my memory over the years. I've always wanted to pay an artist to paint the picture that comes to mind of me laying in the Father's lap.

Standing in the shower that morning as Casting Crowns sang "Come to Me, find your rest, In the arms of the God who won't let go," I saw myself sitting in *Daddy's* lap. All day long that image and God's promise that He "won't let go," kept me upright.

After pulling into the driveway that evening, I went to check the mail. A large envelope was waiting for me. I was ecstatic. I raced to the house, burst through the door, and grabbed my phone. Micah was on his way home, but I couldn't wait. I must have dialed him three or four times before he pulled over to the side of the road and took my video chat call.

"It came!" I shouted, showing Micah the envelope. He was not happy with me.

"Dad, I'm two minutes from home. I'll see you in a minute."

Looking back, I wish I had waited until he was home.

"Here!" I said, jiggling, as he came through the door. I dangled the envelope in front of him as if it were a carrot and he the proverbial donkey.

Reticently he took the envelope and opened it. Inside was a red folder filled with papers. Micah took his time. It was his turn to get revenge. After taking more time than necessary, Micah looked at me and grinned.

"Well?" The envelope, from Biola University, had already announced "You got in!" I was hoping there was more good news in the letter. Micah started reading it aloud. Not only had he been accepted to the first college he'd applied to, he'd received a scholarship that covered nearly forty-five percent of the cost. Celebration was had all night long.

"He did it, Amy," I whispered while I lay in bed that night. "He did it."

On Monday, my principal Kevin stopped by my room. We saw each other often throughout the day, but he didn't usually come to my classroom during my prep-period.

"Do you need to take tomorrow as a personal day?" he asked, full-well knowing it was my anniversary.

"No," I said, trying to sound strong. "I'm going to hit it head on and try to power through it. I have something special planned—actually Amy planned something special back in August—for tomorrow night. I'm going to follow through with those plans."

"Well, if you change your mind, I'll understand." I was really blessed to have been working for Kevin during that school year. He understood grief very well and he understood how to take care of everyone who worked for him.

When I got home that night, I posted about the day and Kevin's visit. One of the youth pastor's wives from our church responded, "Thank you for living out 'Strength in the Lord.' What a leader and Amazing Father you are!!!! May God's peace follow you tomorrow and joy fill your time with the boys!"[51]

I didn't feel like an "Amazing Father" in the slightest. I felt more like a fraud, someone who could keep up appearances until I got home and closed the door. As I contemplated Ana's comment, which I didn't see until after I was home from celebrating my anniversary with my boys, a Twila Paris song began playing in my head.

> Ana, your words are too kind. I feel more like the warrior Twila Paris sings about in "The Warrior is a Child." – "People say that I'm amazing…They don't know that I go running home when I fall down. They don't know who picks me up when no one is around. I drop my sword and cry for just awhile, cause deep inside this armor, the warrior is a child."[52] [53]

After turning off my computer, I laid in bed pondering Ana's words and my response. I found myself hearing God's directive to me once again: "Never grow up, Thom." It had taken quite a while for me to really get God's message to me. I was His *child*.

> *Let the little children come to me, and do not hinder them, for the kingdom of God belongs to such as these. Truly I tell you, anyone who will not receive the kingdom of God like a little child will never enter it.* (Mark 10:14b-15, NIV)[54]

When I put it all together, God was reminding me I was called to have the faith of a child, to be child-like not childish. God the Father was my *Daddy*. He would take care of me. I just needed to climb up into His lap and be held.

I laid in bed smiling, truly smiling from ear to ear. In August, when Amy realized that Disney's new movie *Moana* was going to premiere on our anniversary that year, she told me she wanted to "go see it as a family." Being Disney fans, we often took the boys to see the newest movie in the theater. Rarely did we go on opening night. My plan was to pick up dinner on the way and go "all out" for the movie. Popcorn. Drinks. Candy. The only thing that kept me moving through the day was the thought of the boys' excitement at seeing a movie.

The day itself had been very difficult. Starting before I arrived at work, my phone began pinging. Texts and messages from Facebook were digitally knocking on my phone screen. Friends and family members were sending "prayers," "warm thoughts," and "love" on this day. The sentiment was very much appreciated. Unfortunately, I had stopped at Starbucks to order Amy's signature "2 pump Pumpkin Spice, 2 pump White Chocolate, 2 pump Cinnamon Dolce latte." Just tasting the drink, which was wonderful, started me down a very dark road. When I got to work, I sat in the parking lot for nearly fifteen minutes contemplating whether or not I'd actually go in the building or just requisition a sub and go home. "You are a Child of Mine" was playing on the radio when I decided to go into the building, be an adult, and do my job. (The irony of God's little hints through the day—that I was His child—did not hit me until I lay in bed reviewing the day in my head.)

When I stepped into the house after work, there was laughter. A lot of laughter. It lifted my spirits. Instantly I had hope the evening would be great. I stood for a moment just drinking in the laughter of my children. When one of them realized the garage door was closing and I was home, there was a mad dash to see who could get to me first. The laughter didn't stop. By the time all three had me surrounded in a group bear hug, I was laughing with them. It felt good. What stopped me, actually stopped me—not with tears, but with an overwhelming calm, as if being hugged by God—was the gift my oldest handed me. He made sure to let me know the gift was from all three of the boys. I knew he had used his own money to purchase it, but didn't want his brothers to feel left out of the gift.

I always joked that I was the Beast to Amy's Belle. Little did I know that Disney's *Beauty and the Beast* had debuted six years prior to our wedding date, on our wedding date, November 22nd! I unwrapped the home-made card which told me of the amazing coincidence. Then I unwrapped the twenty-fifth Anniversary Edition of *Beauty and the Beast*! It was an incredible gift. I felt like the best parts of my wonderful, thoughtful, and incredibly servant minded wife had found a place to rest in each of my boys. That night happened to be Micah's turn to shine.

Dinner was good. *Moana* was funny. A few of the songs were catchy. It wasn't *Beauty and the Beast*, my litmus test for all Disney movies, but it was enjoyable.

As I lay in bed that night, I realized that I did not just "exist" or "survive the day." I actually lived and loved. It was the first time I actually had time away from the sorrow and grief. That night was the first night I slept for more than six hours since Amy had died. Just before I fell asleep is when I realized God had been trying to get my attention.

Two days later was Thanksgiving. We spent it with the family. It was the first holiday we'd all spent together since losing Amy. Dinner was great. Lisa was an incredible host. We played games and had a great time. When we got home, I posted on Facebook to let everyone know the Johnson's had many things for which to be grateful.

## CHAPTER 19

# Three Months of Christmas

"Dad, can we start decorating for Christmas on Monday?"

"Monday's only October 31$^{st}$."

"But we don't celebrate Halloween."

It was true. I grew up in a very scary small town in Washington which had ties to the mob, a satanic cult, and large population of Wiccan followers. I stopped Trick-or-Treating when I was eight because I actually had to relinquish my candy to the docs at the ER because of the "pranks" which were not an urban legend in my hometown. On the other side of our backyard fence was the cemetery…the old cemetery where odd things happened on All Hallows Eve. When Amy and I were dating, I had three non-negotiables, one of which was, "My kids will never do Halloween." After hearing my explanation, Amy had no problem agreeing with me.

When Micah was only four months old, local grocery and department stores began decorating for Halloween. He screamed from the moment we walked past any Halloween decorations until we left the store. His brothers followed suit. We started hiding in the back of our home, having darkened the front windows, to watch a family show, often a Christmas movie. Not wanting the kids to feel left out the following day at school, we would give them each a pound (or two) of their favorite candy.

"Sure," I said to my three eager boys. They seemed a little crestfallen. "Now what?" I asked.

"We were prepared to argue more to win you over. We thought you'd say, 'No,'" Isaiah said, acting somewhat as the mouthpiece of the three. It did mean there would be a lot of unplanned work to do over the weekend, but I thought it a good idea. Amy's favorite holiday was Christmas. She spent ten months searching for the perfect gifts for everybody, often finishing most Christmas shopping before my birthday. Amy had some other unique Christmas quirks too. Throw in a couple quirks of my own, and we had a major event when it came to setting up Christmas.

First and foremost, I'm highly allergic to evergreen trees. All evergreen trees. Cedar is the worst. Early in our marriage, we invested in an artificial Christmas tree. When Gabriel was born, Micah, at the ripe old age of three, was feeling a little left out and neglected. In his little mind, since he was having to go to the hospital a lot to visit his preemie, always crying, baby brother, it was only fair that he had his "own Christmas tree." It was true, the three months leading up to Christmas that year had turned his life upside down and backward. We meandered through the holiday décor at Fred Meyer one evening. He fell in love with what I refer to as the three-foot-Charlie-Brown tree. It was hideous. Unlike our seven-foot tree, it *looked* fake. It had colored lights (which Amy despised). And it was so small; it would barely hold any ornaments. But Micah loved it. Since it was on sale, and he was adorable in his request for the tree, and because we felt guilty having lugged him to the hospital almost every night for three months, Amy and I bought the ugly tree, took it home, and set it up that night.

Around that same time, I came across *The Tale of Three Trees: A Traditional Folktale*, by Angela Elwell Hunt. Since Bible college, I had a difficult time separating the Christmas Story from the Easter Story. You can't have one without the other. If so, neither has the power to save us. I was enamored with the book. It eloquently joined both events, along with Jesus' ministry. I have often read it to the boys at Christmas time.

In 2006, while driving home from work, I heard the song "Did You Know?" on the radio. "Did the cross cast a shadow o'er your cradle? Did You know?"[55] I was stunned. For years prior, I had imagined this description in my head. I immediately commissioned a small wooden feeding trough with a cross attached to add to our Christmas décor. And because of the folktale connecting with this song, we soon had a third tree to decorate.

Now enough of my Christmas quirks. Amy has only two worth mentioning here. The year we were married, Starbucks started selling the famous Starbucks mini-cup Christmas ornaments. We didn't purchase any the first two years. When the color of the Starbucks holiday cup changed from purple to the signature red—Amy's signature color—she was head over heels for them. Finally, in 2002, she broke down and bought one for us and one for a friend who also loved Starbucks coffee as much as she did. Then every year since, Amy purchased at least one. Some years there were more than one design. Some years there were also other ornaments: a food truck, a bag of coffee beans, a bronze French press. Her goal was to be able to fill an entire tree with Starbucks ornaments. Needless to say, we have quite the collection.

The other quirk is more of a family tradition. It started out of a friendship Amy made with the manager of a Disney Store in our local mall. Amy was a magnet who pulled in people who were hurting. It was easy for strangers to come up to Amy and tell her of their deepest, darkest woes. I'm not joking. One evening, we were browsing the Disney Store for Christmas presents for our three boys when the manager approached us, offering help. She and Amy hit it off immediately. She walked us around the store helping us look for a certain character one of the boys loved (I do not remember which one). In the process she asked Amy if we'd ever been to "the Happiest Place on Earth." I'm sure it was an upsell the company was pressing. The conversation turned to discussing our Honeymoon at Disneyworld. Then Amy asked the manager the same question. We were immediately watching a woman begin to cry in slow motion. I looked at Amy, helpless. Back then, I hardly knew what to do when Amy cried let alone a stranger. Amy took the woman by the arm and led her around the back of a tall display to give her some privacy. Then she listened. The manager and her husband had planned a trip to Disneyland, but the day before they were to leave, her husband had a physical emergency which sent him seeking medical help. After being admitted to a local hospital, and undergoing an endless battery of tests, the couple, who had two very young daughters and a teenage son, were given the diagnosis: stage three stomach cancer. That was four months earlier.

"Do you mind if I pray for you?" Amy asked. The woman held out her hands and bowed her head. Later we found out she'd been raised Catholic but no longer admitted a faith in any god.

Amy didn't pause. She took the woman by the hands and prayed. I half expected someone to interrupt the ladies, as sometimes happens when God's work is being done out in the open. But no one did. Either I am a pretty terrifying body guard, or God, in His divine will, kept everyone at bay. I'm sure it was the latter, although my middle school students would claim the former. We left the store without buying anything that night. The character we were looking for was nowhere to be found, a fact that puzzled the manager.

"I know I've seen him," she kept saying. "If you give me your number, I can call you if we get something in on the next shipment or two," she offered as we were getting ready to leave. Amy gave the manager her cell number.

"Thank you. Feel free to call anytime," Amy said.

A week or two later, Amy's phone rang. There was something the manager wanted us to come see at the store. We went the next day. It was an ornament. We bought it for the tree, but still needed a gift for one of the boys.

"How's your husband?" Amy asked before we left.

"He's having a hard time with the radiation treatment." So Amy offered to pray with her again and the friendship started. Every month or so, Amy would make sure to visit the Disney Store to check on her new friend. The next Christmas Season, Amy noticed the Disney Sketchbook ornaments and an idea hatched. Our kids happened to be with us making a "wish list." We each picked out an ornament. As we were leaving the store, the manager was entering, returning from her lunch break.

"Amy! I'm so glad I got to see you! I wanted to tell you the good news! Make a Wish Foundation has granted my husband's request. They're sending us to Disneyland in March as a family!" Then she filled us in on her husband's condition. The doctors prescribed a medication that helped him sleep through more of the pain. He was only awake for about six hours a day. Amy hugged her friend.

"I'll keep praying."

"Thank you."

It became a yearly tradition. Every November we would go to the Disney Store and each of us would pick out an ornament. Amy's goal was to have one tree just for Disney and Starbucks ornaments. One tree was the kid's tree and the tree in the front window was the formal tree.

In March, Amy checked in with her friend two weeks after the trip was to have ended. The husband had been so weak. Make a Wish flew medical staff with them to take care of him through the whole trip. He only got to spend about three hours a day in the park, and only three of the five days. On the fifth day, a nurse helped him sit on the balcony of the Disney hotel so he could wave to his family. When he looked down to wave at his family, they were surrounded by Disney characters, all waving up at him. He waved back. Make a Wish had planned an incredible event. When his family returned from the park early that evening, he had slipped into a coma. He died the next day before the family was to fly back home. When Amy returned home to tell me the news she was both emotional and a bit happy.

"Did I tell you she's started going back to church?" Amy asked.

"No."

"Yes, about a month before the trip, she and her three kids started going to church. She even started praying with her husband before he died." She paused for a moment, then finished, "I'm glad God made a way for them to go on the trip. I hope those kids have great memories of their dad's last few days and hours." Looking back at the whole ordeal, it is quite special that my three boys have great memories of their mom's last month, and especially the last few days and hours.

Now back to 2016. Needless to say, it took a week for us to set up Christmas at our house. On November 8, 2016, we made our yearly pilgrimage to the Disney Store to purchase ornaments (this would be our eighth year of this tradition). I had done my research online, trying to figure out which ornament to buy for Amy. I was not fully prepared for what happened.

Going in I was set on getting the latest Belle ornament. Being the Beast in this relationship, I found it fitting that Belle was alone, sitting next to a fountain, reading, almost as if she were waiting for her prince. The Enchanted Rose ornament was already sold out online, and neither were on the sales floor. The kind Cast Member said they were out of the Rose, but she'd look for Belle.

While waiting, my eyes landed on the house from *Up*. Time seemed to stop. There was no sound. Only the memory of the married couple, dancing, walking, laughing—and then just the husband…and later the awkward boy scout who saves the old man. I have three wonderfully awkward boys who daily remind me that life keeps going, that music keeps playing, that laughter and joy can be found in the oddest situations.

The Cast Member returned with the Belle and the bad news that there really were no more Enchanted Roses. She apologized and went to the counter, which I found out later, to see if she could order me one. Then she disappeared. The boys hemmed and hawed, trying to only pick one. Isaiah chose. Gabriel chose. Micah was standing there with two or three in hand when the Cast Member returned, holding the last Enchanted Rose in the store (it had fallen behind some boxes). When it lights up, the Rose looks red with white tips—just like Amy's favorite rose, the Fire and Ice rose.

In a time when many would be wholly mad at God, wishing themselves dead, or even walking away from their faith, this slightly crazy, somewhat balding, extremely sentimental, middle aged man found God in a trip to the Disney Store on a Tuesday night, with his three teenage boys in tow. When it's clear God loves me so much to care about something as trivial as a Christmas ornament, I am not worried about the outcome of the evening's news reel.

The trip for Starbucks ornaments happened a week later. While in my favorite coffee shop, I hatched an idea. I purchased enough ornaments to give to a handful of friends as thank you gifts.

The evening after Thanksgiving, Micah left to meet up with friends to see a movie. Less than five minutes later, my cell phone rang. Micah was crying on the other end. There's that moment for some parents when they hear their child crying—truly crying, not whining—that flips a switch in the brain. That moment was mine.

"Micah...what's wrong?" Only tears were answering me. "Micah! Are you okay? Can you hear me?"

"Dad," he finally sobbed, "I was in an accident. I'm sorry!" More tears.

"Are you okay?"

"I'm sorry, Dad. The car's ruined."

"Micah, I don't care about the car. Are you okay?"

"I can't get out of the car. The door's stuck."

"Are...you...okay?" My tone was even and slow. He was hysterical.

"Just a minute..." then I heard him trying to talk with someone outside of the car.

*God, I need peace to handle this without losing my head. Thank you that he can talk to me. Please give him peace.*

"Dad, I've got to talk with the police. Can I call you back?"
"NO! I need to know, are you okay? Is anything on you broken? And I need to know where you are."

"I think I'm fine. I hurt a little. Just get on the freeway. You'll find me." The line went dead.

Isaiah was in the kitchen helping me prepare for dinner. He heard the whole conversation. He began to panic.

"Isaiah, take a deep breath...good. Now, I need you to call Lisa. Tell her Micah was just in a car accident and you and Gabriel are home alone. See if she can come over. I'll be back as soon as I can. Call me if you need anything. Okay?"

He nodded, but his face was flush. I cupped his face in my hands.

"Isaiah, take a deep breath. Micah's okay. I just need to go help him. Then I'm going to take him to get checked out at the hospital. He's going to be okay...Take another deep breath...Okay, do you think you can call Lisa?"

"Yeah. I can do that."

"Call me and let me know what she says, okay?" He nodded. "Okay?"

"Okay," he replied. I was out the door in two steps, heading for the accident. It didn't take long for fear to attack. As I turned onto the freeway, my mind flashed to a scene of Micah's memorial service. I started to shake. *In the name of Jesus!* I yelled aloud. *No! I won't be afraid!* That was all I could get out before I was coming up on the crash site.

It was very dark and it had been raining. The traffic on the freeway was bunching together when Micah merged. Less than a mile down the freeway, the car in front of him slammed on its brakes. Micah hydroplaned into the car in front of him. When I got to the car, a policeman was talking with Micah. He'd been able to climb out the passenger door. I stepped next to him, introduced myself to the officer and put my arm around Micah. He was still crying uncontrollably.

"It's okay," I started, now hugging him. "You're standing. You're safe. No one is severely injured. This is why we have insurance and you have big, buff angels." I was hoping for a hint of a smile. Micah had settled down quite a bit. We talked with the officer, then he went to finish with the driver of the other car. Our car was totaled. The other car drove away after the police were done with the scene; all four people—two adults and two under the age of four—seemingly okay.

"I'm really sorry, Dad," Micah started.

"I know, Micah. It's okay. You're okay. That's what matters."

After leaving the scene, I called Isaiah and told him I was taking Micah to get checked out at the ER.

"It's just a precaution. He's walking and talking. It might take a couple hours."

"Okay...good. I'm glad he's okay. Lisa's on her way over."

## GOOD GRIEF

Almost three hours later, I drove into our driveway. Micah had been checked for neck and spinal injuries because of the impact of the accident and the location of his pain. He was cleared. He would manifest some nasty bruises, but he would be as good as new in a few days.

"How am I going to get to school on Monday, or work? This is going to mess up everything. I'm really sorry!"

"Micah, it'll all work out. God's got us. Remember?" It didn't completely quiet either of our fears at the moment, but the comment was working like a salve on a bad burn. After talking with my sister-in-law, I checked on the boys who had been getting ready for bed. They both hugged Micah a little tighter when they saw him. Isaiah wouldn't let go. It was clear that the fear I had for a brief moment had taken root in my youngest. After I tucked each of the boys in bed that night, taking a little extra time with each one, I went to the computer to post my Thankfulness. When I climbed into my own bed, exhaustion and relief set in and the tears began to roll.

*God...I don't know what I would have done if...*I couldn't finish the sentence. *I mean if...*

But *'If' didn't happen, my Son,* I felt God say to me.

I curled up and cried myself to sleep.

In the morning, we'd been contacted by someone in our "extended family." They had a car to give us. Christmas really had started early for us. Micah and I both cried, this time for joy. God had not only kept my family from another sudden tragedy, but He'd supplied a need immediately. When Micah returned to school and to work on Monday, he did so in the vehicle God had provided.

By this time, Micah had received acceptance letters from three colleges. (I made him apply to more than just the one he intended to attend to ensure he would be accepted and to ensure he had options.) Days after the car accident, Micah was boarding a plane to Southern California for a double college visit. Micah's godparents, who were living an hour or two away from his destination, acted as surrogates. While in the L.A. area, Micah attended "Biola Bound" with other potential Biola students. Travis and Jenny had asked to keep Micah through the following weekend so he could be present for a "sibling" birthday and a trip to the House of Mouse. It was a perfect week for him to recharge his batteries and take a break from the family stress created by our New Normal. It was also a perfect week for his brothers and me to get a taste of what the following school year might be like around the house without Micah.

When he returned, one of his best friends picked him up at the airport. We'd planned a Christmas party at the house and had invited everyone who had brought us meals, helped with the memorial service, or who were instrumental in other aspects of helping us traverse the prior three months. We'd wanted a tangible way to say "Thank you." We also wanted to honor Amy. She always wanted to throw an "every-other" Christmas party. Her dream was to open our home every two years to family and friends and lavish them with special recipes, music, and laughter. We'd only managed having one such party; something always prevented it.

The party was a hit. We'd wanted to love on others, but at the end of the night, we were overwhelmed by the love we'd been shown throughout the party. God was truly taking care of us, surrounding us with family and friends who were staying with us through the duration of grief.

On December 23, 2016, we attended our first Christmas Eve-Eve Candlelight Service as a family of four. Different friends and pastors hovered around us at different moments of the evening (some before, some during, and some after) to see how we were holding up through the holiday. Part of me felt like Amy was very much gone, while another part always felt like she was just "on her way" and "would be 'here' any minute." I carried two candles that night.

"Dad, why do you have two candles?" Gabriel asked.

"Because Mom's not here to hold her own," I said. Our friends sitting behind me put a hand on my shoulder to let me know I wasn't alone.

There were smiles, a few tears, and some laughter that evening. We all left the church with a full "love bank." We'd received so many hugs that night that we'd lost count. As the evening came to a close, in the privacy of my bedroom, I offered another prayer of thanks. The Christmas Season wasn't turning out to be a *blue* one as Gabriel had predicted. Although our hearts felt as if a large piece of us was missing, we also felt God's presence and hand throughout it all.

On Christmas Morning, I got up and cooked a very "Amy" breakfast. Every year she would go wild on Christmas Morning. She would make pancakes or waffles, eggs, bacon, sausage, and hash browns. While she was cooking, I was usually in another room, reading Christmas stories to the boys. I had a lot of help from Isaiah to pull off such a feat.

After breakfast, we cleaned the table to make ready for another tradition: writing letters to Jesus. In 2009, Amy got the idea to give gifts to Jesus on Christmas. As she was searching for ideas on the internet, she came across the idea to write Jesus a letter. The letters were to contain a summary of the year, thanksgiving for Jesus' help through difficult times, and a pledge for the next year. She loved the idea and thus a new tradition in the Johnson home began. Writing those letters was difficult. We always took out the letters from previous years and read our own. Then we would write a new letter. All of them would go back into Jesus' stocking for safe keeping until the following year. Seeing the pile of Amy's letters gave us all pause. I had to put them away before we could write our own that year.

After the Jesus' Stocking tradition, I walked the boys into the family room and set them on the couch next to each other. Since Amy was so prepared for Christmas, she had purchased some gifts herself before she died. I wanted to make sure the boys knew she purchased those gifts. There were a few tears, a time of reflection, and then the rest of the unwrapping began. Although Amy was not present, we felt we'd been able to celebrate Jesus' Birthday well.

Later that afternoon, the boys and I partook of another tradition Amy had started. We went to see a movie together. When Amy started the tradition, I was shocked to find out that Christmas Day is one of the craziest, most attended days of the year at movie theaters. She and her father had gone to a couple Christmas Day movies while she was a teenager. It had been a fun memory that she wanted to pass on to our kids.

We went to see the animated movie *Sing!* which took place in a world where animals lived like humans. One down-on-his-luck koala bear, who happened to run a nearly bankrupt theater, was holding a singing competition, much like *American Idol*. We all loved it, but there was one small part of the movie that really bugged both Gabriel and Isaiah. It had to do with one of the main characters, a mother pig who was married with thirty-five children. No one supported her dream to participate in the competition. In fact, her husband never heard her excited explanation of the coming event. He was the proverbial checked-out dad. All thirty-five of the children were self-absorbed and "needy."

"Dad," Gabriel said as we pulled away from the theater, "I don't like how those kids didn't appreciate their mom! She was a good mom, like our mom, and they were mean to her." He sounded as if he might cry. Micah and Isaiah chimed in, agreeing with him and comforting him as well. My heart was torn, saddened by Gabriel's take-away, but elated that all three of the boys really knew just how blessed they were to have had Amy as a mom.

Christmas at Lisa's was wonderful, but everyone felt like a piece was missing. We didn't talk about the elephant in the room that night (I don't think), but we did all notice at one point or another that Amy had left a big hole in the family.

When I look back at the whole Christmas experience, I am warmed by just how much God cares about each of us. The Bible says, "And even the very hairs of your head are all numbered" (Matthew 10:30, NIV). God cares that much! People don't number things they have *en masse* unless it is something very valuable to them. I can't imagine God would either. All throughout the Bible, the message is clear: God cares about each one of us, as individuals, all the way down to the smallest degree. Just pick up the Christmas and Easter stories. Read them back to back. It's pretty easy to see that He loves us unconditionally, more than we could ever know, let alone deserve.

CHAPTER 20

# New Year's Scare

After Christmas, my boys took advantage of the snow. They played outside with the kids across the street. They built snowmen, had snowball fights, and even made snow angels. We all seemed carefree. As the days of 2016 raced toward the new year, I started becoming unsettled. I didn't realize how conflicted I was about entering a new year until New Year's Eve.

On December 31, 2016, it hit me that now, when asked, I'd have to say, "My wife passed away last year," instead of "a few months ago." (It's semantics, I know, but it still feels like an eternity has passed in changing the term.) Then, as I stood in my living room, watching the timer count down from "ten seconds," surrounded by my three boys, my sister-in-law, my brother-in-law, and my nephew, I began tearing up. Why? Honestly? Because I had no one to kiss at midnight, no one to hold hands with, and no one to whom I'd ask, as I have for many New Year's celebrations, "Do you still want to grow old with me?" It's silly, I know. Amy was in heaven, partying with her mom, her grandfather, and a few family friends who have followed her to heaven; I was having a pity party. I had always known I would outlive my beautiful wife. I just didn't realize I'd have to grow old without her (a lot can flash through this brain in ten seconds). The ball dropped. "Happy New Year" was shouted around the room. Then my family did something I hadn't expected. They all circled me in a group hug. Then they each kissed my cheek as if they had known what was going through my head. My sadness turned to laughter instantly, and I realized that even though my heart had a hole in it, it was still pretty full of some amazing family and friends, and God was still listening to my heart's cry.

After cleaning up from the party and saying goodbye to Dale, Lisa, and Jeremy, I mounted the stairs for bed. I lay in the bed for quite a while, just pondering the previous four months. I fell asleep sometime after 1:00 a.m.

Wanting to start the new year off well, I had pre-planned the meals for January 1, 2017. The day started leisurely late with bacon, dilled eggs, potatoes, and pancakes. We played with Christmas gifts, played a few games during the day, and even watched a movie. The evening ended with prime rib, haricot vert (Amy's favorite green beans), garlic mashed potatoes with gravy, and a chocolate, hazelnut mousse. All of it was homemade. After dinner, I felt guilty for not inviting family or friends over (we only ate half if it), and I almost had, but I wanted to begin and end the first day of 2017 as a family with a homemade meal that I made (with a lot of help from my redheaded sous-chef). It was more of a test for me. The four months of meals our friends delivered every other day was amazing and it really helped us get our feet under us. I hadn't cooked much and have never cooked multiple meals in the same day—meals that I had to plan, find coupons, and shop for without my wife's help. I'd been a little nervous I couldn't feed the boys real food consistently (not simply Campbell's, Kraft, or drive-in). I needed the day to have happened the way it did. I needed to know I could do it.

When I sat at my computer after the boys went to bed, I posted on Facebook about the day.

> 2017—Day 1—I think I passed the dad test…
>
> No one fought with each other today (much), no one threw a fit (not a real one at least), and all 3 of the boys are talking to each other as they are getting ready for bed; however, I only fed my kids twice today; so maybe I only get a C-…
>
> The last 4 months of 2016 couldn't have been possible without the tidal wave of prayer; our army of friends and family stepping in to feed us and/or transport kids going in different directions; and the phone calls, hugs, tears, and "silent sitting" with us that has literally (to borrow Micah's catchphrase) literally [been what's] kept us going…and sometimes simply kept us upright. Thank you.

It may not have been the best "diet day" for someone trying to stay svelte, but it was a touch of Amy in our day. The house smelled wonderful all day! It is clean (except for the typical teenage bunkers my kids refer to as their rooms)! We were a family today.

So, with one day down, we're ready to tackle another. I'd call that a win.[56]

A very good friend, probably knowing I'm a bit too hard on myself often, replied: "Hey, give yourself high marks! I've never cooked two meals in one day! That daily cooking--being prepared w/ coupons, grocery shopping, etc.--is tough business!"[57] I was encouraged a super-mom found what I was attempting to accomplish difficult.

School resumed the next day. Although I'd just had Christmas Break, I was running on fumes. I felt like I was barely making it through the day. When I arrived back at home after work, I made dinner and then sat down in the recliner for "just a sec." When I woke up, the boys had eaten dinner, put the leftovers away, and had put themselves to bed. I glanced at the time. It was almost 2:00 a.m. I slowly climbed the stairs and tried to get some more sleep.

Tuesday happened very much the same.

On Wednesday, I realized my heart was pounding out of my chest. I couldn't get a steady pulse and neither could the blood pressure cuff I still had from Amy's dialysis kit. I knew immediately what was going on; it had happened two different times ten years before. I didn't want to upset any of my boys. I made dinner, ate with them, and then sat in the recliner, hoping I could get my heart to slow down with breathing exercises.

"Dad, are you okay?" one of the boys asked.

"I'm just tired," I said. When an hour had passed and my heart was still beating irregularly, I started making a plan. I knew it was going to be a late night for me. I made sure my phone was charging, put away the remnants of dinner, and then went back upstairs—slowly—to check my blood pressure. The machine couldn't detect a steady pulse. I called Bob and Susie, my Life Group leaders. I don't remember whom I talked to, but they agreed to pray. Bob was going to meet me at the hospital. Then I called my sister-in-law.

"Lisa, I need prayer," I said when she picked up the phone.

"What's wrong?"

I took a deep breath.

"I think my heart's back in a-fib. My heartbeat is racing and the blood pressure cuff can't read a steady pulse. I think I need to go to the hospital."

"I'll get there as soon as I can."

"I just need you to be available for the boys while I go to the hospital. Gabe and Isaiah don't know what's going on. I told Micah, and he thinks he'll be fine without you coming to the house."

"Alright...are you calling an ambulance?"

"No, I think I can drive. I drove home from work this way."

After putting my youngest two to bed, I gave Micah a pep talk.

"I'm going to be fine. This happened before and they were able to fix things quickly. I'll call you when I can. Lisa said she'd come over if you wanted her to." I could see he wasn't taking this well. I hugged him tightly and then headed to the ER.

They confirmed my suspicions: a-fib...again. I knew the triggers for a-fib, yet I neglected to pay attention. Since Amy's passing, I had only been sleeping five to six hours a night. Combined with the stress of being a new single parent and the coffee I'd consumed since Thanksgiving (probably more coffee than the previous twelve months combined), I was a walking time bomb.

The hospital was able to use the paddles to cardio-vert my heart to a normal rhythm. Within an hour, Bob was driving me home in my van. Micah was seated on the couch talking with Lisa when I arrived. He was so worried and scared, he'd called her. She drove over to be with him. When he saw me walk into the kitchen, he ran to give me a hug.

Holding me very tightly, he said, "I thought I was going to lose you when you went out the door."

"I'm sorry," I said. "I didn't mean to scare you."

After Gabriel was born, I had repeatedly told Amy she needed to be selfish as a mom and take care of herself. After she was diagnosed, I said it a couple of times too. It always caused a fight.

I woke the next morning feeling like a hypocrite. God, in many different ways, reminded me of the many conversations I'd had with Amy about taking care of herself. I promised I would go back to tea and decaf (but only once a week or so). I also promised to make sure I would get more sleep. That was the day I realized I could no longer bring work home with me. I had to find a way to complete all my grading and planning at school. When I came home, I would be home, take care of my kids, and rest. That was also the day I realized I needed to give myself a break. I couldn't keep the house up the way Amy had always wanted it, even though we'd never been able to keep it that way.

Micah and Isaiah both woke up feeling awful. The flu had come to roost. They kept me company while I stayed home with a down day. When Gabriel finally opened the front door after school, he headed straight for his bedroom. Thinking it was odd, I climbed the stairs to check on him. He was asleep on his bed, backpack still on his back. I pulled out Amy's homemade chicken noodle soup recipe and treated us all to a little of Amy's love.

Hopefully, I won't need a third time at this lesson. The divine two-by-four up the side of the head smarts!

## CHAPTER 21

# The Romance Lives On...

I opened my email on February 12, 2017. Top of the feed: "There's Still Time!" I wasn't thinking when I clicked on the message. It was from one of my favorite restaurants.

"We noticed you haven't made reservations this year for Valentine's Day yet. There's still room. Just click on the link below…" I stopped reading and closed the browser. "I hate Valentine's Day!" I yelled at the computer. I pushed away from the desk and stormed into the kitchen.

"But, Dad, don't you still love Mommy?" Gabriel asked as he entered the kitchen from the other direction.

"What?" I wasn't really paying attention.

"Valentine's Day is a day to tell everyone you love them," Gabriel said. "You still love Mommy, right?"

"Yes, sweetie, I still love your mama. Valentine's Day is just hard. I really miss her and I don't get to spend another Valentine's Day with her ever again."

Gabriel crossed the room and hugged me.

"It's going to be okay, Daddy," he said. Rarely did Gabriel call me Daddy before Amy passed away. I began noticing when he used the term. It felt as if God was trying to get me to tune in for a specific message. The message came on Valentine's Day in a very unique, God way.

I have hated Valentine's Day since high school. I always managed to like the girls who thought of me as a brother, and who would usually then go on to date one of my closest friends (college didn't change that experience either). When I met and married Amy, I still hated it: why do men get a pass with chocolates and flowers for not romancing their wife throughout the year? Amy had similar feelings having worked for Hallmark. Valentine's Day was one of the busiest days of a Hallmark store's life. More often than not, her store was full of men who were last minute shopping. In a nut shell, we both hated Valentine's Day.

That didn't stop me from buying flowers or taking Amy out for dinner; I just made it a point to make sure that I didn't reserve those things only for Valentine's Day, Amy's birthday, and our anniversary.

At the beginning of February 2017, while looking for a very important piece of paper, I stumbled upon a love letter I'd written to Amy on February 14, 2002. What a gift!

> "This year I wanted to give you the world, but we couldn't afford it, and then I realized that what I really wanted to give you was five days—five days of bliss, romance, and love."

What followed was a Cloud Nine view of the five best days of our lives together. The five days?

1. February 22, 1997—our first date—"Twelve and a half hours, a dead car battery, $90, and a glass of tea later..." (Temple and Jason should remember that dead battery. Spud and Julie have seen the "glass of tea trick." It was cream soda when they saw it).
2. Easter 1997—the day I knew she'd say "yes" (even though I didn't ask until Wednesday night after Easter).
3. November 22, 1997—our wedding day—I wrote the song "For a Lifetime" with a friend's help. (I meant every word.)
4. October 2, 1998—the day we found out that the doctors were horribly wrong, we could have babies (Micah had been baking for a month already). AND

5. February 9, 2002—a Saturday—"The day was just a normal day with breakfast, errands, tickle fests with Micah and everything else that we do in a day." (Amy knew how to make even the ordinary days special.)

It ended with "This year I'm not asking you to be my Valentine for a day—I'm asking you to remain my wife, partner, lover and best friend 'for all eternity.'" I thought going into Christmas would be the most difficult season to travel through. I was a bit mistaken.

The day before Valentine's Day is Isaiah's birthday. At the end of January, I had asked Isaiah what kind of party he wanted and who he wanted to invite.

"I don't want a party this year," he said while I was driving him to school one morning. Having watched him pull away from everyone in order to avoid the pain of grief, I was worried. I pressed and pressed. I inquired about kids from his new school and even told him his friends from his old school could come. He wasn't having any of it. I was frustrated. I wanted him to have a positive experience. I missed his cues. He truly didn't want a birthday party.

When Isaiah realized I wasn't going to stop asking, he agreed to a bowling party with his friends from his former Christian school. The party was held at the same bowling alley we'd gone to celebrate the night before Amy died. Isaiah had fun and was glad to have had some time with his friends. I was exhausted, having worked so hard to pull off a party without Amy.

Looking back, I think I was afraid Isaiah would completely pull away from every one of his friends. I was afraid he'd look back in retrospect and resent me for not having given him a thirteenth birthday party. Basically, I was afraid. As the years counted on, Isaiah didn't want a fourteenth birthday nor a fifteenth birthday. He no longer wanted to celebrate getting older without his mom.

---

I had a plan for Valentine's Day 2017:

1. Take off February 14th so I don't have to deal with Valentine's Day at school. Done.
2. Take my son to two routine doctor's appointments on my day off. Done.

3. Take my youngest two boys to a party at a friend's house while their older brother is at work so they could enjoy the holiday. Done.
4. Go have dinner at Applebee's by myself (it's where we had our first date; it's where I proposed; it's where I gave Amy diamond earrings on our tenth anniversary; it's where we went when we wanted to reminisce).[58]

I didn't make it to Applebee's.

I had volunteered in children's ministry all day Sunday. Three people told me that I "just have to hear the sermon." I couldn't get it to download on Monday. Tuesday, Valentine's Day, sitting in the driveway of my friend's house after dropping off my boys for a party, I went to the church's website and downloaded the sermon. I needed to change clothes, to "dress up" for my date (silly I know, but I needed to). I was ten minutes into the sermon when I knew I couldn't go to Applebee's. Pastor Keith Jenkins was visiting the church on that Sunday and preached on James 1, Job, and being rooted in Christ during trials. By the time the sermon was half over, I was back at my house, sitting in the driveway, sobbing.

Here's what I knew: I hurt and I didn't always have the answers to the questions my three boys were asking in the middle of their pain. I was afraid, afraid for my boys, and afraid for my future. As I listened to the sermon, I prayed that one day I would have the faith of Job: to ask questions of God; to weep and mourn, and in the next minute to worship like Job did; and to not sin along that pathway.

The Summer of 2016, my lifelong lesson was finally realized: to "count it all joy" when trials show up at my door. I finally understood what God meant in Hebrews 13. I finally found true joy, and I lived in that joy all summer long. Listening to Pastor Keith, my prayer was that I could return to that understanding of joy in the midst of the worst pain I have ever endured.

Pastor Jenkins spoke of "the Knowing People" who sit next to you quietly because they know you are hurting, and because they know you need them, their presence and their arms of compassion, but not necessarily their words. I thought of my wonderful support group of friends and family who have done so for me. After posting about the experience on Facebook, one of "the Knowing People" God has placed in my life responded:

> I keep repeating to myself, remember you are a soul having a human experience. You still need to allow yourself to go through

the experience while holding tightly to the fact that you will be together again. I can't imagine the stress of being a single parent.[59]

There were days when I begged God to take this pain away because I felt like I was seconds from completely losing all ability to function, and that was no longer an option. I lost it once, a week after Amy passed away, and I scared my youngest very badly. I was trying to find her wedding dress. Why? Because I couldn't remember where it was and I needed to see it, to see her in it. (I know it doesn't really make much sense now, but it did then. I had to find that dress.) From that brief window of time, I learned I have to remain strong for my boys. They need me to continue to provide a home, warm meals, and clean clothes for them; to continue to sit and hold them and cry with them; to answer questions (if I can); to continue to love them through their pain, and their anger, and their "numb." Strong doesn't mean stalwart, unflinching, and dry of tears. It means I get up in the morning, do life with my kids, go to work, come home, do more life with my kids, and then fall asleep exhausted. Strong means I wake up the next day, wash... rinse...repeat. I don't go get a drink, or go to a tavern with my co-workers after a hard day of teaching. Not because I think it's a sin to drink alcohol—I don't. For me, with my family history, my impulsivity, and numbness at the time, I couldn't take a drink; I don't think I could have stopped at just one. Strong means my boys will see me own my mistakes. It means they will see me apologize and repair relationship. Strong means they will see me cry, but they won't see me completely lose my grip on reality and hope. I want them to know Jesus is *always* there. Jesus carries us when we can't walk. They need to know we will continue to live—to truly live when this pain isn't so great.

I never made it to Applebee's that night. I was fine with it. I needed to hear Pastor Keith's message. My favorite day in February is the 22nd. The anniversary of Amy's and my first date. I made a mental note to celebrate then. It would be the "20th Anniversary" of that wonderful day.

During the week between Valentine's Day and our "One Year First Date Anniversary," Micah gave me a gift.

"Dad, I'd like to take the boys out for dinner on the 22nd. Would that be okay with you?"

"Um...yeah...let me get you some money."

"No, Dad, this one's on me." He has such a generous heart.

The morning of the day came and I dressed for the "date" after work because I would not be going home. On our first date, I wore my favorite shirt, which, I would find out later, Amy hated. It was mustard yellow. Since the shirt was long gone, I dug through my closet to find the closest substitution. I found an orange plaid shirt. I smiled, knowing what Amy would have said; "It's not as hideous as the mustard poop shirt."

I had given Amy a bouquet of flowers on our first date. Knowing the different meanings of the palette of rose colors, I decided to forgo any arrangement with a rose in it. When I gave it to her, she was thrilled. She thought the white flower was a rose (until she looked a second time).

"White roses are one of my favorite two roses," Amy said.

"Oh, what's your other favorite rose?"

"Fire and Ice." I was stunned. It was my favorite rose, too.

On the way to my "date," I purchased a single white rose. When I arrived at Applebee's, I'm sure I looked silly. A grown man with a rose and no date. I was seated at a two-person table. I set the rose directly across from me on the table. The menu had changed quite a bit in twenty years. The burger I had ordered no longer existed, so I ordered steak. Amy would have loved it. I also ordered iced tea. On our first date, Amy said something funny while I was taking a drink of iced tea. The next thing I knew, iced tea was pouring out of my nostrils. I had been so embarrassed, but I recalled the memory with a grin. Amy had laughed. After we married, she told me that was the moment she knew she was going to marry me. We had been talking on the phone every night for three weeks prior to our first date. I had known eight months prior to that date as we stood talking in the parking lot two nights before I graduated from college.

I didn't stay at Applebee's for five-and-a-half hours like we had done so long ago, but I did sit and reminisce—pondering Amy's hands, her smile, her laugh, her eyes. When the mood music began playing Fleetwood Mac's "Everywhere," I was served our favorite dessert which brought tears streaming down my face on the first bite. I left a little on the plate, feeling guilty for having eaten more than half. It was a nice feeling for a moment, but the tears kept coming. My waitress was wonderful. She never asked about the rose. She didn't strike up a conversation like usually happens. When "Everywhere" finished, I paid the bill. Peter Gabriel's "In Your Eyes" chased me out the door into the rain, which camouflaged my waterfall of tears. All I could think about was being lost in Amy's beautiful eyes.

I sat in the parking lot for quite some time. I pondered our journey to finding each other. I honestly believe that God gives us choices. I also believe that, for a few, there is but one and He moves Heaven and Earth to cross those two paths. Each moment along the way could have been seen as a coincidence if it had happened without the list of others, but it didn't happen that way. More than a few times God proved to us that we were meant for each other "For a Lifetime."

I lost track of time in the parking lot. When I left Applebee's, I traced the path of the remainder of our marathon twelve-and-a-half-hour date. It took nearly an hour just to drive it. Part of me hurt so deeply. Part of me was healing.

When I arrived at home, Micah had fed his brothers and they had played games all night to pass the time. I hugged them all, kissed each one on the top of the head (making Micah bend down to my level), and then headed for bed.

In keeping with the theme, I'm going to jump forward to March 17, 2017. It was a Thursday. Micah and I had been planning that specific evening for months. The tickets had been purchased as soon as tickets went on sale. We wanted everything to be perfect when the four of us descended on our favorite movie theater to watch the release of Disney's live action *Beauty and the Beast*. I had a lot riding on that movie. There were many movies Amy and I had watched together, but none had the same weight in our hearts as Disney's original *Beauty and the Beast*, released in 1991.

My day began with an accidental find; while looking for my sunglasses in the van, I found Amy's glasses. I was caught off guard. Sitting there, tears streaming down my cheeks, all I could think was, "Just one more glance at those beautiful green and brown eyes..." I kept Amy's signature glasses with her signature color of green. Sometimes I would take them out of their case and look at them, dreaming that Amy was looking back at me.

Isaiah climbed into the van a few minutes later. After devotions on the way to school (our daily dad/son activity), he played the song written for the Beast in the movie musical we'd be seeing later that night.

> Now I know she'll never leave me
> Even as she fades from view
> She will still inspire me
> Be a part of everything I do...
> I'll fool myself, she'll walk right in
> And as the long, long nights begin

> *I'll think of all that might have been*
> *Waiting here for evermore*[60]

Rivers were coursing down my face. What a song. The Beast sang what my heart felt. Many times I stood in my house, upstairs, waiting for Amy... to...just...come...home. The release of that song told me I was in for an emotional night.

Most events I tried to plan since Amy passed away usually brought so much stress and emotion that inevitably, one of my boys—usually Gabriel—would hit meltdown stage. Not that night, though. We arrived before the pre-show commercials and trailers. We went all out at the theater. Popcorn. Sodas. Candy. I felt like I was getting an opportunity to see Amy, or at least be with her again. What I got was a trip down memory lane.

The movie started off rather expectedly, until Maurice, Belle's father, first comes on screen. In this version, Belle's mother died in Paris during the Black Plague. Maurice is a gifted music box maker. When he is first seen on screen, he is building a music box and singing.

> *How does a moment last forever?*
> *How can a story never die?*
> *It is love we must hold onto*
> *Never easy, but we try*
> *Sometimes our happiness is captured*
> *Somehow, a time and place stand still*
> *Love lives on inside our hearts and always will*[61]

I was not prepared for Maurice to be pining away after his dead wife. Both songs slayed me that night. I find it interesting that God can use the unexpected things to touch our hearts and remind us that our *Daddy* cares deeply about us and for us.

The portrayal of this Beast was a little too close to home for me. While watching his melancholy rants in the movie, I flashed back to my childhood, full of fear, resentment, and anger. I grew up a beast: scared of people, melancholy, angry, hurt, thinking I was the ugly, fat kid, convinced I was the dumb kid in the smart class. Then I met Amy. On our wedding day, I felt like a prince. She was so beautiful! I sat in my seat in the movie theater holding on to that memory, that moment during our wedding pictures when I first saw her in the one-of-a-kind, crepe and satin dress. I had never seen anyone so beautiful in my life.

At the end of the movie, when Belle held Prince Adam's face and looked in his eyes for the familiar, I thought of Amy's glasses, her eyes so deep I could fall into them, her soft hands cupping my cheeks, that glint that said "I love you"—even without words. She made me feel like a prince.

After putting my boys to bed that night, I sat down and posted about the day. My friend Michelle, counselor extraordinaire, wise beyond her years, replied to my post: "sounds like Amy's glasses serve now as a reminder that the way that she saw you through those exact glasses is the way God sees you."[62] Her wisdom and encouragement has stuck with me. When I read her post the first time, I couldn't help myself but think, *I wonder what God's glasses look like.* I crawled in bed with that question playing over and over in my head.

Then it clicked. I had the answer. I recalled something my youth pastor, and surrogate dad, told me once, a long time ago.

"When God looks at us, because of Jesus' sacrifice, He looks through the veil of Jesus' blood sacrifice. He sees you and me as without sin."

I sat there in my bed in awe. God's "glasses" see believers as sinless. When that thought hit me, and I then turned back to Amy's glasses, my heart was so full of warmth and love that it began to burst.

"She truly loved me," I said aloud to no one but myself. "She… loved…me…"

I know it sounds strange, and it wasn't the first revelation I'd had of Amy's love. I knew she loved me, but the implications of Michelle's comment—that God let Amy borrow His view of me—was earth shattering. His view of all His children who've asked for forgiveness and have allowed Jesus to be Lord of their life is earth shattering. His view of you is earth shattering as well. When Jesus is our King and Lord, God sees us as perfect.

As I've pondered my nearly twenty years with Amy, one thing stands out in neon lettering. She not only loved me, she also taught me how to love. What curriculum did she use to teach me?

> Love is patient, love is kind. It does not envy, it does not boast, it is not proud. It does not dishonor others, it is not self-seeking, it is not easily angered, it keeps no record of wrongs. Love does not delight in evil but rejoices with the truth. It always protects, always trusts, always hopes, always perseveres.

# GOOD GRIEF

> Love never fails. (I Corinthians 13:4-8a, NIV)

I may have been the stupid kid in a room full of geniuses. I may even have been homely to look at; Amy didn't believe it. She taught me not to believe it either. She truly loved me and I her.

A year later, Valentine's Day 2018, my boys were invited to the "Annual Love Day party" at Scott and Mama Mindee's. I had not known the year before that the party was an annual event, nor that it had an official name. When I dropped the boys off, the house was already filling with other teen and pre-teen kids, many of whom my boys knew from church. It was such a blessing for them to go, and to not worry about me...where I was, what I was doing, how I was feeling. Here were two heroes, teaching children (theirs, mine, and other's) that "Love Day" should be about who God has put in our paths to love and those He's placed next to us on our own path as well. The day didn't have to be about having a boyfriend, girlfriend, significant other, or just someone to kiss goodnight after an overpriced meal. "Love Day" doesn't have to be about mourning lost love, whether through death or breakup. "Love Day" can be just that: a day to recognize the love of God in our lives and the people around us we get to love.

I couldn't help but post about my change of heart, how I would look at future Valentine's Days.

> ...I miss [Amy] greatly, but Valentine's Day was not weighing me down in grief this year. My boys were invited to the Annual Love Day party at Scott and Mama Mindee's. When they climbed into the van with these gifts for me (made with their own two hands), I saw a different side of this day I've been at odds with for 30+ years. I noticed the darkness and terror of feeling like a failure as a single dad (this schedule is very hard to keep) begin to fade; in its place a glimmer of hope, which has steadily increased in the past 48 hours, begin to warm me. I'm not looking for attaboys as a dad. I love my boys, and they know it. I just needed to know they knew it. Prayerfully, I'll learn how to master my schedule instead of it mastering me.[63]

Mindee's response helped me see a deeper need for teaching my children specifically about God's love and their self-image, especially on Valentine's Day.

This blesses Scott and I SO VERY MUCH. I started our love day celebrations because of some of the same things you mentioned. I was missing and sad about "romantic love" years ago, after divorce. It was around the time I started to let in the amazing and fulfilling like no other, love of Jesus and he showed a new way to see it. To shift the way people view Feb 14th into a space of "for all above all and from GOD for each of us" The boys were so excited to make things for you, as the person they identify as the most loving, unselfish and always for them in their life. You are so loved and I'm prayerful your share and our party inspires others to spread more of ALL love around this time each year—not just the smoochy and chocolate kind. I love that the Holy Spirit was in the details and little things in your heart that are the BIG things of life. See you soon SuperDad![64]

Thank you, God, for continuing to teach me and for giving me these small glimpses of hope and joy. And thank you, God, for incredible friends like Scott and Mindee who look at life differently, who find joy and hope in the most unexpected places, and who are eager (not just willing) to love on a generation of kids in a way that is so counter-cultural. May "Love Day" catch on and teach many more housefuls of kids the wonderful power of Love, especially God's love.

CHAPTER 22

# Ordinary Days

During my journey through grief, I thought the holidays would be the hardest to endure. I was surprised to find out that ordinary days were just as difficult, often because I wasn't prepared for whatever popped up in front of me. For holidays, I could pull myself together and see the emotion and pain coming like a freight train. If, and, or when I ducked away, people around me knew why. Grief is expected at the holidays. It was the ordinary days I didn't expect, and I have the train tracks on my soul to prove it.

 The first ordinary day I'd like to walk you through actually happened during Christmas Break, but hear me out…all my shopping was complete. Our Christmas Open House had been a success. The presents were wrapped. Everything was done and ready. Christmas Eve-Eve Candlelight Service was two days away and I was looking forward to it.
 When I woke up on the December 21, and stepped into the shower, I realized I needed my new bottle of body soap.
 "Honey! Can you…"
 For nearly twenty years, I had the privilege of doing mornings with my beautiful wife. She knew I was as disorganized as an open file cabinet in a tornado. She still loved me. She would often come into the bathroom to

brush her teeth and talk with me while I took a shower. We were familiar. We were doing life together. We were two halves of a whole.

I made a few of those mistakes, calling out to Amy, or making a mental note to talk with her when I got home, or pulling out my phone to text "I love you" or "I miss you."

The ache was significant. Deep. Choking. I must have been in that shower for over half an hour. The boys had all been through the morning shower ritual before me. When the hot water turned to lukewarm, I picked myself up off the floor and began actually taking a shower. I didn't finish before the water turned icy cold. I had been in there for a very long time.

❦

Why is it always in the shower lately that I completely lose my composure and break down sobbing? I will be knocking off the terrible smell of sleep and sweat and boy when I think of something I wish I could do, say, or have related to my Amy-zing wife and the next thing I know I'm leaning against the wall of the shower convulsing. I guess it's the best place to hide my tears. They mix in with soapy, dirty water and flow down the drain. I wonder if God's cleaning my soul with tears while I'm cleaning the outside of me.[65]

❦

In the middle of February, I was in my car on my way home from work. I was listening to Christian radio, something I don't usually do. I am often listening to a book on .mp3 or using my Spotify account to listen to music. That morning, I'd forgotten to download the next book in a series, so I turned on the radio. The DJ was interviewing Mandisa about her new album hitting store shelves in three months. I was in and out of paying attention to the interview. There were many things racing through my head, things that had to be finished before I went to bed. At one point, Mandisa began introducing songs from the upcoming record. She talked about a long depression and the toll it took on her and her relationships. She talked about having a hand full of pills ready to swallow when someone knocked on her door. When she began talking about the first song she wrote for the album, I was a little more intrigued. She said she'd been mad at God, and had written the song in the depths of despair. For her, she was challenging

God. When the words of the song began to play, I pulled over to the side of the road and began weeping.

> *You could've healed her*
> *You've done it before*
> *You could've sent the angels down*
> *And turned it around*
> *Wouldn't that have meant so much more?*
> *Instead You took her*
> *Left a young family behind*
> *And I'm wondering where You are*
> *You seem so far, while we're all here asking why*[66]

The chorus was haunting. I recognized the pain Mandisa was singing about and the weight that often caused me to struggle to breathe. I closed my eyes. Amy was clearly waiting for me behind my lids. I could see her face as the chorus played.

> *Prove me wrong*
> *Prove me wrong*
> *These waves will take me under*
> *My heart will not get over*
> *And this pain won't make me strong*
> *Prove me wrong*[67]

By the time the second verse began playing, I was screaming out in pain. This woman, who I had never met, was singing about the pain in my heart. It seemed impossible.

> *Would it be wrong if*
> *I asked You for proof?*
> *I wish that I could just believe, without questioning*
> *I'm just being honest with You*
> *And they say Your ways are better*
> *But I still don't understand*
> *And You can't hold me together*
> *And this can't be Your perfect plan*[68]

When the song finished and I could safely drive home, I pulled back onto the road. I arrived at about the same time Micah did. He'd heard the same interview and song. Later when the CD hit store shelves, we purchased it. Nothing seemed to have been closer to our hearts than that album. We would later find much healing related to the rest of that CD.

When Micah was only two years old, I came across the book *Raising a Modern Day Knight* by Robert Lewis. The premise of the book centers on the steps boys take between childhood and becoming a godly man. Using the ceremonies from Medieval Europe that a boy would go through to become a knight, the book discusses the need for making the road to manhood a purposeful, distinct, ceremony-based path for boys to become godly men. Amy and I changed our whole approach to parenting. Just before Micah turned twelve, we designed a family crest and had it printed on canvas for the trip. Micah's biblical manhood weekend happened at the beach. I had asked two other godly men to join me in the weekend event. It was a success; one I think made a lasting impression on my oldest. His mother thought so too. Two weeks after Isaiah's birthday in 2017, Todd and I took him to the beach for his overnight trip focused on godly manhood.

When I decided to approach Todd in early January about being part of Isaiah's godly manhood journey with me, I was terrified. When I had planned Micah's, Amy was there to help sculpt the event, to bounce ideas off, and give her opinions. This time, I was doing it alone. The real reason I was terrified, though, was because Todd is a busy man. He has two boys of his own, one in college, the other in high school. He pastors a large group of children in third, fourth, and fifth grade at our church. And more important to me was the fact I would be asking him to take time away from his wife. For me, I felt like I might be asking too much. I also felt very guilty asking for more from Todd. He'd been the first call I'd made on that dark day in September. He'd been to my house countless times to help do various things. He'd spoken at Amy's memorial service. He'd taken my calls at all hours of the day when I needed parenting advice. As I listed it all in my head, I had nearly talked myself out of asking him to go. *God, what do I do?* I knew the answer already, but I was still scared.

The entire emotional monsoon happened on a Sunday morning while I was volunteering under Todd's leadership. Right after asking God my rhetorical question, I took in a deep breath and looked up from the floor. There was Todd walking toward me. Service was over and most of the families had left. Only a few of us volunteers were still in the building. Todd stopped to talk as he always did when he wasn't "on duty."

"How are you?" he asked.

I fought the tears. I didn't want him to think I was in the middle of grief, because I really wasn't. I was simply terrified to ask a friend for help. It sounds ridiculously stupid, I know, but I can't change the reason for my fear.

Without thinking, I opened my mouth as words tumbled out before I could stop myself. He immediately said, "Yes."

"Are you sure? I don't want to take you away from Julie or your boys."

"Yes…I'm sure. I'd love to go. In fact, I'd be honored to go." We met over coffee in his office once or twice to make plans. Then the weeks flew by and it was time to go.

The drive to the coast was filled with laughter, conversation, and a dinner stop. When we arrived at the beach house, we settled in and then officially started the events of the trip. Isaiah was a bit nervous, not really understanding all that would happen. Once we told him the plan, he was excited. Since the concept of the book had been Medieval knights, we watched Disney's interpretation of *The Lion, the Witch, and the Wardrobe*. After the movie was over, we talked with Isaiah about the intentionality of becoming a man, using the metaphor of the knight. We asked him many questions about the movie and about his own knowledge of the road ahead.

In the morning, we all pitched in to make breakfast. After cleaning up, we headed out for a walk on the beach. After Todd and I talked with Isaiah about the armor of God,[69] battling against laziness, and every man's war with lust, Todd peeled off, heading back to the house, leaving Isaiah and me alone for the next phase.

As Isaiah and I kept walking down the beach, I was intentional in talking about different struggles that come up in the lives of boys on the path to becoming a man. Every once in a while I would stop and hand him a flat polished stone with a specific scripture engraved in it. Then we'd begin the walk again. At one point, Isaiah began picking up pebbles on the beach and throwing them out into the ocean.

"What's wrong?" I asked, sensing the tone change.

"I'm just trying to throw my anger away, out into the ocean."

"What's the anger about?"

Isaiah stopped and looked at me directly. I knew what his anger was about, but I wanted to know if he would tell me.

"Mom's death," he finally said. "I wish she was here, but I don't want to be angry anymore." He began picking up pebbles and chucking them out into the surf again. Our walk and talk continued.

When I had given Isaiah all five of the intended stones, we stopped.

"Why did I give you five stones?" I asked.

"I don't know."

I then began telling him the story of King David as a young teenager. When I got to the part about David picking up five smooth stones from the dry riverbed, a light went off in Isaiah's eyes. He jumped in and finished telling the story for me.

"This road to godly manhood is similar to King David's road from a teenager to be the king of all Israel. Along the road, he had to slay Goliath. There will be Goliaths along your road too." I stopped to let that sink in a bit before we turned around to head back to the house.

"Dad, I think I know one of the Goliaths," Isaiah said finally. I started to walk back toward the beach house slowly.

"You do? What do you think one of your Goliaths is?"

"Mom's death. Getting over it."

"Honey, I pray you won't ever 'get over' Mom's death. I know it's painful now, but grief doesn't ever go away completely. If we let it control us, then there is a problem. But, we never want to be rid of the pain altogether."

"Why?"

"Because then we begin to forget her."

There was silence for quite a while as we headed to the beach house. Just before we were back at the house, Isaiah reached his arm around me as we walked.

"Thanks, Dad, for bringing me out here."

The afternoon was filled with more planned activities. We played games to help teach being a good loser and a good winner. Todd and I talked about different passages of scripture we both thought appropriate to the topic. And we talked through the family crest Amy and I had created. When our time was coming to a close, we packed our things into the van, and then sat on the couches in the living room for the final activity of the ceremony.

Todd and I took turns blessing and praying over Isaiah. It was a perfect trip.

Todd has continued to be a tremendous support and incredible friend to me, but the one thing I thank God for most is his unique heart for each of my three boys. That trip cemented him as one of Isaiah's mentors. Micah and Gabriel were already dialed in to Todd's leadership and oversight—at church and outside of church. Isaiah had been a bit harder to pin down, more reserved and hiding in the shadows.

---

Leading up to Spring Break, I was feeling anxious and claustrophobic in my own house. Everywhere I looked were piles of things I needed to take care of, but for one reason or another, they had gone neglected. The biggest problem area was my bedroom. Shortly after Chris removed all the medical equipment, other stuff began to take its place. If it had belonged to Amy, and we didn't know where to put it, it went in my room. From her side of the bed to the bay window was packed and piled with stuff. I couldn't get into the walk-in closet. Amy's vanity style dresser was piled so high the mirror was useless. There was little room to do anything in the room.

I started feeling like a failure as a father again. I'd been requiring my boys to clean their own rooms, but had not been able to keep up with mine. Each time I'd bring up cleaning "your room," I was one step closer to instigating World War III. It began to really eat away at me.

I decided to start being a better example for the boys. But that meant I needed to clean out the closet so that my bedroom could begin to find order. Each time I entered the closet to begin thinking about reorganization, I was hit with the realization of having to pack up and get rid of Amy's clothes. I would stand there, trying to create a plan, but the room would begin to spin, the air would grow thin, and I would need to sit before I fainted and hit the floor.

One day Lisa asked, "Do you need any help over Spring Break?"

Usually, when asked that question, my response was, "No" or "I don't know." Lisa was ready for that. She'd been in my house regularly. She knew how I needed help. I'm sure God had already told her I needed help with Amy's clothes.

"I thought I could do it myself, but I really need help getting Amy's clothes out of the closet."

Lisa connected with Mary. A plan came together. They chose a day to come over to sort and pack Amy's wardrobe.

> Last night, in preparation for today, I started picking up my bedroom and looking through drawers that haven't been opened

since September…since Amy passed. I found her jewelry (most of it). I found her stack of "40th Birthday" cards that everyone mailed her just after she announced her diagnosis. And I found the cards and art that the boys have given her over the years. It was an overwhelming find, full of many tears, smiles and…pauses. Mixed in the bunch was an Easter card I'd given her many years ago. It sings when you open it. I put it all back.

In less than an hour, Lisa and Mary will be over to help me sort through Amy's clothes. Please pray. I'm a bit wiped out just thinking about it. I've saved all the camp T-shirts and sweatshirts (Gabe and Isaiah will be able to use those in the future). Chris turned her jeans and a couple of shirts into beautiful blankets. I don't know if there will be any other "saves," but I do know that this will be hard.

A huge thank you goes out to my wonderful Micah who just left to take his younger brothers to a movie. It would be too hard for my Angel with Autism to watch/know what is happening.[70]

There was a huge outpouring of love and friendship among my Facebook community. I felt bolstered as I walked into this space of time.

Amy's step-mom and sister arrived around 1:00 p.m. I had been collecting nice boxes for them to use. When I walked them both upstairs to show them what I needed help with, the room started spinning again. I was exhausted already. Mary and Lisa looked at each other.

"We got this, Thom," Lisa said.

Mary added, "Go ahead and do what you need to do downstairs. If we need help, we'll holler."

Although my initial response was to argue with them, I breathed a sigh of relief and descended the stairs. After a couple of hours, Amy's clothes were sorted. What was saleable was nicely folded in the boxes. What was a little dated and should be taken to a thrift store was packed in large black plastic bags. The things not worth the trouble were tossed in the garbage.

When I ascended the stairs, there was order to my room. I could put my clothes in the closet, along with some bedding and other boxes that were filling up the walkway around the bed. A lot of work happened in that entire day, and I slept really well that night, knowing a mountain I was trying to make a mole hill had been tackled for me.

September 21, 2017, was an "ordinary day." The doorbell rang. I was in the back of the house. When I opened the door only a gift bag could be found. The gift bag contained a vast array of things that didn't make sense to me, so I posted a picture of the contents and asked Facebook friends to help me figure out the clue. What follows is the second post of the night after God had flipped me on my ear. The contents of the bag are described in the post.

> The Mystery continues…
> About an hour after receiving this mysterious gift, I hopped into the van to go and retrieve Gabe and a couple friends from youth group. On the way, "No Longer Slaves" (Bethel Music) began playing on the radio. When it finished, Laura Story's "Blessings" immediately followed. Both songs were used in Amy's Memorial service. At the end of the second song, I turned off the music, tears welling, and I knew God was trying to get my attention. I parked the car and waited in the church parking lot for a while (I was 20 mins. early), staring at the pictures I had posted earlier tonight…and the puzzle began to come together.
> You may think this is a stretch; that's okay with me, but here goes.
> [Two of] Amy's favorite colors were bright red and neon green. Amy's favorite way to wrap gifts? Gift bag and tissue paper. How was my gift packaged? Bright red metallic gift bag and neon green paper.
> The first thing I pulled out of the bag had been the toy car. I've been praying and stressing and then off-loading the stress at the foot of the Throne and praying some more about car needs—some for the van and acquiring a second set of wheels for Micah when he returns in May. Did you notice the "second set of wheels" in the picture? I've literally asked God to provide a "second set of wheels for Micah."

The next 2 items I pulled out were rocks. One is a smooth polished, beautiful green stone while the other is a rougher, light tan stone, with a couple cracks and a few veins of dirt (but it's also been through a rock tumbler—so it's a bit smooth). There we were, Amy and I. She was finally made whole (smooth) and she's perfect now. Me, I'm a bit smoother than when Amy first married me, but God's still got a lot of work to do.

The pink card came next. "Build a Better World" it says. It's a coupon for a free trip to a Tualatin Hills Parks and Rec swimming pool...for a youth! Gabe has been asking me to take him to the pool for many months—actually to get passes like we had when he was much younger. It's always been, we can't afford it right now, or it doesn't fit into the schedule. Guess what shares a parking lot with Gabe's new school: a THP&R Aquatic Center (with a lot more amenities than just a pool). It may not be a Season Pass, but it's a day pass none the less.

Then came the yarn. Isaiah is the crafty one, always asking for yarn, fabric, needlepoint thread, etc. to work on his latest passion: knitting and sewing. He just created a baby's dress and bloomers for a newborn. Guess what color the outfit was. Guess! Bright red and green—the same green as the yarn and tissue paper. And the yarn was neatly rolled together (not a mess) like Amy taught him to do with his yarn. She was so thrilled to find someone willing to teach him to knit, crochet, and sew!

The rest...well, I just had to laugh at the glue. Today, not yesterday, nor the day before, but TODAY, I answered a colleague's inquiry of "How are things going?" I said, "I feel like I'm coming apart, trying to chase down all the pieces that need to be stuck together." (I wasn't complaining. I was just talking about how crazy our house schedules have become.) I opened the glue initially to see if there was a clue under the lid; sitting in the parking lot, God reminded me it's the royal purple glue that dries clear. Guess what my favorite color is.

I think you're getting the picture. The other 3 items are much more personal; but know this, God has my number, and He's meeting (or will meet) the needs in my household: physical, emotional, and spiritual.

Ten minutes after receiving the gift initially, the doorbell rang again. When I opened the door, stuck to the outside of the screen door was a sticky note telling me the gift givers were two of the little kids who live across the street. I knew that when I got in my car. I knew that when I was sitting in the parking lot of the church. I knew that when slowly but surely God began to get my attention, piece by piece by piece. Isn't it funny how God can get your attention with the littlest of things?!? Earlier this week God reminded me "I'm no longer a slave to fear." When I'm focused on Him, God's "mercies in disguise" are the answers to our prayers—our "Blessings." Doubt can't stay. Broken hearts are knit back together. And God polishes us with tears.

For those of you who stuck through this entire post, thank you for indulging a sentimental—soon to be—old man who finds God in the oddest of places. Good night.[71]

I don't know if God speaks to everyone through simple objects like He does me, but that moment was one that continues to remind me that God is no only on the Throne, but totally in control.

---

The boxes containing Amy's clothes stayed in my room, nicely stacked—and somewhat in the way—for a few months. Initially, I thought I could take the clothes to a consignment shop. As I called and called different shops in the Portland Metro Area, I kept getting the same message. It wasn't going to be worth the effort. Most of what I had would not be accepted because it was more than six months old.

As Spring Break turned into Summer and Summer turned into Fall, I began to get antsy about the boxes still in my bedroom. I'd asked a few friends about where I might be able to donate Amy's clothes so they would be given to women who needed them, not sold. I was coming up empty handed. Late in November 2017, I made one last desperate call before just dumping the whole lot off at Goodwill. It had all been God's timing. Women connected to our church had a ministry that could immediately begin giving Amy's clothes to women in need. It was such a relief.

When I pulled back into my driveway after dropping off Amy's wardrobe, I took a minute.

*God, thank you for caring about the little things. Amy wouldn't have wanted her clothes to be sold at a thrift store if they could go to women in need. Thank you for honoring her and helping me find the right place for them.*

A peace descended over the car. It hadn't been a difficult thing to move the clothes in boxes and give them away. For me, I wasn't giving away Amy's things; I was blessing people with Amy's clothes. That made all the difference.

---

There are random moments, in unassuming days, while doing the mundane, when memory—friend or foe, timely or un-, ready-or-not-here-we-come—wields its head to remind me of the joy, beauty, grace, and devotion of my loving wife, Amy. I never want to forget those moments, those random, unassuming, ordinary moments where I encountered her love, her presence, her laugh, her touch, for a brief moment. Sometimes I see her in the three faces I hug every day. Sometimes it's in the love notes from me to her that I stumble upon in the oddest of places…realizing that she kept each one. Sometimes it's simply driving down the road, spying something about which she commented once upon a time.

# CHAPTER 23

# The Mom Mafia

"Pray? Why should I pray?"

It would seem that many believe God is not, or maybe no longer, in the prayer answering business. Some have even given up on the activity, believing that God has stopped listening to them. They didn't get what they wanted, so either God doesn't exist or He hates them! Sadly, pop culture and music have taught for generations that God either doesn't exist or He has left us to our own devices, electing to watch "From a Distance."[72] Some have even gone so far as to ask, *What if God was one of us...just a slave like one of us.*[73] It would seem to be easier to bring God down to our level than to expect us to try and reach up to Him.

When it comes to prayer, it is my experience that God does answer prayer. When I feel I have not gotten an answer to a prayer, I try to find out *why*. According to the Psalms, God has a path for each of us to take; those paths will end up serving His divine plan. "He guides me along the right paths for his name's sake" (Psalm 23:3b, NIV). In the Lord's Prayer, Jesus instructed His followers to pray God's will be done, not their own. "Your kingdom come, your will be done, on earth as it is in heaven" (Matthew 6:10, NIV). Later in the Garden of Gethsemane, Jesus shows His followers that we are to be praying the will of God over our own will. "Father, if you are willing, take this cup from me; yet not my will, but yours be done" (Luke 22:42, NIV). Jesus was facing the worst way to die at the hands of man, yet He did not prioritize His will over God the Father's will.

When God took me through each of these verses, I was battling a sickness within my own body, years before I ever met my wife, completely full of fear. I was looking at a possible six months to live; I wasn't looking at my Creator. However, God met me in the Valley of the Shadow of Death and taught me His paths are righteous, His plans are perfect, and His will is above all.

As I've spent years since learning about prayer, I've learned that not only does God answer prayer, but He often answers it in unexpected ways. Like the Prodigal Son[74] or the Syrophoenician woman,[75] I used to come to God asking for scraps. But I've come to learn that God is a good God and a fantastic Father. Jesus said as much.

> Ask and it will be given to you; seek and you will find; knock and the door will be opened to you. For everyone who asks receives; the one who seeks finds; and to the one who knocks, the door will be opened. Which of you, if your son asks for bread, will give him a stone? Or if he asks for a fish, will give him a snake? If you, then, though you are evil, know how to give good gifts to your children, how much more will your Father in heaven give good gifts to those who ask him! (Matthew 7:7-11, NIV)

So, I started asking for bigger things, a little nervous at first, but more boldly as God answered my prayers. There was a desperate prayer, whispered on that fateful morning as my middle son lay wailing on the body of his mother. *God...It* was all that would come out for what felt like an eternity. *God...I* started again, *I can't do this alone*. It was a prayer uttered in total fear and helplessness. I knew I was an imperfect father; I knew that the job of raising children had been given to *parents*...plural, not singular. It's a difficult job to raise children, and nearly impossible to do by oneself.

Shortly after Amy's Memorial Service, it became evident I had been right so long ago. I could not parent my three boys alone. They needed a mom. I can be a lot of things: a teacher, a life coach, a counselor, a cheerleader, a chef, a chauffeur, and a vast array of other jobs. But a mom, I could not be. When I began praying for God to bridge this gap, I was asking God to bring someone, even if it were a different someone, to each of my boys to fill in as a *surrogate* mom. What God delivered was much more than my feeble mind could fathom. I have come to lovingly call this godly group of servant warriors the "Mom Mafia."

Let's take a minute to unpack this term. First of all, I realize that the term *mafia* usually has a negative connotation and often brings with it a concept of fear. Movies show us what happens when someone goes against the Mafia. Usually something like cement shoes or a small meal of lead are served to the offender. That's not the image that comes to mind, however, when I use this term. Let's be honest though…who is not at least a little afraid of their mom? There is wisdom in having a healthy fear of moms—a *respect*, if you will, that acknowledges her position, her place, and her power in the lives of her children.

Second, I've noticed that no one fights more fiercely than a mom. Moms stop at nothing to take care of their children. NOTHING! Don't believe me? Get between a mother bear and her cub. She will be nicer to you than a human mama looking out for her child. Don't get me wrong, dads fight too…we're just usually not as good at it. Moms have an innate sixth sense. Whether or not children are with their mothers, moms know if something is wrong with one of them. They know if their child is doing something to put themselves in danger. They can sense it. Dads do a great job of teaching their children to take chances, daring chances, that sometimes put our children in harms' way. It's how we are wired. We don't always see the threat present. We're not always looking down the road at the possible consequences, especially if we were young when our young were born.

Last, moms know what their children need from them. I simply believe (and have seen evidence in my own children and in my twenty plus years of teaching) that children need two parents. Children gain something from each they cannot from the other one. It's the way God designed things. In the broken world in which we live with the high number of single parents, there are many children growing up without dads who desperately need a male role model, a mentor, to step into that role. The children growing up without a mom need something altogether different.

Soon after Amy died, each of my boys showed a need for "mom talks." I wasn't offended. I just knew I needed to find a mentor mom who could step in and take over, for lack of a better phrase. They needed the calming voice, the gentle hand, the knowing look that only a mother can provide. Micah needed advice. Gabriel needed someone who spoke autism and could help me decipher his heart. Isaiah needed the creative encourager and cheerleader. All three of them needed a woman's intuition too, especially related to trouble on the horizon with new schools, with moving away to college, and with relationships. Especially with relationships.

Selfishly, I knew I couldn't be by my boys' side as much as I used to be. Single parents know. There's only one of me, trying to cover two jobs. It just doesn't work. Amy was a stay-at-home mom who worked from home to supplement my salary and help pay the bills. There was always someone at the house when the boys woke up and *usually* when they came home from school. Through most of their schooling, Micah and Isaiah were delivered to and picked up from school by Amy or myself. Amy usually met Gabriel at the bus stop or at the porch after school. All three of my boys were used to having a parent—usually Amy—within earshot. Being only one person, I just could not be everywhere at once. I began looking for godly mothers who were willing to pray for and with my boys, and were willing to also pray for and with me.

In the beginning, there were days I just sent out a text asking for help. Other days, I would post to Facebook anonymously announcing the great deeds accomplished by the mom(s) who stepped in to help parent or guide my child(ren) on a given day. I couldn't name each one and list each of the amazing things these women have done for my boys and me, but I am going to highlight a few of the women and a few of the miracles for which they were a part. Why? One, because these women need to be honored. They will tell you, "I didn't do anything incredible." They may even say, "Amy would have done it better." But the drastic effect each of these women have had on each of my boys has been so far past what our human expectations have been. They have all become heroes to me, my kids, and hopefully their own kids who have witnessed their selfless gifts to our family.

Because I respect these women significantly, I want to highlight a few of the miracles of healing and help they brought to our family without embarrassing them outright and naming them directly. The following accounts are here to show you the power of a praying "mom" and the incredible selflessness of a handful of women whom God prompted to forever redefine the term "Mom" in my children's lives. Don't get me wrong: my children have not and will never replace their mother with anyone else. These women simply linked proverbial arms in obedience to their Lord and Savior in an effort to fill in the gaps left in the wake of Amy's departure.

My prayer is that you are encouraged by their selflessness and possibly challenged to step in and fill in the gaps for other single parents.

<hr />

First and foremost, the two I often turn to for help are ladies who cannot remain anonymous: my sister-in-law Lisa and my mother-in-law Mary. When a Mom Mafia prayer request goes out via text, they are the first to receive it and often the first to respond back: "Praying." As an aunt and grandma respectively to my boys, these two women have seen and/or heard it all. They have spent countless hours on their knees, warring in prayer over my boys. Both Lisa and Mary have taken my boys to doctor appointments, attended functions mothers would be expected to attend, standing in the shadows, beaming with pride over my boys. They were there before Amy's death when we celebrated a great accomplishment or witnessed a tragedy in the lives of each of my boys. Both have stepped in individually to teach, to train, to assist, to listen, to dream, and to do life with Micah, Gabriel, and Isaiah. Neither has allowed distance to hinder their divine appointment in the lives of my boys. I can't even begin to wrap my head around the incredible, amazing, godly roots these two women have nurtured in my boys' lives.

Lisa, having been schooled by her mother in Spiritual Warfare Prayer 101, has taught me much about praying the heart of a mom over my boys. She's helped me wade through Gabriel's disconnected conversations and find the problem with which he was wrestling in order to help him stand back, arm himself, and then power ahead. Communication with Gabriel is one of my biggest challenges, especially right after Amy died. He was so fragmented in his communication. Often his stories were very long and seemingly unconnected. Lisa painstakingly reminded me how to listen, how Amy listened, to each of my boys...not just Gabriel. Lisa has also identified the war on the spiritual plane when the fighting in the house didn't seem to make sense. She's made countless last-minute ventures to my house to help get Gabriel off the bus and sit with him until Micah or I could get home. And, when I realized bills needed to be paid, about a week after Amy's death, Lisa came over to help me write a budget, figure out what was where, and teach me about finances in a way I understood. Money management has always been very difficult for me. I'm not sure if it's the ADHD or the Executive Functioning Disability or both, but I've always struggled to keep in my head how to stretch a dollar and make sure everything was covered with money left over at the end of the month. Lisa, a book-keeper by trade, stepped in and began teaching me how to budget (something no one ever taught me). She helped me find the bills—all the bills—and create a habit to ensure they were all paid every month. Amy used to do all of that. When we got married, I handed her my checkbook (which had never been balanced) and said, "With your history in banking, this is better held in your hands than mine." That's not a healthy model for married people to have regarding finances because someone can end up where I was: clueless about the bills needing to be paid…right now! Lisa was very patient as I have continued to ask questions and learn how to budget and save for "surprises," which usually are not at all fun to deal with when they present themselves. She also began schooling me in the costs of raising a high school senior-soon-to-be-college-student, and the hidden costs of college kids. Her knowledge and care have been endless.

Knowing Isaiah's passion in the kitchen, Mary came over to help Isaiah bake one of his mother's favorite cookie recipes the week she passed away. She patiently coaxed and worked alongside Isaiah, reigniting his passion in the kitchen. She's picked him up a couple times before family meals and whisked him off to her house so he could help with the big meal. He loves the time in the kitchen with her because she speaks his language and loves him right where he's at with the gifts and talents God gave her.

When Gabriel was struggling to find something of his mother's to hold onto physically, Mary stepped in to help. As Gabriel watched Isaiah in the kitchen, he grew jealous, thinking Isaiah was going to take over Mom's role. Every once in a while, Gabriel doesn't realize his own limitations and strengths. Cooking is not one of his strengths. But with a careful grandma's eye, Mary found a way to give him what he needed. She sat with Gabriel, creating a menu file of his favorite recipes his mama used to make. He put it in his room. When he is sad, he will sometimes take out her recipes and talk to his mom as if she were sitting on his bed.

Mary and Lisa both have taught me how to ask questions of my boys in order to help them identify their challenges and successes. They have spent hours on the phone texting or talking with my boys, checking in on them from afar. And they reminded me that it is perfectly normal to have the "mama bear" rise up within me to defend my boys.

Amy was the baker in the family. She was incredibly gifted in that area; she could create magic in the oven. Shortly after we were married, she started to create the perfect chocolate chip cookie recipe for me. I like chocolate chip cookies that are a little soft in the middle. I like them to be tall and chewy, not spread out and flat. I like them to not be hard…ever! Each time she made cookies, she would ask, "Is this batch closer to the perfect chocolate chip cookie?" It took her six months, but she nailed it.

When the kids were little, she would spend time making their birthday cakes or cupcakes, and I would frost them. We took a cake decorating class together shortly after we were married. I excelled at the decoration; Amy excelled in the creation and taste department. So we worked together. Shortly before Amy's diagnosis, her baking slowed. She resorted to buying birthday cakes because she just didn't have the energy. It was one of the first signs something was wrong.

One of her dear friends knew of Amy's love for baking. She herself is a master baker. Her delicious, decadent desserts have graced many tables since, like Amy, she was given the heart of a hostess, taking care of those in need around her. This Mom Mafia member was the first to sign up on the "Meal Train" website and one of the first to bring us a meal the week after Amy's death. She arrived with a phenomenal meal, snacks, and baked goods. "I know they're not as good as Amy's," she had said as she handed me the box of goodies, "but I hope they remind you of her." They were incredible. We talked for a few minutes, and Isaiah began to ask her about baking. There was a spark. Just before she left, she made her only request.

"If it's okay with you, I'd like to bake the boys' birthday cakes this year to honor Amy." I was a bit shocked and relieved. I hadn't even thought of birthday cakes without Amy, but just the mention of this gift helped me know that I might pull off birthdays, even if just a little, like Amy did.

When each of the cakes arrived, we were all stunned. Each was a masterpiece, created with flavors unique to each boy. Gabe wanted "anything chocolate, like Mommy would have made." He also wanted it to be red because it was one of Amy's favorite colors. The cake was tall, covered on the sides with shaved chocolate, with a simple red design. It was perfect. Isaiah wanted "chocolate cake with Bavarian Cream filling," because it reminded him of his mother. Our baker extraordinaire friend delivered it with an incredible blue design, Isaiah's favorite color. The cake also came with a blessing, the same blessing Amy and I have prayed over our boys countless times:

May the Lord bless you and protect you.
May the Lord smile on you and be gracious to you.
May the Lord show you His favor and give you His peace. (Numbers 6:24-26, NLT)

Micah didn't know what kind of cake he wanted. What I knew, however, was that one of his favorite memories with Amy (and one of his last) was standing over the outdoor fire pit making S'mores. Our friend had never made a S'mores cake, but she was up for the challenge. Again she delivered a masterpiece. With each cake, each boy lit up like they had been homeless and this was the first birthday cake they had ever seen. I was encouraged by the specific, detailed, unique decisions made by my friend's observations and research of my boys. She didn't just deliver a vanilla cake with white frosting and a little color in the lettering. She delivered works of art that spoke to the heart and identity of each of my boys uniquely. I've witnessed many a mother with a gift like that for her own kids. This blessing, this miracle, was for my kids from someone who was not their mother, yet who knew their mother very well.

The offerings to our family did not stop with the birthday cakes. This woman of God stepped in while I was out of town to give Isaiah a "Day of Baking" gift where she showed him things she'd learned in the kitchen, some of which Amy hadn't had the time or opportunity to teach him. What happened was an incredible day of baking. He knew most of the terms and techniques, but he hadn't baked with a mama in a very long time.

This member of the Mom Mafia is very humble in her amazing gift. I've eaten things she's made that I would pay money—a lot of money—to purchase over and over in a store. She doesn't bake for money, however, she bakes to take care of those God has put in her path, encouraging her own son to hold a bake sale every year to help fund an orphanage halfway around the world. God is using her gift to touch thousands, possibly tens of thousands, because she gives Him back the gift He gave her.

After the Memorial service was over, Micah was approached by one of the Mom Mafia.

"You have to buy those shoes," she said, referring to the bowling shoes Micah had borrowed and wore for his mother's memorial service. "I don't care what it takes. Let me know if you need more," she said, handing him some money.

The day after Amy's memorial service, I took Micah back to the bowling alley that had lent us the bowling shoes. He asked the manager if he could buy them off the establishment. What he got was a rude and grouchy reply from a manager who was at his wits end due to a lack of staffing for the day. Micah returned nearly in tears. He was defeated and discouraged. Enter a *mama ready to protect and serve*.

Two weeks later, Micah had an afterschool "snack date" with this Mom Mafia member. She took him for pizza where he recounted what had happened at the bowling alley. After pizza, they went to the bowling alley which happened to share the same parking lot. A different manager was working that day; in fact, she was the same manager who had been working the last night we'd been a family together and had gone bowling. Micah was caught off guard when he learned her name: Susan.

"Of all the names in the world, God meets you here with a woman named Susan. Jesus and your grandma are going to help us get you those shoes," she'd replied. Then they stepped to the counter to talk with the manager.

Susan listened to Micah's story with compassion.

"We hardly have use for a size 17," she said, scanning the checkout screen. "In fact, we've only had two people ask for them in the last six months." Then she checked the date. Micah had been those "two" patrons. "We'll need to keep them until new ones arrive, but I'll call you as soon as they do."

Two months later and still no word about the bowling shoes, this persistent *mama* took Micah back to the bowling alley. Susan was not on shift that afternoon, but the owner was.

"I'm so very sorry," the owner began after hearing Micah's story. "I don't know why the shoes weren't given to you on the spot. Here." She handed Micah the shoes.

"How much do I owe you," my friend asked, having promised Micah she would be paying for this "present" from her.

"Nothing," the owner responded, "they're on the house. I'm sorry you had to come back in so many times."

You would have thought Micah had been given an amount of money he could not fathom. Those shoes are still one of his most prized possessions, reminding him of his last fun night he shared with his mother and the tenacity of a woman who knew he needed something tangible to help him heal.

That night I sat down and penned a "thank you" via Facebook, naming this woman a hero for the day and for our family. Her humble response still brings tears to my eyes:

> Oh Thom...I don't even have the words or know how to respond other than to say I'm the one who has received the blessing here to be able to be a part of this story. I'm humbled and honored and full of love and joy right in the midst of the sorrow. Truly, this is the least that I could do for a boy who lost his mama...[76]

A few months later, while walking the aisles of Costco, this woman of God saw coats and thought of my boys. It hadn't even crossed my mind in the haze of grief that my boys needed new clothes, let alone coats (they were growing at a crazy rate when I look back at pictures). At Thanksgiving Service, she handed my boys new coats and declared she'd *adopted* us as part of her family. She wasn't overstepping. She wasn't pushing their mama out of their hearts. She was simply wrapping her physical arms around my boys because their mother could not.

This family friend, lovingly referred to as an *Aunt* by my boys, has continued to check in with Micah, even after he headed off for college. She even sent him a care package that only she could have sent. It arrived the minute—literally the minute—he needed it. Her mama's heart and her proclivity to defend the young and teach them how to grieve, to heal, has continually brought me back to the description of Aslan, in *The Lion, the Witch, and the Wardrobe*, by C.S. Lewis. The series is an allegory, aligning Aslan to Jesus, showing readers just how powerful and good Jesus is. In chapter 8, Mr. and Mrs. Beaver are educating the Pevensie children about "the King of the wood and the son of the great 'Emperor-beyond-the-Sea.'" Mr. Beaver is taken aback at the lack of knowledge the *Son of Adam* and the *Daughters of Eve* have regarding their Lord and Master.

> "...Aslan is a lion—*the* Lion, the great Lion."
> "Ooh!" said Susan. "I'd thought he was a man. Is he—quite safe? I shall feel rather nervous about meeting a lion."
>
> "Safe?" said Mr. Beaver; "don't you hear what Mrs. Beaver tells you? Who said anything about safe? 'Course he isn't safe. But he's good. He's the King, I tell you."[77]

This member of the Mom Mafia is always described as *good* by the many kids (besides my three) who call her *Auntie* in our church. She has the heart of a mama, though she has no children of her own. God even saw fit to wind her heart strings around those of a young woman who was without a family giving her a "child" who refers to her as a mama. My friend fights, like a lioness, for the needs of many children God has put under her charge, especially those in trauma who need a warrior to help them return to a normal way of life. She guards them as her own. She prays for them nightly, warring in the spiritual realm, contending for their souls and their hearts. Her example reminds me of the way Jesus has gone to fight for us, with tenacity, with tenderness, with an undying endurance, and without ever giving up on us.

One of the people responsible for lighting the passion my boys have for drama is another member of the Mom Mafia. She is another lovingly known around our church as *Auntie*. What made this godly warrior part of our family so easily was her relationship with Amy. They were really good friends who cared deeply for each other, who prayed for each other, who laughed with each other. Amy trusted her with the things moms wrestle with over their children and she trusted Amy and I with the same. Having herself been a single parent, this godly woman has come alongside me to encourage me, and deliver brutal honesty when needed. Sometimes God's called her to open my eyes—when I was doubting my abilities as a father, struggling with teenage boys who were being teenage boys, continually saying, "I have no idea what I'm doing with these boys; I don't know why God saw fit to take their mother and leave me as their only parent." This mama bear looked up at me one morning after service and flatly said, "Stop that. You know God called you to be their dad. Stop acting like you're clueless. You know what to do! God's equipped you." It stopped me for a moment. For a moment it was as if Amy were standing there with us. She would have said the same thing to me; in fact, she's probably in Heaven asking God for permission to use the two-by-four He has sometimes used to get my attention!

Sometimes God has aimed her at one of my boys. They all highly revere and love her. They also have a healthy fear of *Auntie*. They know she'll shoot straight with them. They know she'll listen to them, let them cry, and then give them practical advice to help them slay whatever dragon is in their path at the moment. As each of the boys struggled with a different aspect of grief, *Auntie* was there to help.

Micah transferred into an arts focus high school in the middle of his junior year. That first semester was challenging, but he made it through with his mom's encouragement and wisdom. His mom died the day before he was supposed to begin his senior year. Just the thought of going back to school threw him in a tailspin. "There were so many things I wanted to do with her, Dad. She was supposed to be there." What should have been an exciting year of "lasts" with his mom became a terrifying unknown. He floundered. When Micah had to find a community member as a mentor for his Senior Capstone project, he turned to the woman whom he had dubbed *Auntie*. It meant he'd have to spend quite a bit of time with her working for most of the year on this project. When he'd come home, he was glowing. He'd been taken care of by a mama who knew his heart, who shared his passion for theatre—especially musicals. When it came to graduation, Micah wanted this member of the Mom Mafia to sit in his mother's seat. After Micah landed in college, she's been the consistent phone call he makes, to keep in touch, to seek advice, and to fill his "mom time" need.

But this champion of motherhood didn't stop at Micah. Later when Gabriel began acting rather mean toward me. I recognized it as his grief reaching the surface. After weeks of him yelling at me that he'd wished I'd died and not his mom, I began to wear down and my calm patience was nearly gone. The boys' *Auntie* saw the behavior and mile away. "Can I help you, Thom?" she asked, and with a nod from me, she was off to talk at a heart level with a boy whose heart was rent with grief. Gabriel was met with a loving, but firm, no nonsense heart to heart from a warrior mama.

It hasn't all been correction, though. When Gabriel was cast in *Peter and the Starcatcher*, he needed his own stage makeup kit. *Auntie* swooped in for the rescue with a little aid from one of the other Mom Mafia members. They taught him how to put on the makeup, how to care for it, and how to clean his face correctly.

She's even made herself available to Isaiah as well. When he went through the darkest time in his grieving process, I was actually afraid something terrible might happen to him. Whenever conversation would come around to his mom, Isaiah would just vanish. When there were too many emotions, his fight or flight kicked in and I found myself having to go find him. When I sat with him at a counseling appointment, where his counselor explained to him why he needed to tell me where he intended to be—and not because

I was *stalking him*, as he put it—she directly asked him, "If you can't talk with your dad about something, who do you think you could talk with?" This no-nonsense, warrior mama was his first reply.

A single mom who raised her kids to adulthood, a woman who has earned the time to rest and enjoy the joys of being a grandparent, accepted God's challenge to insert herself into my boys' lives, with Amy's and my gratitude and blessing, so she could help shape them after her friend was called heavenward. Her sacrifice and gift of friendship speaks volumes to the sheer weight God asks of His kids to help those around them in need.

When I asked Micah to describe this member of the Mom Mafia to me, his description stopped me in my tracts. I thought immediately of the story of the prodigal son—not that Micah is a prodigal at all, but because his words reminded me so much of the heart of the father in the parable.

> "I always knew, no matter what, that when I called, texted, or even showed up at her house, I was accepted and loved, even when I felt like a failure."

That's how Jesus is. He told a tax collector, "I must stay at your house today" (Luke 19:5b, NIV). He let a harlot spend her most precious perfume to prepare Him for his soon coming burial.[78] And He hung out with fishermen.[79] Stinky. Smelly. Probably foul-mouthed fishermen. Why? Because He loves us *no matter what*. He made them all pull their weight and challenged them to be better men and women of God than they had been before He walked into their lives. That's what *Auntie* has done for my boys.

---

One of the things moms are often known for is creating memories out of the mundane days. Many moms across the globe spend significant amounts of time not only creating memories with their children, but also cataloging those memories in tangible and intangible ways. One of the Mom Mafia stepped into this vacuum in a very unique way.

This mama knows pain and heartache that comes with parenting. Having had a very traumatic birth with her son, she and her husband chose to only have one. Their son was born with disabilities they determined were not going to sideline him...or them. They were told by doctors that their baby would probably not amount to much more than a living mass who was unable to do anything for himself. Yet, along with their determination, God closed the gap between what was and what could be with tremendous blessing. God saw to it that this mama would have the time and patience and wisdom to teach her son things we all take for granted. The things that most children pick up in a few hours, days, weeks or months took this mama three, four, and sometimes ten times the expected amount of time. God was with her through it all. He has blessed this young man with an incredible education from a college prep, private, Christian school and given him his own small business to run. He has managed many people who work with and for him in that business. He is a miracle in his own right, but his mama has been a miracle to my family from before the birth of any of my children. She saw us through the harrowing birth of our twenty-seven week and two-day son, as well as through the other two difficult pregnancies and births. But what makes her even more the miracle is how she creates and catalogs memories with and for my boys and me.

This mama bear has attended both of the musicals in which Gabe was cast. Both times she brought flowers and words of praise only a mother could bring. She reclaimed a suitcase that was very special to Micah which was previously owned by Amy's mom, making it a beautiful piece of Christmas décor for him. She's even helped Isaiah learn how to make special quilts and beautiful art projects.

Every year, this member of the Mom Mafia takes my kids and teaches them new types of crafts while strengthening their other creative skills as well. The first Christmas after Amy passed away, she helped each of my boys make commemorative Christmas ornaments with Amy's non-precious jewelry. She spends time with my boys, individually and as a group, helping them to commemorate their mother in beautiful, astounding, and creative ways to boot. And her gifts to my family have been designed to bring out the good memories of their mom. One year she took three different solid color shirts and Amy's denim to make denim and fleece quilts with patches. Each of the quilts has a different color woven into the pattern of quilt patches: 1) Micah's is green, 2) Gabriel's is red, and 3) Isaiah's is royal purple. Each of the boys loved seeing their mother in the color this mafia mom used for their specific quilt. The next year we were given handcrafted glass cases, filled with the roses and hydrangea flowers from Amy's memorial service. They remind us of the enchanted rose in Disney's *Beauty and the Beast*, Amy's and my favorite Disney movie.

She has the heart of a mother bear and is very protective of my children. Her dedication to my health and well-being has been life-giving as well. She has helped me to know when and how to slowly transition our home from a mausoleum of pain to a place that honors my late wife, but also allows us to live and move throughout our days without soul-crushing grief. It's not easy to know when to part with stuff belonging to a loved one who has passed on, stuff that is not needed by anyone else in the family, nor is it of any emotional value except that it had once belonged to someone who was loved. Being thrifty and creative, this countryfied city mama has helped to sift through those belongings, dispersed the no longer needed ones where they were needed, and transformed some into things of unequal value for my boys and me as an honorarium to her good friend and fellow mama.

Two other women who were good friends of Amy's, and who both have taken turns as the worship director for Children's Ministries in our church, have been granted by the boys a significant role in each of their lives as well. Yes, they've been present and supportive of all three of my boys, but specifically they've been able to help me understand the language and thought processes of Gabriel. When he was really young, Amy and I realized Gabriel had a terrifying capacity to absorb more stimulus than any neuro-typical kid, or even an adult. When he speaks, it is usually with glee and excitement. Often, his stories get crossed and he is easily confused, as is his audience. But he has a heart of gold. Knowing his heart and his need to be heard, both have taken time to stop—to actually stop what they were doing, even when in a hurry—to listen to my boy's heart.

I am often terrified or embarrassed at the things which have come out of Gabriel's mouth. I have been concerned he would say the wrong thing to the wrong person and the storm would start. I know I shouldn't worry, and these ladies are proof why. Both know the innocence inside of Gabriel. When he's said something "worrisome" or embarrassing to most people in polite circles, these two members of the Mom Mafia have taken it in stride. But they didn't stop there. Both have taken the time to also teach, follow-up, reteach, and encourage Gabriel through a stage of discovery in social norms. I cannot count the times I have laughed at the situations these women have handled, because what he says is often hilarious, while yet being a smidge (or more) inappropriate. Nor can I count the times these two have sought out my boy to build relationship with him, not just letting him come to them.

Both have also built deep relationships with my other two as well by using their gifts as moms and musical powerhouses to encourage my children to be heard above the noise and to worship with abandon, no matter who's watching them. The fearlessness these two have taught my children is astounding. Whenever they've had the opportunity, they pour into my children, without neglecting their own. I simply don't know how they do it. Most of the time I can barely keep up with my own children. Adding someone else's kids would take away from my own. It's the curse of single-parenting. There's just not enough of me to meet all the needs. So God has seen fit to wrap these amazing pillars of faith around my boys and me to help cover the gaps and do the job of being surrogate moms for my boys.

❦

One of the Mom Mafia has six kids who call her mom in a blended family—both she and her husband bringing three of their own to make this full house. Since our family started hanging out with theirs, it was clear that this woman, who is equipped with an amazing depth of joy and wisdom, was one God had handpicked to affect them for the long haul. She is known by many kids who call her *Mama*, many who aren't even hers. Just being near her, in the same room, my boys come away bubbling over with joy. If she could *Mama* all the children who find themselves without a mama, she'd do it. Yes, she is wise to her limitations and she takes incredible care of her own Brady Bunch. Her husband, a good friend of mine, calls her blessed, and his eyes twinkle when he talks about her. Her children, born and step, are testaments to her ability to mother. Is she perfect? She'd be the first to yell, "NO!" Does she have a calling and a passion to change the lives of kids God puts in her path? The answer is evident in the passion and respect for which my children speak about her.

Within days of Amy's death, this Mom Mafia member was helping me navigate "how to get everyone to school and home" since only one of my boys had a school bus that transported him to and from school. When Isaiah started disappearing because he was overwhelmed by grief or the situation he found himself in, or both, she helped me find a family locater app that would help me know where each of my boys was in real time. She helped plan and organize a "road rally" and surprise party for Micah's eighteenth birthday. She checks in with the boys weekly and has even set a monthly lunch date with one of them who has struggled a little more than the other two regarding his identity in our family and in God's family. What amazes me is her passion for God and her ability to juggle a husband, a home, six kids, and her own business, let alone my three boys, and she does it all with skill and apparent ease. She may not have hours in a day to give my boys like Amy used to, but she gives my boys what they need when God puts them in front of her. My kids love being around her kids, and it would seem the feeling is mutual. She reminds me of the woman in Luke chapter twenty-one who only had two coins for her offering to God, yet she gave them willingly. I am more amazed by the miracles God performs around me and in the Bible with what would amount to two measly coins. Do not think God can't use you because you only have a little to give. In God's economy, a little can be multiplied to the point of needing doggy bags for the leftovers.

The last member of the Mom Mafia I need to highlight is a woman whose gift of hospitality is on par with my departed bride. This Mama, as her kids call her (and mine have sometimes as well), sits near the CEO's chair of the Mom Mafia, if not in it. By God's direction, she spent many years "doing life" with our family. This woman knows my kids almost as well as if she were their own mother. Not a week goes by when I am not approached or texted: "How are things going?" She is a prayer warrior at a level many will never encounter. Even fewer have the passion and skill to navigate spiritual battles she has fought. I truly believe that when demons hear her name, they cower in fear because they know Abba God is her Father and she is not afraid to enter into war when necessary. Her relationship with God the Father, through Christ Jesus, with the prompting of the Holy Spirit, is a model of faith, grace, and hospitality. There are many things I could use as an example of God's blessing and miraculous grace and wisdom from having spent so much of life together with this mama warrior, but I'll limit it to one that highlights the true heart of a mom, with the focus of keeping family together.

It was August and Micah was leaving for college in just a few days. His Graduation and Going Away party were happening at the house after church. It was an open-house-style event. Many people were invited. I was grilling hamburgers and hot dogs. Many brought sides or salads to share. It was a family affair. At one point during the day, Micah asked me privately if he could stop the party to thank me publically. I couldn't even speak. Instant tears. Throwing parties takes everything in me. I'm an introvert from the word go. I can fake being an extrovert, and many would classify me as one, but I am not. All the coordination and planning were Amy's expertise. Cooking was mine. And this party was highlighting the fact that my family would be "missing" a member, physically, in a matter of days.

"Micah," I was finally able to squeak out, "I know you're thankful. It's just not important to me that you do this. Your mom could have done this so much better. I'd like to go out thinking I did at least a decent job. If you stop the party and all eyes are on me, I won't be able to function. It'll just be tears, and there is so much still left to do." He seemed to understand. I could tell he was a little disappointed.

At the height of the party, when the most people were in attendance, and a few were looking as if they were wanting to leave, this mama called an audible. I didn't know that she had prompted Micah to publically say something before everyone left. He wanted to get my permission first, knowing that the day was a hard one for me. When Micah told her that I had asked him not to say "thank you" publically, my friend stepped into motion, showing her ulterior motive.

"I know we are here to celebrate the accomplishments of a wonderful young man, and to wish him goodbye, but there is something else we've got to take care of," she said aloud in a mama voice to which all hearts are quick to listen.

I was standing in the kitchen; she was on the opposite side of the counter in the area most easily heard and seen. She looked right at me.

"Come here, Thom," she said. I was caught off guard. I'm not good in the spotlight. I'm usually extremely nervous or awkward. As I walked around the counter, I realized that everyone who was at the party had crammed themselves into my dining room and family room to witness what was about to happen. No one was in the back yard anymore. Putting a hand on my shoulder, she soldiered on.

"This man is an incredible dad. He's had a hard year, and yet here he is, trying to do Dad things and doing them well." I wanted to crawl under the couch or become invisible. I felt far from the description she gave. "We all wanted to bless you, Thom." She handed me a handmade, black folder, the cover of which read, "Operation 2017 Family Weekend."

"We thought it would be important to create a way for you to get a glimpse of Micah's strange new world. Moving him in will give you a cursory peek, but we thought you should personally experience the college community, so we are sending you to the Family Weekend event in October." I was overcome with many different emotions. Fighting the urge to talk Micah into staying home was a daily task. I knew God was sending him away to college for many reasons. I knew he would stay if I asked him to stay. I also knew I couldn't do that. But the thought of not seeing my oldest son for months on end after having just lost Amy a year prior was choking me. My friends and family, spearheaded by this powerhouse of organization and hospitality collected money, air miles, and hotel vouchers in order to send me to visit my son just two months after he would leave for college. This giant in the Faith knew it was going to be difficult for me to say goodbye. She also knew that I didn't have the funds to go on the parent's weekend myself. She asked God for a net-breaking miracle catch of fish. She never doubted God would answer her prayer, and He did.

Moms who have the faith to breathe mountain sized requests for their children and never waiver until they see God meet the need are one of the truest mirrors of what it means to be like Jesus and walk in faith. This Mom Mafia faith giant would describe herself as an organizer. I would describe her as a servant warrior, as a mom, and as a friend.

Some of the things the Mom Mafia has helped me do seem "obvious" tasks that any good parent should know instinctively how to do, which makes me look pretty inept. However, with the added layer of grief, the learning curve on single-parenting is extremely steep. The needs of the moment aren't always obvious during the grieving process. These women have helped me to stand in the moment and know that with God's help, sometimes through them, my boys would be bathed in prayer, kept safe, and loved uniquely as only a group of mothers could love.

When I've written down the names of the women who've been the core of the Mom Mafia, I realized that God was using each for a different component of Amy so that her shoes could be filled uniquely...with two exceptions. God's list:

- ✓ A mom of the details and hospitality
- ✓ A mom in search of Joy in spite of chaos

- ✓ A single mom whose kids are now adults
- ✓ A working mom juggling kids, husband, and career
- ✓ A mom in the same station of life
- ✓ A crafter, frontier mom
- ✓ A singer mom
- ✓ A piano teacher mom
- ✓ A baker mom
- ✓ An aunt with the lion heart of a mom
- ✓ A sister, who raised boys

The exceptions…

- ✓ A grandma, loving on the next generation of kids, and
- ✓ A sewing, creative mom who could teach Isaiah what Amy could not

There are many others I could mention who have participated in the mafia of moms from time to time. From a pastor's wife with her own three children to raise, to a long distance mom who popped in on Micah at Biola as much as possible, to a woman raising three young boys who organized "Care Packages from Mom" each month for Micah's first year of college. There are many more situations I could tell, and still a few more women I could honor, but I've said enough to prove the point I think God has been trying to teach me. It's a lesson He's been working on for quite some time, and each time it comes back into view, I understand things at a much deeper level. What's the lesson? We were not created to be islands. It's pretty simple.

In the beginning, God created Adam and Eve, two people, two halves, who when put together make one whole.[80] "It is not good for the man to be alone; I will make a helper suitable for him" (Genesis 2:18, NIV), God said. He didn't stop this message at Creation; He teaches us about community all throughout the Bible. "Encourage one another daily" (Hebrews 3:13a, NIV). How can we encourage each other if we are not around others, if we have not surrounded ourselves with people who will also encourage us?

> Two people are better than one, because they have a good return for their labor: If either of them falls down, one can help the other up. But pity anyone who falls and has no one to help them up. (Ecclesiastes 4:9-10, NIV)

Who do we surround ourselves with? "Walk with the wise and become wise; associate with fools and get in trouble" (Proverbs 13:20, NLT). The command is to find wise people with whom to surround ourselves. God also said, "As iron sharpens iron, so a friend sharpens a friend" (Proverbs 27:17, NLT). God's five-part directive is pretty clear to me:

1. Man was not meant to be alone. Seek relationship. Strive to be known.
2. We need to be present to help our friends when they are down. They weren't meant to be alone either!
3. We need to be encouragers. Sometimes it only takes the loving word of someone who loves us to quell the hurt boiling up to the surface, masked as anger or rage.
4. We need to surround ourselves with wise people who will help us become wise. Wisdom begets wisdom. Folly begets folly. Choose well!
5. We need to be gracious receivers of the help God sends our way. If He thinks we need help, who are we to tell God He's wrong?

To children, God says, "Obey your parents in the LORD, for this is right. 'Honor your father and mother'—which is the first commandment with a promise—'so that it may go well with you and that you may enjoy long life on the earth" (Ephesians 6:1-3, NIV). In order for my children to honor both me and their mother, they need me to do my part. I have to be honorable. The one way I found to be honorable is to teach them what I can, and when I need help—especially a *mom's touch*—I have surrounded myself with godly, wise women, lovingly known as the Mom Mafia. God used these women to help put my broken family back together in a way that enlarged it and gave us stability. He also blessed my boys with a mafia of moms in which to confide or call for some motherly advice.

Before I close this chapter, I have to mention the husbands of the married women who are part of the Mom Mafia. I am friends with all of them. What astounds me almost as much as the heart these women have for my boys is the encouragement and strength these men have shown me. Many of them have stepped into a ministry role with me or with my kids at one point or another. All of them have welcomed my boys and me into their homes, into their families, to be loved on by mamas whom God has gifted with love and compassion specific to my boys. I know there are some men who would be jealous or threatened by the time and support these ladies have given to me and my family. These men have shown the opposite. They have stood alongside their wives, and me, as we work to raise my boys.

There's an old African saying, "It takes a village to raise a child." When I first heard it, I was annoyed by it. Little by little God has shown me that He's in charge. It's His job to ultimately raise my kids. Often times He uses me. Sometimes He uses someone else with skills far more superior than mine to teach me or my boys what it means to be godly, and to follow the will of God in this world. It truly takes a village.

# INTRODUCTION TO CHAPTERS 24, 25, AND 26

Wanting this book to be genuine in its approach, and to reach out to as wide of an audience as possible, I asked my kids to help me write it. Chapter 24—"If I Had a Time Machine..."—was written by my oldest, Micah. Chapter 26—"From Caretaker to Child"—was written by my youngest, Isaiah. The words contained within them are entirely theirs. The English teacher in me gave them a grammar check, but the words are all theirs. Something I find incredible about both of these chapters is hidden in what you will not see. I told both of the boys separately about the book I was writing. I then asked them if they would consider writing a chapter of the book. It went something like this...

"The book is about grief. It's going to focus on what God's been teaching me through the death of your mom. Would you like to write one of the chapters from your perspective?"

Both boys hemmed and hawed, wanting to, then not, back and forth. I didn't nag. Both boys came back to me with a definite, "Yes, I want to write a chapter." The process for each of them was different, unique to his own personality and experience. Neither had read more than a chapter or two of what I had written before beginning to write their chapters. However, there is a theme present in both of these chapters that is seen throughout the book. I hope these two chapters speak to you as much as they did to me.

Chapter 25—"Smelling Bricks"—sandwiched between these two chapters, focuses on my middle son, Gabriel, and what God has brought him through and taught him during the same period of time. Although Gabriel has autism, he is very outgoing and relationally centered. Unfortunately, autism is often described as a "communication disorder." Many times, my kids, family, friends, or I will find ourselves trying to follow the pattern of

Gabriel's thinking from point A to point B by way of points F, P, H, R, P (again), and Q. The purpose of the chapter is to give you a glimpse at his experience from his own perspective. To get that, however, the process looked differently than those of his brothers. I have spent hours combing through conversations I wrote down or posted on Facebook in order to capture every specific word Gabriel has spoken about his experience. I even interviewed him over the course of writing this book, a little here and a little there. Then I sat down to compile the chapter as his "ghost writer." Much prayer has bathed this process. I pray that the chapter is true to Gabriel, his experience, and his personality. I also pray I've untangled his thought process just enough to help you see life through his eyes.

Micah was nineteen years old when he penned his chapter. Gabriel was fifteen when I interviewed him. Isaiah was only fourteen when he put proverbial pen to paper.

## CHAPTER 24

# "If I Had a Time Machine…"

"If you had a time machine, what one thing would you go back and do?" If you asked me two years ago, I would have immediately said, "I would have taken my mom to the ER the night before she died." There would be no hesitation, just bring me the DeLorean and let's do this thing. Mind you, that's if you disregard the whole space-time continuum, black hole paradox, or whatever they talk about in all those Sci-Fi TV shows. Now, if you asked me, I would give you a different answer. What is it? Well, just bear with me.

I learned a phrase from society over the past eighteen years that I have grown to hate: "I'm good." You know how it works, right? Someone asks you how you are, and you answer, "I'm good. How are you?" To me, it is one of the most disingenuous things to say. Granted, the other person might not want to hear how you *actually* are, but either way, the whole interaction feels very meaningless. Let's start with the question: "How are you?" Whoever is asking it could be genuinely interested, but generally, they aren't. They are just asking to be polite, to show friendliness. The answer is almost always, "I'm good." Whether the person answering is actually good or not is irrelevant. The assumed answer from the asker is "I'm good." The answerer takes the bait and gives the expected answer: "I'm good."

Over the past two years, I have learned to be a lot more honest with my answer to that question. My answers are generally brief, because that's all they need to be. If whoever asked me doesn't really want to know, they can walk away after I say, "Today's been a struggle, but hopefully it will get better." But those who do want to know might ask me more about my day. Those are the people who should be held dear in life, the people who ask you how you are because they want to know. Hold them even closer if they act on the information you gave them, or didn't give them. Sometimes, they might know what you're feeling even before you tell them.

So "How am I?" Let me lay out the story of Mom's passing in my own words. Included are some fantastic examples of what I'm talking about: people whose actions said a lot more than a "How are you?"

Mom died the day before my senior year of high school started. The last day of summer. That kind of thing can really set a tone for the coming school year. A lot of things happened that day. The event itself happened early in the morning. Dad had to go to work (he didn't). I had evening plans with my friends (I cancelled, without giving an excuse).

The summer was pretty great. Actually, it was fantastic. I think it was one of the best summers I have ever had. Then came a rude awakening. September 6, 2016. The last day of summer. My dad woke me up early that morning. He came into my room, said he needed my phone immediately, and I needed to go to his room. It was way too early. He grabbed my phone, and I sat on my bed for a minute before standing. *Why is he getting me up so early? There wasn't any panic in his voice.* And then I went to his bedroom. We found her, not breathing. He had used my phone to call 911. Long story short, the CPR didn't help. The paramedics were unable to help as well. My mom passed away in the night. It was the day before Senior Year. That hit pretty hard. I didn't know what to do with myself. We had just finally got her on the kidney transplant list, and now they're telling me she passed away possibly because of a blood clot? What?

It took me awhile to tell anybody. A lot of people might immediately call their friends. I couldn't. I just couldn't. I had previously made plans with a few of my friends for that evening. I cancelled on them. I didn't give them a reason. I just said I wasn't going to be able to go. I couldn't even talk to them over the phone. I was only able to send a five-word text: "Can't make it tonight. Sorry."

Four hours later, the friend who'd put together those plans called me. I didn't even realize. He left an awkward voicemail. He just didn't know what to say. I could tell he was crying. My friend from school was the only one I was able to call. And I wasn't able to call her until late that night. We had plans to meet for coffee and go to the Senior Sunrise event at school. I had to deliver the news and tell her I couldn't go. And here's what they did for me.

After calling and leaving me the awkward voicemail, my friend immediately rounded up the gang we had originally made plans with that night. He filled them all in on the situation, and instead of having the Nerf war they were planning, he forced me into his car, and we met the gang in our church parking lot. We just sat and talked and ate bulk WinCo candy for three hours.

My school friend said she was picking me up the next morning. She convinced me that someday I'd regret missing the opportunities that only came once. After Senior Sunrise, we went for coffee, and I went home (thoroughly confusing my classmates who had seen me at the school earlier). After another day or two of being home, I went to school. The occasional teacher would say something about my mom here, or my senior advisor and I talked a little there, but nobody really addressed it. That's because nobody really knew. The staff was all emailed, but I don't think any more students than I could count on one hand knew. And it was like that for a long time. Then, I started opening up a little to some of the people around me, but still, it hasn't been a big part of things. It still takes me a long time to broach the subject.

In May, just before my high school graduation, I presented my senior project. I attended a public option school, designed specifically for students with an interest in the fine arts. My assignment, which the school called a Capstone, was to be a forty-minute presentation about my journey through the arts, and more specifically, the school. There was just one problem for me: I had only attended the school for a year and a half. I transferred there in the middle of my junior year. I did not have enough experience to be able to fill a 40-minute time slot. I needed to come up with something. So I created a presentation so incredibly unique to my creative ability: I wrote a musical about my life. Yes, it was ambitious. Yes, it took a lot of time and planning.

If you know anything about writing, you know there has to be a beginning, middle, and end. The beginning, or opening number in my case, has to wow the audience. The audience needs to feel what I like to call "The Three Es: Engaged,

Engrossed, and Excited." It took forever for me to be able to figure out exactly how my musical was going to start. I am a huge musical theater nerd. So, I took to my trusty music streaming service, and listened to countless musicals. I needed some kind of inspiration. It could have been anything: an opening number, a great plot device, even the title of a song. It was approximately late January when I had a vague sense of what I wanted to do. At that point, I had decided I was not going to write my own songs. I did not have enough instrumental capability to compose songs, but I did feel fairly confident in my ability to write lyrics. So I took existing songs, tweaked a few lyrics, and made a musical. I guess you could say it was a jukebox musical, except they were all musical theatre songs, so it would not appear on a jukebox. That made the whole process so much easier, but I still did not have an overarching plot line. I also had officially chosen only one song: "She Used to Be Mine." It was the most important piece of the puzzle (but more on that later).

As the weeks went on, I finally was gaining some traction. I had picked some more songs, and was starting to write a script. I still had no plot line, but I knew I had to get working. I was listening to music on the way to school when it hit me. The song I was listening to discussed a wedding rehearsal, and everything was going wrong. That was it! My overarching plot line was a Capstone rehearsal! I was so inspired I wrote almost the entire script in one day. Most of the things I had written previously were thrown out; I had kept only "She Used to Be Mine."

When I was finished (or when I thought I was finished), I breathed a sigh of relief. I left it alone for a few days, and then it came to me. Did I really write a 40-minute musical? So I rehearsed my Capstone in my living room one night. Mind you, it was not written as a one-man show, I just played every part. Over an hour later, I performed the closing number, and just about cried. I had to cut a third of my senior project. I had no idea what I was going to do. I had to cut major events out of my life story I was telling. I went back to the drawing board, which was just a bunch of post-it notes on my living room wall. I took every single post-it note off the wall. I slapped the "She Used to Be Mine" post-it up in the middle, and started building around it. Important life events such as Mom's death, and the difficult birth of my little brother Gabriel, things I wanted to touch on went up first. Then came some comedic moments, scenes crucial to keeping the rehearsal plot afloat. Finally, there were the songs.

Throughout the different versions, there were approximately thirty songs total I had considered, including a great Disney medley I had concocted.

In front of me, I had the list whittled down to eight songs. It was a difficult decision. I did not have time for them all. I scrapped three of them, including a touching tribute to my little brothers I am still disappointed I did not have a chance to perform. The Capstone still didn't feel right. Something was wrong. I thought long and hard; what was it I needed to do? It became time for me to settle in on a final draft. So on a whim, I replaced two numbers: the opening number, and the poorly-placed song I had thrown in just to give my mentor, Auntie Jody, a song. The new opening number was much shorter, and was again reprised as the finale. Auntie Jody was given a comedic relief song, which was easily most of the audience's favorite part.

The day came, and I was terrified. It's not every day you write a musical about yourself and have to present it. It went well. I mean, as well as it could go. The whole joke was it was a rehearsal, so we pretended to mess up (and in some cases, actually messed up) as we told my life story in a musical format. The time came. I had to sing "She Used to Be Mine" (I told you we would come back to this part).

"She Used to Be Mine" is a song from the musical *Waitress*, with music and lyrics written by Sara Bareilles. The song in its original form didn't necessarily fit the theme of my Capstone, but with a few minor tweaks to lyrics, it fit like a glove. With the lyric changes, the song became a story about a boy (me) whose life went down a different path than the one he had dreamed for himself. He looks upon his younger self, and wishes he was the young kid who once was fearless, but realizes he isn't that kid anymore. The bridge and chorus of the song sum up the emotional journey I was trying to highlight.

> *And be scared of the life that's ahead,*
> *Fear growing stronger each day,*
> *Until someone reminds him to fight just a little,*
> *To bring back the fire in your eyes,*
> *That's been gone*
> *But it used to be mine.*
>
> *He is messy, but he's kind.*
> *He is lonely most of the time.*
> *He is all of this mixed up and made into a pretty good guy.*
> *He is gone,*
> *But he used to be mine.*[81]

It was the most vulnerable I had been in front of a sizable group since Mom's memorial. It felt so nice. It was a great time to reflect, and a great time to let everyone know who I was. As the Capstone continued, I kept talking about how people grow, myself included. I opened up to the audience, talking about things I had never before told anyone. I went into much detail about Mom's passing, an event only about five percent of the audience (including my family) actually knew about. It was never something I wanted to talk about with people. I didn't want everyone to constantly give me their condolences, causing me to think about Mom's death all the time, and I certainly didn't want anyone to think I was trying to gain attention with sympathy. It was oddly therapeutic. By the time the Capstone was over, laughter, sweat, and tears had poured out of nearly everyone in the room. I was thrilled it was over; after all, it was one of the most stressful things I had ever done. It was over.

Now you are probably wondering why I told you all that. Well, it helped me cope. The whole process helped me realize exactly who I was. There's a sense of lost-ness (lôstnəs. *Made up Noun*: a feeling, or sense, of emotional wandering that is restless and endless) that came with Mom's passing. I learned what I needed to from this endeavor. This assignment was never meant to be a burden; it was meant to be an experience from which to learn. That I see who I was. Who I have grown to be.

Capstone was only the beginning to a roller-coaster of a weekend. The following Sunday was Mother's Day. My first Mother's Day without my mom. That in and of itself would be a hard day. But there's a twist. May 14th is my birthday. Yep. It was Mother's Day and my 18th birthday. God definitely has a sense of humor. The day was really difficult for me, and I elaborated on it in my blog, *In Constant Search*, a week later. Here's what I wrote:

> I don't know about you, but sometimes, I like it when things are all about me. Like birthdays. Birthdays are a great day to make everything about you.
> 
> I've never really liked it when my birthday falls on Mother's Day. I've never gotten to celebrate my birthday on Mother's Day; Dad used to say "your birthday has been relocated to a different day." And this year was an interesting one. My birthday fell on Mother's Day. It was my 18th birthday. It was my first Mother's Day without Mom. So the whole time leading up to it, I managed to find every

way to slip it into conversation to make everyone feel bad for me. It could be about me this time! Here's what happened instead:

The night before was prom. So I was out really late and only got around 4 hours of sleep. So, let's just say I wasn't the perkiest of people that morning. I had a harsh sing-songy awakening and went back to sleep. When I finally woke up, I rushed to get out of the house to take a little brother to church, without any time to stop and get a coffee, or even have any breakfast.

Now, I love church. I love getting to talk to people and learn more about God, but let's be clear: I WAS NOT WANTING TO BE AT CHURCH THAT MORNING. But I put on a smile, and went, and I served. After serving in Children's Ministries, I went to my own service. I left shortly after our youth pastor told us all to text our mothers and tell her what we love most about her.

On my way home, I stopped and grabbed a coffee (caffeine! Finally!), and went home to be treated to a special brunch made much like Mom would have done. Shortly after brunch, Dad piled us into the car with cards and flowers galore to go treat a few moms who had made a huge effort to love on us these past eight months (a.k.a. the Mom Mafia). And while it was super thoughtful and kind, I really didn't want to. Birthdays are a great day to make everything about you. All I got so far was a brunch. And we didn't even sit around the table; we watched a TV show. So I was a little miffed. Well, a lot miffed.

We spent the next 3 1/2 hours delivering Mother's Day treats. And when it was time for dinner, Dad asked what we were gonna do. Traditionally, we go to Red Robin, but since times were a little tight, we were going to do a homemade meal. [Being] disappointed, [I] said that I wanted ravioli, and when Dad decided that we were going to Red Robin, I felt guilty and said ravioli was fine. But it wasn't. I was really angry that whole time. I wasn't having a lot of fun. It was my birthday. I was trying to block out the fact that it was Mother's Day and just have a grand old time. But I spent my day grumpy and tired. And then there was dinner and a movie. I wanted to watch the movie my little brother had just gotten me, but we didn't have time for that. We had another Mother's Day delivery to make, so I had to settle for a TV show instead. I couldn't even pick a movie to watch for my birthday? Wow. I was peeved. But I tried not to show it (at least to the people who weren't my family).

Later that night, Dad was apologizing. He didn't know how to balance the day. He didn't want to under-celebrate me or Mother's Day. I said I was fine. But I wasn't. Later that night, I wrote a blog post. A real honest blog post, one that wasn't very nice to anyone (including myself). It was a big, passive-aggressive, my-birthday-sucked-but-its-my-fault-'cause-I-was-angry complain-fest. And I spent a good time crying about it. I felt bad. I had done all of these nice things, and I, in the moment, didn't mean any of them? I felt like a horrible person. I cried and cried, and wrote and wrote. And then Dad read it. I knew I couldn't post something to that extent, and I didn't even want him to read it. I felt so terrible, like I was the worst person in the world. It was my birthday; it was supposed to be all about me. But it wasn't to everyone else. Just me. Dad did his best to comfort me (we grabbed ice cream from the Target up the street and started watching a really funny movie), but even now, I still feel really bad.

And now here we are, with me regretting every word that I type because I really hated that day, and I don't want anyone to know how I was (and am) feeling. And now I don't know what to do with myself. I mean, where am I supposed to go from here? It's not like I get a do-over.

I feel bad because every Mother's Day thing we did, I meant from the bottom of my heart, and I would feel like it showed on any other day except that day. Because *my* birthday was supposed to be all about *me*.

So, I guess the lesson is, don't always think the world revolves around you? I don't know, I'm still trying to figure this lesson out. But I do know one thing: I hate it when my birthday is on Mother's Day.[82]

That was definitely one of the hardest days I've had since Mom passed away. As you could see, I was definitely not in a good frame of mind. I still feel bad I had that kind of outlook on that day, an "it's all about me" mind-frame. I wanted...no, I needed to feel loved that day. Little did I know, fast-forward a week and the birthday surprise began.

I knew I was having a birthday party the following weekend. I begged for an *Amazing Race*-style birthday party where me and my friends would all go adventuring into the city. I didn't have high expectations. Fifteen of my closest friends met at my house for this party. The house was barely decorated, half-cleaned, and yet, the scavenger hunt activity was really well put together. I was pleasantly surprised. I haven't had the biggest, best track record for birthday parties (after all, my sixteenth birthday party was postponed by three months), and I knew that Dad had a lot going on. I was quickly given information that some of the Mom Mafia (I'm sure you've heard of them?) had assisted in creating the game. It was a great time and I had an absolute blast (even though my team definitely did not win). The last clue led us to the parking lot of my church. It made no sense. I was incredibly confused. We were all invited into the children's ministry building. It was at this point I realized I had no idea what was happening. As I walked in, I was greeted with a red carpet, a full meal spread, and my friends who joined me for the game. I kept walking down the long hallway, and along the hidden wall in the room were *over* forty-five more people who had come to surprise me. There were mentors, family friends, families I babysat for, so many people I loved. So many people who loved me. The evening went on, and it was a total blast. We even ended with my favorite pastime ever, an impromptu lip-sync battle (which I obviously won since I'm insanely good at them).

I realized in that moment, that even when I thought I was alone, I wasn't. I was loved, and always will be loved, even from people whom I don't get to see very often. Over this journey since Mom's death, I've learned vulnerability is key. I felt terrible a week prior to this party because I thought I was a horrible person for being sad my mom wasn't around anymore. It blinded me from realizing just how many people had come around me and my family in our time of need, to support us and love on us.

At the start of senior year, I was incredibly sad Mom would not be around for any of the "last things" I would encounter. She didn't get to read my essay for, let alone the acceptance letter from, Biola University. She didn't get to take me on a road trip to visit the campus like we planned. She didn't get to see my Capstone or even my graduation. She wasn't able to plan my eighteenth birthday either, the birthday where I finally became "an adult." She didn't even get to help me move away to college. I struggled with it for a long time. I thought there was something I could have done for Mom the night she died. At the end of senior year, I had finally accepted there was nothing I could have done.

Have you ever broken your foot? Well, in sixth grade, I broke a very small toe bone in my left foot (which then became the entire side of my foot because my little brother accidently flying squirreled it), and it hurt worse than anything I had felt before. I went to my dad, asking, begging if there was something he could do to fix it. He told me to walk it off (he thought I had just sprained my ankle). When I was finally taken to the doctor (my dad thought I was whining about nothing and sent me to basketball practice instead of the doctor), I was desperately hoping the doctor would have some way to fix my foot right then and there. But to my disappointment, the doctor couldn't just wave a magic wand and, *Bibbidi-Boppidi-Boo*, my foot would be fully healed. I wore a cast because I needed support. I used crutches because I couldn't stand on my own. I rode around in a wheelchair when I had other people who could push me in the right direction. And even when my cast was off and I didn't need any help getting around, my foot still was not the same. Even though the doctor told me the bone was healed, it still had the remnants of a break in it. My foot would never be 100 percent healed. There are times when my foot still hurts where the break happened. Other times, I feel like I was never hurt.

So it is with Grief. Grief is a masterful thing. Just like my foot, it can hurt worse than anything you've ever felt before. It will get worse before it gets better. You might go to the Father, asking, begging for some way for Him to fix it. You desperately hope "the Doctor" will snap His fingers and everything will be okay. Yet it won't. You might feel alone, like the best thing for you to do is just to sit in your room alone and cry. But just like with a broken foot, sitting around and doing nothing is not the best thing for you to do. You eventually have to try to walk, even for a little bit. You can't just hide in a hole and watch as many CSI reruns as possible. You need support because there are moments when you can't stand on your own. You need a team, a trusted group who can comfort you, and be with you in the good, the bad, and the ugly. You need friends and family who will encourage you, and push you in the right direction, even when you feel abandoned and alone. You'll find yourself wishing things could go back to the way they were, and you just want the pain to stop. You want to stop hurting. The truth is, you won't. You'll get used to your new normal. You'll learn how to move on and to cope. You'll have good days and bad days. There will be days it won't even cross your mind; there will be days you just want to cry and nothing else. And that is okay. It's all okay. Grief looks different for everyone.

## GOOD GRIEF

If I could sum up everything I've learned in the past year and a half, it would be this. There are three big questions you'll find yourself asking in times of Grief:

1. God, where were you?
2. What could I have done to prevent this?
3. Will I ever stop hurting?

When you first ask these questions, you think you know the answers. I thought I did. I still wrestle with these questions. I realized it didn't matter where I thought God *was*, but where He *is*. I realized that even if I could have prevented my mom's death, what happened happened for a reason. I realized I won't ever stop hurting, but I will be able to find joy and peace in the situation. Questions come faster than answers. So do not lose hope. He *is* always with you.

Oh yeah, I almost forgot. If I had a time machine, what one thing would I go back in my life and change? I wouldn't change anything. You know, a wise friend who spoke at my mom's memorial wrote me a letter. I hadn't been given the chance to read this letter until after I had started writing this chapter. I won't be going into very much detail, as a lot of the things said were very personal, but I will give you a glimpse of how it started.

> "Micah, if you could get into a DeLorean and travel 'back to the future' and meet your Mom when she was a teenager- you would recognize so much of yourself."

So that's my answer. I'm honored by the fact this friend thought I was so much like my mom. She was incredibly kind-hearted and a phenomenal woman. So, if I did get one chance to use a time machine, I'd meet my mom when she was a teenager...or I'd attend the opening day of Disneyland, because, I mean, who wouldn't?

THOMAS MICHAEL JOHNSON

For her last birthday, Micah took his mom
to see her favorite musical: *Newsies*

CHAPTER 25

# Parenting Without the Autism Whisperer

*Gabriel Johnson*

Yesterday, in the middle of a storm I didn't think would end (major car issues with both vehicles), as I was crying, my little Gus, who has his mama's heart and Jesus's eyes, put his hand on my knee (I was driving) and said, "Daddy, Jesus is here. It's okay." Then he chose a song from his Spotify account to play and said, "I think you need to hear this." What played? "Jesus Take the Wheel." As we both sung with Carrie Underwood, I marveled at the profound insight, compassion, and empathy that God put into a little boy with autism, a little boy who they said wouldn't walk, or talk, or have a quality of life worth living. Amy and I have always marveled at Gabe's spiritual insight and direct connection to the Throne of God. I see Amy in him every day; I see Jesus in him every hour. To have the faith of a little child...

P.S. It wasn't until I began writing this post nearly 24 hours after the fact that the irony hit me. For those of you who are worried, I didn't fleece God to see if He'd actually drive my car.[83]

※

When out in public, those people who don't know you tend to think you should have arrived at all the needed parenting skills if you have more than one child. At least, that has been my experience while in public when "autism shows up," as we have begun calling the situations.

Autism is a hidden disability. People cannot identify a person with autism as they can other disabilities. A wheelchair is an immediate indication of a walking disability. A long, white stick extended in front of someone walking is an obvious nod to a vision impairment. A person with Downs Syndrome is also quickly identified. But autism has no outward physical identifying traits. We—Amy and I—used to never say anything about Gabriel having autism while we were out in public. We've always treated him like he was a normal child, because he is; all children come with their quirks—that's just how it works. As Gabriel has aged, there have been more and more people who speak up in public, wondering why our middle child "is the way he is." Sometimes the question is legitimate, couched in concern and wonder. Other times it is derogatory, people wondering "what's wrong" with our child. To the latter, we've simply said, "There is nothing wrong with our child." We believe that wholeheartedly: there is nothing wrong with Gabriel. God just decided to make him unique.

Unique. I love that word. It brings with it the idea that something is special, valuable, one of a kind. Unfortunately, said in public in many circles, the word *unique* is a way of labeling someone as odd, off, or different (not in a good way). In my world, however, *unique* is a word I often use to describe each of my kids, and my students too. I have spent a significant portion of my twenty years as a teacher/professor working with exceptional[84] and twice-exceptional[85] students. What I have learned from my years in the classroom is that God has made each of us unique in more ways than I ever really understood. Each of my boys is unique, and each of them came into the world a little differently than the other two. Each of them has different interests and strengths, and each of them has their own *genius*. I'd like to redefine *genius* for this chapter. For me, *genius* includes not just exceptionally smart, but also exceptionally creative, exceptionally musical, exceptionally innovative, and the list could go on, but I think you get my point.

Psalm 139:14 says that we are "fearfully and wonderfully made." It also goes on to say, "Your works are wonderful, I know that full well." Science tell us that no two people have the same fingerprint or genetic code, not even identical twins. When God created each one of us, He created only one version. There is no Thom 2.0 running around in this world, no matter how much my youngest looks, thinks, and sounds like me. And since each of us is different than everyone else, it only seems logical that each one of us has our own unique *genius*. I've watched the Olympics and have been very impressed by the *genius* God has given each of the athletes. I have watched bakers create pastries and decorate cakes in ways I can only describe as *genius*. Why not use the words *creative* or *artistic*? As a Language Arts teacher and writer, I've come to find those two adjectives bland, common, and a bit dull. When someone is described as *creative* or *artistic*, the listener thinks of someone gifted with some type of art. Be it musical, dramatic, or picturesque, we think of art. I've watched my students and each of my kids. I've even watched friends and family members. I've taken stock of the gifts, talents, and genius of each. Why? If I need work done on a car, I call my father-in-law. He understands and knows cars inside and out. If I need help with my taxes, I call my accountant friend who understands the tax laws of our country better than I understand grammar! If I need help putting on a play, or an event, or if I need to find...I could do this all day. We are all unique. We all have a special, individual, and exceptional *genius* that was hand-crafted just for each of us.

When I decided to have three chapters focused on each of my three children, I knew that writing Gabriel's would be *unique*. He loves stories, but he's not the writer his brothers are, so writing his own chapter was not an option. He loves talking about his mama, but his wires can often get crossed and the listener can get very lost. He loves people, but he is often misunderstood by people around him who do not know him, truly know him.

Because this book is not fiction, I could not "don the character" of my son and write from his perspective in order to give you the same experience with his chapter as you will get with my other two. I pray that this chapter will challenge you in your understanding of grief, sorrow, and healing. I pray your eyes will be opened to a larger understanding of who God is and exactly of what He's capable. It's hard for our minds to wrap around what would seem to be the impossible, but God is good at the impossible.

---

"True love's kiss has to bring her back, right?" Gabriel's eyes were staring at me, expecting only one answer: *Yes*. Amy's body was on the gurney in the front room of the house. We had all sung a worship song or two. We had heard scripture. We had prayed. It was time for the morticians to take her from the house. That wasn't enough for my little angel. He was not about to accept this jarring reality without exhausting every imaginable possibility. He bent over his mother, one foot on the floor, the other on the gurney next to Amy, his body laying next to hers. He had kissed her on the forehead, because that's what you do, right? Prince Eric kissed Princess Ariel and she got her voice back. Prince Phillip kissed Princess Aurora to break a sleeping curse. Prince Florian kissed the beautiful Snow White on the forehead while she lay motionless in a glass coffin. The prince kisses the princess and breaks the curse. And Death is a curse. Therefore, shouldn't a kiss of true love break Death's curse?

It took me a beat to catch Gabriel's train of thought. Then it all made perfect sense. Amy was Gabriel's favorite person in the whole wide world. She could do no wrong. She could pinpoint his favorite things. She could talk his language. His day started and ended with Amy. With no malice or pain, I can truly say, it would have been easier for him had I died than his mother. About eight months before she died, Amy started deferring all issues to me when it came to Gabriel.

"Mom, I'm mad at Dad."

"Okay, go talk to him."

"No, I want to talk with you."

"No. You need to talk to your dad. I can't fix this." Then she'd drop the payload. "The Bible says we're supposed to go straight to the person and work things out."

Grumble. Mumble. Wait twenty minutes.

"Mom, I'm still mad at Dad."

"What did he say when you talked to him."

"I didn't talk to him. I want to talk with you."

"Nope. Talk to your dad."

It was one of the most difficult things Amy had to do. We recognized that Gabriel had been "checking me" as if trying to become the Alpha male in the house. He would often puff up his chest, stand as tall as he could—even use his tippy toes, and then scream when trying to talk to me. But it hadn't always been like that.

When Gabriel was born, I was his world. He wanted nothing to do with Amy if my voice was within earshot. He didn't crawl for five or six months after a "typical birth" but when he did, I could not get away from him. We made a game of it. He would laugh. His baby laugh was one of the best sounds I've ever heard. He would chase me until I let him catch me. Then he wouldn't let go. He was a strong baby. It took three grown men to hold him down when he was eight months old to get a blood sample and give him a shot. Two of us were using a lot of our weight to hold him down (without hurting him) and he still would get away from us.

He wasn't just strong; he was also a determined toddler. If he wanted something, nothing was going to stop him from getting it. He wanted to see what was so exciting about the thing Mom set pans on when she was making dinner. He was going to reach up and feel whatever it was, maybe even pull it down and look at it. We spent ten minutes dissuading—rather, trying to dissuade—him one night. When it was time for dinner, we gave the call and walked to the table with hands full. Gabriel darted around us and his hand alighted on the red hot coil in mere seconds. From then on, Gabriel would stand guard to the entrance of the kitchen refusing to let his baby brother enter the kitchen while Mom or Dad was using "The Hot" thing on the counter again.

"'Zay, you not go in. You touch it," he was pointing to the stove, "and The Hot burs hard." (He couldn't say *burns* at that age.) When people came over to visit, Gabriel gave them his tour and spiel: "The Hot burs hard. You don't wanna touch it. See?" He'd hold up his hand to show the burn marks at first. About the time they left, Gabriel was done worrying about The Hot.

Not only is Gabriel strong and determined, he is also full of hope and joy. In middle school, Gabriel coined a phrase that is both humorous and ominous in the same breath.

"Mommy, I can't wait to grow up and get a car," he said one night.

"Well, Gabe, what happens if you grow up and you can't drive?"

"Well, I'm almost a teenager. What could go wrong?" The two years before Amy died, *What could go wrong?* became his mantra. If there was something difficult he had to face at school, "What could go wrong, Mom?" If he had to walk himself to the bus stop alone because Amy didn't have the strength to walk out with him, "What could go wrong, Mom?" If he was angry with me and wanted to take care of his mom himself (as precious little boys are want to do) to ensure that she was "the safest," "What could go wrong, Dad?"

But that morning—September 6, 2016—something had gone wrong. It would take nearly a year for him to understand and accept what "God's timing" meant.

"True love's kiss has to bring her back, right?" Gabriel was not romantically in love with his mama. At the physical age of thirteen, he was only as mature as an eight-year-old boy. Eight-year-old boys want to grow up and marry their mamas. Why? Because she is the most incredible, amazing woman they know. If she's good enough for Dad, then she's perfect for me. Right?

Sometimes Gabriel would surprise us and say the deepest, most profound things, but usually he was a little boy with little boy faith. "Let the children come to me....I tell you the truth, anyone who doesn't receive the Kingdom of God like a child will never enter it" (Mark 10:14b-15, NLT). It was that simple to him. Amy was incredible. He was supposed to take care of her. She was sick. Like Snow White or Aurora, the beautiful, magically sleeping princess was she. The handsome prince was he. "True love's kiss has to bring her back, right?" Translation? *Why is God taking my mommy?* It's a difficult conversation to have with a young child. Slather that child with a layer of autism, no matter how highly functional, and figurative goes out the window.

Whatever you tell Gabriel, you must be aware that he will believe you. Unless you tell him you're kidding, you're being sarcastic, or you're pretending, in his mind what you say will come true. His faith is that of a little child. He knows God is going to come back to get him and take him to heaven...to see his mama again.

Does it feel a little repetitive? That was intentional. It's call *perseveration*. Perseveration is the acute focus on an issue or item with the inability to let go of it. When I was a kid, I remember Hugo the Abominable Snowman from *Looney Tunes*. He was a little different, but he wanted to be loved. He wanted to have a pet. And when he caught that pet he was going to "name him George." To show the pet love, he said, "I will hug him and squeeze him and pat him and pet him and rub him and caress him."[86] What was the problem with that scene? Hugo wanted a pet bunny rabbit. Bugs Bunny had set up his frenemy, Daffy Duck, to take the fall. "But I'm not a bunny!" Daffy kept repeating. Hugo would hear "bunny" and he was coming full circle: "I will name him George and I will hug him and squeeze him and pat him and..." The repetition had us all in stitches as kids. Most of us thought Hugo was just dumb. But Hugo was far from dumb. He was based on a character from Steinbeck's *Of Mice and Men*. Lennie Small is a mentally disabled character in the book. He has the body and strength of a fully grown adult man. He is simplistic in his view of the world, though, and perseverates over soft things—they calm him. In the book Lennie is unable to control his strength when his emotions are at the extremes and he has the capacity to bring a significant amount of harm to those around him, although without intention or anger. Just accident. He's guilty of loving something to death…literally. He does not understand the fragility of life. He just wants to "hug it and squeeze it and make it mine!"

After having a child with autism, I look back at Hugo and Lennie and I see my Gabriel: the body and strength of a grown man, simplistic in his view of the world, unable to control his own strength, a capacity to bring significant harm to those around him unintentionally, a bottomless vat of love to go around, and a protective streak that is unending. When Lennie is confused and afraid, the unthinkable happens. When the "bunny" is taken from Hugo, the unthinkable happens.

"True love's kiss has to bring her back, right?"

In his view, Amy was taken from Gabriel. I did not know what would happen. I knew it would be difficult. I knew it would be extreme. And I knew it would be painful. I also knew my son had a heart of gold. He would stand up to protect whomever needed protecting, even if he was not the right person to do so. God gave him one last piece of *genius*: his capacity to love and have empathy for others. People with autism do not typically seek out interpersonal relationships, let alone have the capacity to feel and express empathy or love devoted. Gabriel is different. Our pediatrician calls him an "anomaly." God called him by the name of an angel.

Three times I have heard my innocent, lovable boy scream—the type of scream that can only cause pain to all who hear it. The timbre and pitch is one every human knows innately that the unthinkable has just happened. Pain beyond what one person could bear has taken over and the heart of the wailer lays in pieces. While Gabriel lay on the gurney next to his mama, screaming, I was panicked, looking around for answers to questions I didn't know I would be asking. The night before the memorial service, when Gabriel watched the video of Amy's life, screaming, I was frozen in fear, unable to comprehend how to help him make sense of something I could barely understand. When Gabriel sat in the dark screaming "Why did she leave me?" I held him not knowing how to console him. Why? Because I didn't know his language as well as Amy did; I didn't know how to "speak autism" as well as his mother could.

Gabriel is extremely literal. When he was little, if you told him he could fly and then described jumping out a window and flapping your arms to catch air, he would have felt you were mocking him, wanting to hurt him, because he would have jumped…and then broken a few bones. Or he would have thought he'd done it wrong and then tried again some other time after the casts were removed.

When he was really little, I felt like Gabriel understood everything I said. As he became an elementary student, I felt like he was speaking Arabic while I spoke Greek, with neither being the wiser. Amy stopped me one day.

"Thom, you didn't listen to your son." I got a bit offended.

"Yes, I did. He wants me to be in the story he's writing. I told him it was okay for him to write about me."

"No, that's not what he asked you." I opened my mouth to object, but was cut off. "Yes, he said those words, but you don't know what he means." She raised a cautionary finger. "He was watching a show this morning. The main character said to his new friend, 'Why don't you come into my story and play?' Then the two characters jumped into a book and began to play together…as…the…story." Amy watched his every move. She noted every twitch. She interpreted every word. She untangled every story wrapped up in the string of words he often would say in conversation. She was his translator. That night she taught me my son was inviting me to be part of his story, to come into his room (his book) and play.

I made it my mission to learn to speak autism fluently. Like any other foreign language, it was far from easy. There were many bumps, groans, and outright loud bursts of anger. I interpreted them all personally. Amy would step in just before I boiled over and gave in to anger. Each time she could show me the trigger. I was never the cause. I just happened to be the one receiving the unintended pain as Gabriel fought to find his voice. I began learning patience late, but I don't regret starting. It has sometimes taken all of my willpower to remind myself how to look at Gabriel and see his heart.

And he has a great big, God-sized heart. It's one of the first things people tell me they are impressed with regarding Gabriel. He loves deeply. He cares about everybody, even if he's just met them. He wants people to be happy and to not be in pain either. If you could sit down and talk with Gabriel, you would find it challenging, almost like talking with Yoda. But once you understand him and listen to him, you will find he has many profound things to say. Some of them don't always make sense, but hang around long enough and you will hear pure, sweet love gushing out of my Gabriel. Then the next minute he might have you in stitches.

About three weeks after Amy's death, we were visited by the leader from our church who oversees "Grief Share"—a ministry for people who have lost a loved one. The wonderful woman brought with her a basket of goodies only a mom could provide. After setting them on the table and taking a seat, she asked a question we had all heard many times. However, this time her question was aimed at my boys and Gabriel's response was extremely profound.

"What do you need?" she asked.

"We need prayers, dignity, and hope," my angel said without hesitation. We were dumbfounded. His words were perfect and timely. Five months later, his conversation was more comical:

> Driving in the car tonight, alone with my middle angel, (Matthew West singing in the background), Gabe looks at me and calmly says,
> "Dad, you don't look like an idiot to me."
> I tried to find out what provoked that comment. He simply said,
> "I want you to know you're loved. You're my favorite dad, and Mom had a heart of gold."
> There are times when I wish I understood the workings of an autism brain. Tonight wasn't one of them. I tried very hard not to laugh. I was successful; however, the darkness had a big job concealing my grin. Apparently I'm not an idiot![87]

Wanting to give you as much as I can from Gabriel's perspective, what follows are my questions, his answers, and my musings from our multiple interviews.

"What has been the hardest part of life without Mom?"

"The hardest thing about…when Mom died…it's been trying to do our jobs that we have to do. Like chores. I can't get past all the work."

Literal. "Hardest part" is interpreted as physical effort. Frustrating.

Washing the dishes has been one of Gabriel's chores for a while now. He's mastered taking out the trash. He's mastered vacuuming. Dishes? Nope.

"You told me to put everything I could into the dishwasher. I did that!"

"But I've shown you how to load the dishwasher. You can't pile things on top of each other. They won't get washed. Do you remember me showing you that?"

"Yes...but..."

Instant anger, hot face, sweat, and steam.

"What have I told you about 'Yes...but...'?" I asked in anger. The conversation did not go well. Argument. Frustration. Everyone lost. I walked into the other room to take a minute.

*What did you tell him to do?* I heard God ask me.

*Really, are you taking his side?* I was really mad and God was my next target.

*What did you tell him to do?*

*To 'fill the dishwasher' and 'fit as much as possible in it.'* I heard it. Gabriel had done what I had asked him to do. autism would agree that he had done what was asked. Autism would prevent him from understanding the nuances of my direction.

*Did he do what you asked?* God asked. My frustration disintegrated.

I don't like losing arguments. Even if that argument is with the Creator Himself. Nobody likes to lose. But I'm glad God is patient. And He's willing to help me understand the boy in front of me, not the disobedience I feel is staring back at me. Truth? Gabriel did what I told him to do. The problem was my directions. I've told my kids since middle school, communication usually breaks down with the sender. The sender is responsible for the message and how the message is received. We don't like to hear that. We want to send a message and then blame the receiver for their reception of it, but it doesn't work that way. If we want to truly communicate, we have to go the extra mile and check for understanding. It's Teaching 101!

I found myself going back into the kitchen to talk with Gabriel. First to apologize, then to re-instruct...again, but without frustration.

---

"What do you miss most about Mom?"

"I miss her cooking. Her scrapbooking. Sometimes I miss seeing the memories we had together."

Gabriel was born with sensory issues. There are certain textures throughout his childhood that have caused him agony. It's hard for me to fathom, but I've had to accept it, know it, guard against it, and help him problem-solve. The biggest texture Gabe could not handle was anything resembling a sponge. Think about how many things resemble the texture of a sponge. Keep sponges away...no problem! Wait! Bread has the same texture. Cake has the same texture. Muffins have the same texture. On his first birthday, Gabriel stuck his fingers in the frosting of his piece of cake and was done. It was sticky! And the cake texture...What we'd worked hard to have turn out perfect went up in smoke. Bread caused him to scream and cry as if someone scary was threatening him. My son didn't eat a sandwich until he was eight years old! Did we make him eat it? Nope. We had tried that many times. We happened to be at the farm I grew up on one Summer day. Grandma was preparing lunch for us. She made the boys "something special." It was a grilled cheese sandwich. Amy and I looked at each other. I headed for the door to retrieve Gabe's food from the car.

"Wait!" It was a loud, muffled, whisper. I followed Amy's hand. She was pointing at Gabriel. Gabriel was sitting at the table, his back towards me. The grilled cheese sandwich was in his hands. I actually watched him take a bite. I cringed. Amy cringed. We were both waiting for the emotional blowup indicating World War III had begun. Nothing. He ate the whole sandwich like he'd been eating them his whole life. At one point, he simply looked over at one of us to see if we would react. We were stone-faced, trying desperately to not break and show emotion that would cause him to change his mind about bread.

A week later when Lisa was at the house, Amy made him a grilled cheese sandwich. She wanted to show Lisa the impossible. Lisa was not ready for what happened. Gabriel dipped his sandwich in her tomato soup. As one does. Lisa was caught off guard and began laughing. She had just witnessed a miracle.

Amy never forgot Gabriel's favorite foods. She made them just like he liked them. She made sure the house was filled with foods related to his needs (as well as the rest of ours).

Months into counseling after Amy's death, it was clear to me that Gabriel needed a creative outlet. I didn't know what that outlet would be. Every time someone in the family begins to really enjoy a creative outlet, Gabriel wants to take it over and be in charge of any and all activities related to the newly acquired interest. Micah wants to be a playwright. "I'm going to write plays, Dad! I'm going to write one where Mommy doesn't die. It's going to be the best play ever." Isaiah likes movies. "Dad, I'm going to see all the movies and then I'm going to make them. Please help me...I mean right now!" I love superheroes: comic book, TV, and movies. "I'm going to grow up to be a superhero just like you, Dad. Then I'll show you. I'll be able to do more than you can do." Each time it comes across as bragging. Each time we've all struggled with not letting it bother us, even when he's RIGHT THERE in the way, preventing us from doing what we wanted to do. "Daddy, I'm going to write a book like you're writing. I want to write about Mom's life. You can be in it too. What should I write? Will you put some stories down on paper for me? They can be a part of my book."

As I dug a bit, trying to find the switch to flip, I grew more and more frustrated.

"Daddy, when are we ever going to scrapbook again? Mommy helped us start the Disney albums from our trip. When can we finish them?"

"Not right now, Gabe. I'm trying to cook dinner."

"When are we going to scrapbook again?"

"Not right now, I'm trying to figure out what type of sports or clubs you should do at school."

"When are we going to scrapbook like Mommy used to?"

It was as if I were Daffy Duck, and Hugo was brushing my "fur" backwards. I was so irritated.

*God, why can't he leave it alone? Scrapbooking has too much pain in it. There are too many memories from when I used to help Amy scrapbook. He needs a creative outlet. Show me what that is so he'll stop bugging me about scrapbooking, please.*

Sadly, it wasn't as obvious to me as it has probably been to you. What is Gabriel's creative outlet? He has two of them. First and foremost, he finds fulfillment being interested in the things his friends and loved ones are interested in or actively doing. Why? Because it gets him time with that person and he gets paid in the joy of working together. Who'd he learn that from? Yours truly! Doesn't God have a sense of humor? When Amy and I got married, my only hobby was writing. Actually, I loved writing. I also loved cooking, but I didn't know how to cook much. She fixed that. We cooked together. "Let's take a cake decorating class, Thom." Sure. I didn't want to take the class. I wasn't "artistic." My cakes would look bad. Did they? Yes, they did...at first. Then I started having fun with it. Then I started entering contests and offering personalized cakes for parties. I even did one wedding cake. One. Never again. But it was fun, and I did it because Amy wanted to do it and I wanted to spend time with her. We did many things like that. Gabriel watched and learned.

His second creative outlet…scrapbooking. How could I have been so dense? I was focused on my grief, not his as a father should. It took me a few months to drum up the courage to pull out Amy's supplies and begin scrapbooking again…without her. Tears. Many tears. But wait, this was fun. *Thank you, Gabriel, for reminding me how to connect with you.* Now we scrapbook together. I'm working on patience and it's getting to be a lot more fun again. By scrapbooking, Gabriel's been able to keep his memories.

❧

"If you got to talk with Mom one more time, what would you ask her?"

"If I could ask Mom one more thing, it would be, 'Why did you have to be on dialysis a lot more?' I also want to know, 'Why did you have to get sick at Superplay? Why didn't you have dinner with us once we got home?'"

I realize I had just asked a loaded question. The discussion was just as difficult. When we told the boys Amy was sick, Gabriel had the most difficult time understanding what was happening to Amy's kidneys. To some degree, if it is out of sight for Gabriel, it is out of mind. If he can't see it with his eyes, then it's abstract. Gabe, autism, and the abstract form a trio of confusion. Because Gabriel saw less and less of his mother toward the end, he didn't see the yellowing skin, the sunken eyes and cheeks, and the pain she lived with daily. By the time Gabriel saw Amy, she had make-up on and was focused on giving her best to her boys.

Sometimes I get frustrated by the chaos autism causes. There are times when the world can clearly see what needs to be done, or what a certain outcome of an issue should be. When Gabriel looks at the situation, he is clueless to the problem. When it came to Amy's sickness, he struggled. Of my three boys, Gabriel has the best immune system. He does not get sick very often. To him, it would seem appropriate to choose *when* to be ill. I'm still working with him to understand the Fall of Man.[88] In his mind, Amy *choosing* to be ill at Superplay just doesn't make any sense. It was a night of celebration. It was a night for his mother to champion him while he tried to knock ten pins dizzy. Then, for her to have not eaten dinner with us was the breaking point. When you celebrate, you eat food, right? Dinner that night became something the boys could make without me. We'd planned a nice dinner, but when we arrived home, Amy was in need of all my attention.

What he's really asking is, "Is it my fault?"

"Why did she leave me, Dad?"

For him, the stage is Betrayal. Amy was his world. He was struggling to understand why he feels betrayed. Why should he feel betrayed by his favorite person? She always took care of him. She always made his days special. She was always next to him when he needed her. But on the other hand, having feelings of anger at Amy causes Gabriel to feel like he's betraying her. That's a confusion he doesn't know how to resolve.

As we talked, I got the sense he had an underlying question. It was one I could not bring myself to ask if he was feeling: *Does she still love me, Dad?*

---

"If Mommy could have been here for one thing to do with you this past year and a half, what would you have wanted her to do?"

"This may come as a shocker. I would want her to have seen me in *Peter and the Starcatcher*. I would have wanted her to see me and meet the cast."

The answer to this question still cuts me to the core. I had done what angers me when other people do it—I expected *less than* of Gabriel. He is a genius in his own right. He is a people person, a servant, and a devoted young man. There are many things Gabriel can do because we let him try; we didn't tell him he couldn't do something. We encouraged him to try whatever he was interested in trying (except growing up to become a princess—he had a hard time understanding the difference between a princess and a prince—he gets it now.) In the middle of my grief, I looked at Gabriel and saw autism staring back at me. I didn't see a capable boy who has wowed the doctors since birth.

It was a Tuesday morning in March 2017. Things were hectic. I was about to leave the house for work, and I wanted to have left already. Needless to say, I was stressed.

"Dad," Gabriel said, stepping between me and the door, "I want to try out for the school musical."

It took me a moment to register what Gabriel had just said to me. I should have been supportive and happy. Both Amy and I had acted in high school. I had a small part in a professional production before Gabriel was born. Micah wants to write musicals. He's written some amazing short films and stage scripts. He even was given the privilege of writing and directing a one-act play in high school. Isaiah is interested in acting. We all love watching movies, and then talking about the acting and the characters. It should not have been a surprise to me when Gabriel said he wanted to pursue a role in the school musical. But I didn't support him. I had been getting frustrated that Gabriel was always trying to "one up" his brothers. I was frustrated that in whatever his brothers showed interest, Gabriel was "more interested" and "more full of knowledge" about the subject. Sometimes it's difficult to differentiate between a desire to be accepted and lying.

"When are the auditions?" I sighed.

"Today after school."

"Gabe, you're going to have to pass. Maybe you could be in the stage crew." I was relieved he'd waited until the last minute to tell me. I didn't want him to have his hopes shattered. I didn't know how to tell him that his autism would prevent him from acting. Now, before you get angry and put down the book, know this: God hit me with a two-by-four that night to get my attention.

"But, Dad! I want to be in the musical."

"Honey," my tone was condescending, I'm sure. I was now later than I was when I realized I was already late. "There is a lot that goes into an audition. You need to have a monologue memorized, ready to perform. You also need to have a song practiced and ready to perform. We don't have the time to do either. I'm really sorry." I actually wasn't, but I didn't want to hurt Gabriel's feelings.

"But, Dad!"

"No, Gabriel. The answer is 'No.'" Now I was past irritation. I left for work, frustrated that I was sending my son to school in the frame of mind that often turned aggressive toward male authority figures.

That night I took the boys to youth group and had about two hours to myself. Since Amy's death, it's been hard to have alone time…at least, without guilt. There's always something that should be done with one of the boys. Always. I don't remember what I was doing that night. But what I do remember is what happened when I arrived at the church to pick the boys up from junior high youth group.

My cell phone rang. I didn't recognize the number. Most times I don't answer my cell when I don't know the number. That night, I was on *autopilot*.

"Hello."

"Hi. Is this Thomas Johnson?"

"Yes, this is Thom."

"Hi, Thom. I'm Gabriel's drama teacher."

Oh...did I forget to mention? Gabriel was in drama class at school. He was doing well in it, too. God had set him up for success. All I saw was a boy with autism trying to do something the "normal" kids were doing.

"I was calling to ask if Gabriel could audition for the school musical tomorrow after school."

"He's at youth group right now and won't be home until after 9:00 p.m. There's no way he'll get a monologue memorized or practice a song and be ready by tomorrow."

"That's why I called. I've seen Gabriel in drama class. I think he would be great in the play. As for the music, I don't care if he sings the ABCs. I just need to hear whether or not he can sing."

"He can sing," I stammered.

*What's happening here?* I was overwhelmed. *God, how do I say, 'Yes,' let him get his hopes up only to be dashed by a 'No.'*

God was silent.

"Um...yeah...I guess that's fine. I can pick him up on my way home from work. He'll be very excited." I was speaking words of excitement as if they were mind-numbingly boring. My head was spinning. Anxiety was building. Against my better judgement, I agreed, nervously, hoping that Spring Break wouldn't be filled with the autism meltdown to end all meltdowns.

*He's yours, God,* I whispered Friday morning, knowing that the cast list would be posted sometime that day. I felt myself begin to prepare, almost as if I were standing in front of an overstuffed closet that would dump its contents on me when I opened the door. I was nervous through my lunch and prep period, knowing that Gabriel would be waiting with bated breath. I received an e-mail from his Special Education (SpEd) teacher during that time, which I hesitantly opened, extremely wary, but alas, there was no news about the play. It wasn't until I was in the middle of my fifth-period class when my phone buzzed. At the break, I checked...

Gabriel's wonderful drama teacher cast him in *Into the Woods* as the Steward. It was a small speaking part, but he also had a small solo to sing. (The next time I saw Mr. Hauser, he said, "He sang very well. I was very impressed.") We—Amy, the boys, and I—had watched *Into the Woods* a week before she passed away. Gabe knew the lyrics for all the songs!

Gabriel's SpEd teacher shot me another e-mail, "I've never had any drama teacher take a chance on one of my kids before!" (She's been teaching longer than I've been alive—literally. She started teaching one month before my birth.) Needless to say, I cried...a lot! Take that, autism stereotypes! And the doctors had said, "Your son will just be a vegetable, not able to hold up his head, roll over or even speak."

I sat at my desk, crying. My sixth-period students were returning and I was crying. In the span of a moment, I realized just how intricately God intervened in Gabriel's life in order to have a connection to his mama. She loved musicals. She loved *Into the Woods!* although she'd only seen it the one time. For Gabriel, it is one of his last memories with her. I also realized in that moment I had put God and Gabe in a box. I was afraid and asked God to be the bad guy. *You tell him!* had been my approach. I didn't think Gabriel could do it.

Preparation for the play was exhausting for both Gabriel and me. But it paid off. Gabriel was wonderful. The play was a hit and he'd caught the drama fever. Four months later, Gabriel was auditioning for *Peter and the Star Catcher!* during the first two weeks of his Freshman year.

This play was much more taxing on Gabriel, and likewise on Isaiah and me. Play practice was every night after school, not three nights a week. Practice didn't end until 5:30 p.m. I would pick Gabriel up from practice and he would be ready for bed. I had to pull out every trick in the book to keep him awake until we arrived home. Dinner was quick because Gabriel just wanted to sleep.

Something I didn't factor into the decision of allowing Gabriel to do this play was the loneliness that would descend on Isaiah. The school district installed a two hour early release every Wednesday. Isaiah arrived home at 1:00 p.m. every Wednesday and at 3:00 p.m. the other days of the week. Gabriel and I didn't make it home until 6:00 p.m. Sometimes I would make it home from school before I had to pick up Gabriel, but at least three days a week, the rush hour traffic prevented that from happening. Being in a new school, with new grade-level curriculum didn't help me either. I often lost track of time, adding to my late arrival. Isaiah told me he thrived on the alone time, but it soon became clear the nearly twenty hours a week alone had a much more negative effect on him than he let me realize.

"I don't want you to worry, Dad. Take the time you need at work. I understand." When it dawned on me that his "permission" was acceptable from a spouse and that my thirteen-year-old was trying to "take care of me," I course corrected and fought to get home between 4:30 and 5:00 p.m. The loneliness had already taken root at that time. It would take me and Isaiah's counselor months to help him pull out of his shell again.

Near the end of the practice schedule, Gabriel began having trouble with his cast mates, specifically with the girls. Everyone knew he had autism, but no one really knew Gabriel's brand. I have often said, "Once you've met someone with autism, you've met one person with autism." It sounds a bit odd, I know, but this is what I mean…most people I've met or worked with who have autism do not like to be touched, want to be left alone more often than not, and are pretty happy with a rather small friend base. Gabriel is the most "un-autistic" Autistic person I've ever worked with or met. He thrives on relationship. He enjoys music. He likes hugs. He readily says, "I love you," to his friends and family. The problem with that is two-fold. First, high school girls usually understand "I love you" to mean something more than what it means for Gabriel. Secondly, Gabriel thinks that anyone who is around him is a friend.

Needless to say, I had a few meetings with Gabriel's drama teacher. He is an incredible teacher who knew Gabriel was not trying to cause problems, and he could figure out that he was missing some information. Once I connected the dots, Gabriel's drama teacher helped the cast understand Gabriel on a better level. It was a big success.

On opening night of the play, Gabriel's godmother Chris and I sat side-by-side watching with awe. Gabriel was doing very well. Every once in a while I could tell he was having a hard time and needed a stimulus break, but Chris couldn't tell. Neither could the rest of the audience. Since Gabriel had been cast as part of the Chorus, his drama teacher and cast mates had devised a plan to help him out and give him the necessary stimulus breaks he needed when the need arose. They executed it perfectly and Gabriel was allowed to shine in a very unique way…in spite of autism.

*Peter and the Starcatcher* is Micah's favorite play. He wanted to fly up from college to see it, but it just wasn't feasible. The night before opening night, Micah told me that although the play was a comedy, the end would be hard for me. I didn't take him seriously, but I should have. I found myself fighting sobs and a runny nose through the last ten minutes. My grief surprised me by showing up when I least expected it.

> I realized today what instigated the spiral of darkness. At the end of Gabe's play (*Peter and the Starcatcher*), one of the main characters tells Peter Pan, "After a while, you will begin to not hurt anymore and

you will forget." To which that character's daughter sternly stated, "No! It has to hurt. That's how you know it meant something." I keep telling my boys that the pain will not go away, it will just get easier to bear, especially if you keep giving it to God.[89]

The comment was really hard to swallow. I was at the play to celebrate my Angel with Autism. I was not at the theatre to deal with grief. I left the theatre struggling with loneliness and the beginning of Depression. I hid it well from Gabriel. He was elated.

"I wish Mom could have seen me," he said when we were in the car on our way home.

"I'm sure she did, Gabe. I'm sure God let her look down from Heaven and watch."

The doctors told us he would be a vegetable. They were wrong. I've known they were wrong for a very long time. Sadly, however, each time Gabriel has come to me wanting to try something at which I'm not sure he'd be successful, I've tried to steer him away from that task or activity. That night proved to me Gabriel is more capable than I've previously thought. When I evaluated my actions, I was ashamed. When Micah or Isaiah want to try something new, I always stand behind them and encourage them to succeed beyond expectations. I had not done the same with Gabriel. I made a vow that night to give Gabriel the same treatment in the future. Doubt is no longer a common word in my vocabulary or a common emotion in my head. It just isn't any more.

"What do you do to remember Mom?"

"Watch her favorite movies. Sometimes I dream about her. She sees me and I see her again. I get a little sad. Her scrapbooking is also a part of the dream, too. She does it with me. Sometimes I draw a picture about her, or write in my journal about her, or write my own story about her. Sometimes I dream about what her memories were back in the past. Sometimes I dream about her Memorial Service, about when we talked about her when she died."

It was nearly all one breath. It's been a journey watching Gabriel process, grieve, and heal. Sometimes I think he's a lot further along the road of grief than I am. Sometimes he has a Chernobyl scale meltdown, and I realize he's just like the rest of us when it comes to grief. The steps are there. Denial.

Anger. Betrayal. Depression. Acceptance. It just takes a bit of listening and relationship to realize Gabriel is on the same path we all are on together.

"Daddy," he had one last comment to make before going to the community swimming pool, "I wish I could just stand in her shoes for a day. I just want to be her for a day. Because it would tell me a lot about her, what happened in her life."

The gravitas of that statement still has me mesmerized, weeks later. When I take the time, look carefully, and ask questions, I find I "speak autism" a lot better than I once thought. It's still a process. We're still in process. I love him dearly, and he loves me too. He really loves me. I keep reminding myself that he sees the world in "black and white." He struggles to understand the gradation of meaning in the English language. For him it is what it is and that's it.

As I've struggled to connect more with Gabriel and understand how his mind works, I sometimes end up worried about him. I know many people love him and know him and he is accepted for who he is, as he is. It is truly a tremendous group of people with whom God has surrounded our family. When my stress level gets high regarding Gabriel, God usually steps in to show me He's in charge. When that happens, my heart is full.

Gabe's first "play date" in more than five years came to the house to play games…whichever games Gabe wanted to play. Gabe texted him an invite. The reply was nearly instant. Schedules finally synced. They are in the same grade. Both love drama and musicals. And both have been in the same cabin at Summer Camp for many years. Patient, caring, understanding, laidback. I sat in the front room listening with tears streaming down my face. Gabriel's friend, who is "neuro-typical" (essentially, without special needs), came to be with Gabriel. Gabe doesn't have many friends, but the ones he has are incredible. Every time I turn around, God shows me someone else who speaks "Gabe" very well. I worry that people will be offended by him. I should probably stop worrying. He's wanted to be treated as "normal" for years. Every once in a while, he gets that wish. The play date was one of those days.

---

"What has God taught you about grief these past two years?"

I spent a long time defining grief to him, then he answered.

"God's in charge. God's got Mommy in Heaven, and I'll get to see her again someday. I miss her, but she's not gone, not really."

I couldn't have said it better myself.

After my interviewing of Gabriel was over and just before the book was finished, he gave me a piece of paper. He'd written something on it.

"It's for your book, Dad. I thought you could use it."

"Did you write this?" I asked, clearly knowing he did by the handwriting.

"Yes," he said, "I thought it was important." Then he walked away.

I looked at the page. I couldn't decipher it. I had to take a picture of it and email it to his older brother. Micah immediately called me and dictated the script:

"It's hard to be without Mom so much because our hearts are so sad. She has showed us how to be inspiring people. She loved us so much in our lives."

That she did, Gabriel. That she did. You are very inspiring. I couldn't have said it better myself.

Amy and Gabriel at her dad's wedding
Picture courtesy of Leah O'Connor, LC Photography LLC

## CHAPTER 26

# From Caretaker to Child

*Isaiah Johnson*

You know, being a child is a great thing. You get to run around, not care about certain things going on in the world, get infinite hugs from your parents, and generally just have a good time. Well, that's most people's experience, and it definitely was mine for awhile. In August 2013 my parents told me Mom's kidneys weren't working correctly. A year later, my mother had to start dialysis to help her kidneys. I remember those first few months when she didn't have a machine to do it for her and we had to sit there and wait for an hour while gravity did the work. I remember sitting next to her, talking about different things, and laughing at people on TV. Mom never wanted me to worry about her, so she tried to distract me by making it fun.

When she did get a machine, I adopted the role of her "caretaker." Every night, I would go upstairs and set up her machine. Every morning, I would go in after breakfast and clean up the supplies from the previous night. It worked for me, and, looking back on it, that was my way of coping with the fact that she had an illness that I was powerless to stop at the moment.

September 6, 2016, was a nightmare for me. The first thing I remember was feeling embarrassed when my dad woke me up that morning. He had come into my room, the train wreck that it was, at 8:00 in the morning. I wake like a zombie, but when I heard my very boisterous dad gently rock me awake and whisper, "Isaiah? I need you to wake up," I knew something had gone terribly wrong. I pulled back the covers. There was a sick feeling in my stomach as I quickly dressed and followed my dad and my half-asleep brother Gabriel downstairs.

There was a collection of people in our living room. My aunt, uncle, grandmother, and grandfather were all sitting or standing in the living room. Two of the pastors from our church were there as well. I knew something was terribly wrong. I took a seat on the couch next to Dad and prepared for the worst. Honestly, I remember the first thought going through my head was: *This outfit really clashes with this couch.* Seriously, a death in the family, and here I was being a fashion critic.

"Boys," my dad said, his voice cracking. "Last night, Mommy went to be with Jesus." This statement caught me off guard, but my oldest brother Micah didn't seem to be as fazed. My other brother, however, was a different story. His eyes held a look that seemed to say, "What do you mean?" I, in my grief, decided to answer Gabriel's question.

"She's dead?" I cried, the anguish in my voice and fear in my eyes seemed to hit my dad as much as if I had punched him. I broke down in tears, unable to speak after that, becoming a blubbering, sobbing mess in my dad's loving arms. He held me so gently that for a moment I thought he had died too. I heard Gabriel start talking, expecting him to break down as I had. But, out of everyone in the room, he seemed the calmest. I can't remember exactly what he said, but I remember he said something so out of the blue we all couldn't help but laugh. I turned to Micah, wrapped my arms around him in a death grip, begging him not to leave.

"Daddy, can we go see Mommy?" I remember asking. His reply was simple, sweet, filled with the loving touch of a father, but I felt like he had just smacked me across the face.

"No." That response drove me over the edge. I ripped away from my brother's arms and ran to the other room, collapsing on the other couch, sobbing into the pillows, punching them. Everything in this house was the last vestiges I had of my mother, apart from my own memories. I screamed into them, my anguish pouring out through my voice box. Dad followed me into the room. He sat down next to me and let me cry, then he apologized, his face streaming with tears.

"They are going to bring her down so we can all say goodbye," he said.

Eventually, the people from the morgue came and went up to my parents' room, where I could only guess was my mother's final resting place. They set her on a gurney, like you see in those TV shows about doctors. They covered her with a quilt so only her face was visible and then brought her down the stairs so we could say our last goodbyes.

It was difficult to stand in that room with my mother's cold, lifeless body, even though her face held only an expression of peace, bliss, and even joy. I was in so much pain that I couldn't bear to look at her for more than a few seconds at a time. I remember Gabriel throwing himself over her body, planting a kiss on her forehead, then turning to my father, telling him, "True love's kiss has to bring her back, right?" I remember, in that moment, feeling helpless, broken, and responsible. Responsible, because I knew she wasn't feeling great the night before, and I did nothing. I did nothing to prevent her death. Sometimes I still feel that some small part of this was my fault.

Mom died before I woke up that morning, and I was starting a new school the very next day. I remember being so afraid of all the uncertainties, and scared that something would happen to my father, too. That night, the habit of preparing her machine was so ingrained in my brain that I remember walking upstairs to go and set up her machine. I had been Mom's caretaker for just over two years. I had everything ready when I remembered. I was in shock, and had just gone back to what felt natural. I sat there and just started crying. My mother, my anchor, the one person who I truly felt understood me, was gone. I had been thrown from caretaker back to child. It felt like someone had thrown a car into reverse at 60 miles an hour.

This was just step one in my process of denial. In the coming months after she died, I went to go see my therapist to try and get help dealing with the pain that came into my home that fateful morning. I remember my therapist would try and get me to talk about my feelings, and I would just sit there, motionless, speechless, and when I did finally talk, I was quiet, meek, afraid that I would say something to disappoint her. She would give me "homework" to try and get me to talk about my thoughts, make friends at school, or journal about my feelings. I remember my dad had to force me to do these assignments because I was so far in denial and shock that I would go out of my way to avoid doing them. My therapist would assign me things like, "write in your journal about that time you two made cookies for your class on your birthday," or "talk to a friend at school about your feelings." I was so scared to do these because it meant admitting that Mom was gone. It also meant admitting what I felt. Looking back, I wish that I had done these assignments, especially the journaling because I think it would have helped me understand a lot more what I was feeling.

In those first few days, and even the following weeks, I developed a sort of protective instinct for each of my family members. I "shielded Gabriel" as much as I could from pain, which meant trying to shove him into an isolation much like my own. I was "trying to protect him," I told myself. Micah, I left alone. We had never had the best of relationships, and I didn't want to make things with him even worse. I begged my father every day to get better, to breathe, to think of something else, to do anything but dwell on what had befallen our family. I questioned his every move, telling him what to do, to "just calm down," and "stop crying." Honestly, I just wanted him to calm down, to come back to being my father. I wished he would just take a moment to stop being a "zombie."

With my new-found "calling to protect" my family, I completely disregarded myself. In my madness, I didn't think about what I needed, and I suffered for it. At one point, I got fed up with everything. I constantly felt like my brothers hated me, and that my father didn't even remember that I existed. Like I said earlier, Micah and I had never had the best of relationships. We were always fighting, "locking horns," as my dad would put it. Gabriel would always side with Micah, which tended to happen even before Mom died. Typically, I would have one or both of my parents on my side, but with Mom gone and Dad spaced out, I was alone. It was two-on-one, and fight-or-flight kicked in. I chose flight. I grabbed my shoes, my coat, and my phone and I ran from home. I didn't know where I was going, just that I needed to get away from everything. Luckily, my brother thought quickly, got in his car, and drove after me before I could get very far, but it was still terrifying for the both of us.

I was attending a new school that year, where I didn't know anyone. It was an option school, built specifically for the "gifted academically." I felt a need, a pull to go there on the first day of school, despite our recent death in the family. I think that I was just trying to fit in at the school. Everyone notices the kid who comes in on the third day of school. They don't notice the hundreds that come in on the first day. That night, I was sleeping, not dreaming, just an endless void of black. I woke up suddenly and walked down the stairs to the room where my father was sitting. I just sat in his lap and told him, "I can't do this. I can't go to school!" It felt like my heart was tearing out of my chest to say that, even though I knew I should've felt no guilt at all.

Before Mom died, I was that really weird kid who loved school. I had a lot of friends, despite the fact that I had a tendency to remind the teacher to collect our homework. Most people that I know would disagree with me, saying that school is a "nightmare." The classes, homework, projects, and the fact that you get no sleep generally makes it seem like it drags on and on, never stopping until those joyous weeks that you are on break. When my mom died, I lost my love for school. I felt like a walking zombie, just going through the motions until I could get home and hide from the world and cry myself to sleep.

When I did finally go to school, I adopted the role of the stereotypical new kid. I sat alone at lunch intentionally. I avoided all contact with people. Generally, I kept to myself. Those first few weeks, I was in shambles. Every day, an internal battle raged within me. Do I go to school or not? Do I tell Dad that I need to come home or not? Do I try to talk to people today or not? The answer to most of those questions was always "No!" I hid not only from the world, but from myself. I didn't want people to judge me for grieving. I wanted to have a normal life, one that wasn't filled with grief. I denied my emotions, and I was a mess. Let me give you a piece of advice. Don't put up the walls that I did. If society frowns on you for crying and expressing yourself, tell society to shove off. Feel free to sob and wail. Feel free to laugh and dance. Feel free to spend the night curled up, listening to heartbreaking music and crying until you can't cry anymore. Just don't hide.

Eventually, I left my shell. I decided I would finally try and make some semblance of friends, even if it was only to not be seen as the awkward, new, loner kid. Most of the kids at my school were welcoming, but I didn't feel that I could trust them to know I was suffering. I didn't want them to think I was weird because I would spend my nights crying and my days fighting with myself. I thought all the kids at my school were going to be shallow and that they wouldn't understand where I was coming from. I was so focused on me that I didn't realize that someone else, walking the very same halls, could have been going through or had gone through the same thing.

My dad tells me I am an "extroverted introvert." What he means is, when I am surrounded by people I know and cherish, I am bubbly, fun, and talkative. But I have an energy bar, like in a video game. Eventually, I need my alone time, to "recharge." When Mom died, that extroverted part disappeared. I was hiding most of the time, trying to never talk to anyone. I spent most of my time just reading or crying in my room. However, when surrounded by people I knew and loved, I became animated, albeit only a facade.

In those first few months, I forgot how to be a kid. I know that sounds silly, but it's true. Whenever anyone tried to talk to me, I would push them away. I never wanted to do anything fun with my family. I only came out of my room for bathroom breaks and some meals. One day, while I was at school, I couldn't handle dealing with my emotions, facing the world, maintaining this mask that I had worked so hard to build. I asked my dad if he could send my aunt to pick me up from school. I was having a terrible day, and I felt like I had to go back to something that felt normal, my life before Mom died. I decided to visit my friends from my previous school. That was a nightmare. Sure, they made me genuinely laugh, but, even being around people I had known for years, I still felt like I had to put on a mask, to hide what I was truly feeling. I didn't want people to judge me or think I was a wimp. I wanted to make a good impression, but that didn't work. I was always hiding from everyone.

You know, there are those things that you see pop up in your social media feed like "How to deal with Grief," and things like that. They outline the "Five Stages of Grief." While those are true, and they do have some merit, not everyone goes through all those stages linearly, or in that order. Most people hop around the stages, or are in many at once, or feel like they aren't in one at all; they are just in this proverbial limbo. That's kind of how I felt. I wouldn't let myself grieve. I just sat there, trying to stop the constant onslaught of "Honey, you need to grieve" from literally everyone around me.

I know that this chapter has been one story after another about how I had a terrible experience and you are probably thinking I have a really dark chapter right now. But I'm going to let you in on a little secret. It gets better. Let me repeat that. It. Gets. Better. Maybe a song you hear on the radio reminds you of someone you lost. You just start singing along and you just feel like they are with you in that moment. Maybe you are making something and it feels like they are watching you and congratulating you from Heaven. For me, it meant my Mom was just there at school, proud of me, encouraging me, loving me. It never felt like she was truly, completely gone...until I got home and remembered, she was gone.

Just because you spend your first few nights unreachable doesn't mean you are trapped in grief for the rest of your life. It also doesn't mean that when you feel fine, grief won't come back at some point. Take my experience for example. Sure, I've given you my "woe is me" speech, but it wasn't like that forever. Eventually, things got better. I started to do the things I would have done before my mother died. I began baking again, singing Broadway tunes with my family every once in a while, dancing a little with my brother or alone in the kitchen or even while Dad drove the car. It felt like I was loving again…with all my heart. At one point, everything seemed fine. I was on the bus ride home and I saw a specific shade of red. I don't even remember what shade of red it was. But I do remember thinking, "She looked beautiful in that color." Instantly, I was sobbing. My friend put her arm around me to comfort me. I wish I hadn't taken so long to start feeling emotions in front of people. I wish I had just said, "Hey, this is who I am. If you don't like it, I don't care." I wish I could have trusted people more to tell them how I was truly feeling.

Life is all about change. At the end of everything, there will be death. Until the Second Coming of Christ, that's how it is going to be. There's no avoiding it. And as long as there is death, there will be people grieving. They don't deserve to go through the pain alone. Let them know they are loved. Send them a care package or take them out to dinner. If someone is hurting, comfort them. If they just need a shoulder to cry on, give them one. If they seem fine and just want to spend all day watching Netflix and baking cookies, be there. Watch Netflix and bake cookies with them, or at least be there for "quality control." If someone is trying to hide their pain, be there. Notice they are hurting and help them through it. They could be contemplating things that no one ever should. Be there. Don't be afraid of things they might say to you. If you feel they need it, get them more help. Be there for the people who need you, and the ones who "don't." Just be there. The pain does get better. The waves of grief do lessen in intensity, and while there may be a freak tidal wave every once in a while, you will be fine. Just because someone you love died does not mean that you have to stop living. Keep feeling. Keep living. Don't hide. It's what your loved one would have wanted.

GOOD GRIEF

Amy teaching Isaiah how to make applesauce

# CHAPTER 27

# The Story Continues

I love stories. God wired us for story. Somewhere in our being, whether it be in our DNA or simply in His image, we were created to connect to stories. Everywhere I look, I see stories. In the grocery store, at the gas station, or in a pew at church, there are stories to be seen. Some of them are fiction, some of them are true life, but all of them are stories. Growing up, my grandfather told me, "Find out what you love to do, and then figure out how to get paid for it." What do I love to do? Write stories and teach. It was a no-brainer to become a Language Arts and Social Studies teacher. Still wondering about God wiring us for story? Just parse out the word "history"...*His-story*. Look at the Bible. It's full of God's story. The last place I thought I would learn about God's story, however, was in my classroom. I teach in a public school. I know what I can say and cannot say when it comes to "Religion" —as the rule states. I was in for a big lesson.

At the beginning of May 2017, the school year was quickly coming to a close. I started teaching my final unit for Language Arts: *The Outsiders*. I had never before read the novel, but the entire seventh grade was set to read it. It's a story about three orphan brothers in 1965. One is an adult, one a high schooler who dropped out to help pay bills, and the youngest a middle schooler. It's an American classic. I was up for the challenge of teaching a new novel. I was not expecting the lessons in grief I would learn and share in my classroom.

The month of May was also very crowded outside of my classroom. During the first weekend, Micah was performing a play at his school he had written, cast, and directed himself. It was a huge honor. His school does a "One Act" weekend. Usually it is filled with student-written work. However, that year, his was the only student written work chosen. I had been telling him that his writing was special, that he had a future in writing, but what did I know? I'm just Dad. When Micah's theatre teacher read the script, which he'd written for a class assignment, Micah found out Dad was right. He worked many hours and weeks preparing for that weekend, sometimes forgoing enough sleep, sometimes skipping meals to get there, but his sacrifice was rewarded. The play was a hit; he received high praise from the school and was invited to star in the summer musical *Smile!* Coming off that emotional high, Micah powered on, working to finish school.

Unfortunately, his schedule did not get any easier. The following weekend held Micah's Capstone project, Prom, his birthday, and Mother's Day all in three days' time. I was gearing up for a breakdown, hoping, praying it would be after the weekend finished.

I had taken that Friday off of work so I could see Micah's Capstone project. He hadn't wanted me to read the script, but he had given me an idea of its contents. Sitting in the audience, with my other two boys and Micah's godmother, Jenny, I was beaming. I'd had the opportunity to see Micah perform in church and summer camp dramas, but I'd never seen him do any other type of acting. When the audience is third through fifth graders, the acting bar isn't very high. The previous weekend I'd watched his genius come out in the One Act Festival; he could clearly write and direct, there was no question in my mind. Watching Micah perform his Capstone to a large audience, many of whom did not know him personally, proved to me he was gifted at arresting the attention of an audience. The four of us family members in the audience were swiping tears through the entire event. I dared not look directly into Micah's eyes not wanting him to see my emotions of pride mixed with grief, pain, and awe. I didn't want to throw him off balance.

Dinner that evening with Micah's godparents was incredible. Travis and I go all the way back to high school. He's my best friend. His wife and Amy have so many similarities in practicality, design taste, and other things that they became good friends too. Sitting there, watching the interaction between them and Micah, recalling December and their willingness and openness to help Micah on his college visits, my heart was full. Amy and I had chosen well. They had both been so purposeful and available to Micah throughout his childhood, but especially since Amy passed away.

The next afternoon, Micah said, "Dad, um…I have a problem." What he had thought to wear to Prom was not going to work. We raced to the men's store, and luckily found the perfect suit coat and pants for him, with an hour to spare. He took one of his friends to the Prom. They had a blast. When he arrived at home, I knew he was empty; his emotional tank had no reserve to deal with the next twenty-four hours. I didn't, however, know any way around the next twenty-four hours for him. We all had to just go through them. I could not, in good conscience, plan a birthday party for Micah on Mother's Day. I didn't want Micah's friends to try to pick between their mothers and their friend whose mother had died. I felt it was a no-win situation. I also knew that although he never told us, Micah loved having birthday parties. He loved being surrounded by his friends and playing, or singing, or watching a musical. He was the life of the party. Whether it made me a bad dad or not, I rigged a surprise party for him, full of all his heroes, his friends, and his mentors, but he'd have to survive the week first.

On Mother's Day, after church, the boys and I came home, ate lunch, and made a game plan. We had eleven different Mother's Day gifts to deliver. I tried to make the drive fun. I played music. I tried trivia. I asked the boys to reminisce about things each of the Mom Mafia had done with them over the past few months. Talk about a balloon popping conversation. Tears and aggravation blossomed. It was a very rough day…that got better, or at least I thought it was getting better as the day continued into night.

The responses the boys and I received from delivering those Mother's Day gifts were overwhelming. There were hugs all around. At least an entire box of tissues was used by each of us. That evening and the next few days, the responses poured through my Facebook page. What follows are three of the many.

1. I read my mom the sweet cards I received from your kind, handsome, brave, strong sons on Mother's Day, and we sat amazed thinking about their mature thoughtful words…You're raising good men, Thom. Keep up the good work and we'll be supporting you and praying along the way.[90]

2. Words cannot express the depth of love and beauty that I was shown this afternoon. Amy Johnson you cannot be replaced, but your boys did you proud! I think I will forever cherish the love notes…thank you Micah, Isaiah, and Gabe!![91]

3. CONFESSION: My most cherished gift yesterday was not from my family. They were wonderful to me yes, because God made them wonderful (and he lets me help too sometimes) = My Mom Kathy and I gardened away the afternoon. The kids made me creative, messy, stupendous gifts and completed unselfish acts of service for me. My Prince made me feel like a Princess (although quite honestly he manages to do that most every day). But still…

   My best Mother's Day moment came when Thom and his terrific tribe of tall, kind and handsome, witty, thoughtful boys showed up at my door with flowers and hugs to tell me I mattered to them. This would matter anyway on any given day but yesterday was Mother's Day. Their own Mom watched it all unfold from her cozy Mickey Mouse kitchen in heaven. Her first time hugging them on Mother's Day with her memories and wisdom and legacy instead of her batter splattered hands. Yesterday was also her first born Micah's 18th Birthday. A double dose of tough stuff to man up to without your Mom to straighten your tie for church or make your favorite breakfast like only she can.

   And yet, there they were surprising me at MY door. Turning their sorrow to sweetness. Leaning on faith and Jesus and each other to make a hard day feel like a candy cabin at summer camp.

   Amy—Let's have a moment Mom to Mom. There is nothing I pray more for my children than to learn to take the lies and temptations of the enemy in their lives, knock it on its backside and drown it in a bucket of Gods truth, silver lining and timing. Selfishly, my second prayer is that I have all of my own lifetime to do this, teach this, watch this and love them through this. It's such a hard job. The world is so mean to them sometimes. The fact that you and Thom managed to make this their character and mission in such a short period of time?! Well sweet no bake peanut butter cookies on an Isaiah frosted red velvet cupcake! You are the Mother of my dreams.

> Truly as I know these words fall from my lips to Gods ears, what a Mom you were, are and will be for generations to come.
> Life is not about the years you get, it's about the love you give. Johnson boys, my family is gigantically inspired and impressed by you and your Mama's heart. I promise…she is so so so proud of your courage to do hard things. Keep it up![92]

As one might guess, the delivery and hugs surrounding the vases of Mother's Day flowers, and a few more personalized gifts, brought our emotional tanks to a dangerous low. I had thought going into the weekend that the boys and I would be pumped up by the love. It felt more like we were wrung out and left in the wind to dry. Aimless and full of pain.

From Mother's Day/Micah's birthday through the rest of the week, I watched Micah's emotional limp increase. He wasn't sleeping well. He was really irritable. His brothers were on his nerves. He was trying to finish large projects for school. When Friday came, the meltdown happened. I was relieved. I knew his birthday party would be a hit since his pain, grief, and anger had found a voice. It was a long, hard night, and I got to hold my "little boy" again while he wrestled with all of the stress related to the end of high school, his mom's death, his own guilt for not having wanted to celebrate Mother's Day at all, and (in his mind) the "anti-climactic birthday party" set for the next day. I'd told him I'd arranged for a few of his friends to have a road rally (which he'd requested), with cake after the teams finished. Micah was overwhelmed when the car he was riding in from the road rally pulled up in the church parking lot and he was directed to walk the red carpet leading into the chapel of the third through fifth grade building. A significantly large array of Micah's close friends, mentors, and pastors were there to wish him well. Without the help of the Mom Mafia—many of whom were all in attendance—I would not have been able to pull off such a party. It was an enormous success, ending with an "impromptu lip sync battle" (totally planned by myself and one of the Mafia moms) which Micah actually won!

When his birthday celebration was over, Micah's emotional tank was running over the brim of his soul.

"Thanks, Dad. Now I understand why last weekend had to be about celebrating the Mom Mafia and not me. I'm sorry."

I hugged him.

"There's no need to be sorry. I just didn't know any other way of celebrating you with everything that was happening last weekend."

"Thanks. It was perfect." And it had been. I was afraid many people wouldn't be able to come. I was wrong, and Micah finally got the giant birthday party Amy and I had always wanted to throw for him.

In between Micah's big weekends, on May 8, 2017, my maternal grandmother, with whom I shared a birthday, passed away. Although I hadn't seen her in nine years, she and I had a special connection. We had kept in touch through Facebook and the occasional phone call. Growing up, she would often come into town to celebrate a special birthday treat—just her and I—near or on our birthday. I felt close to her. I spent many weekends with her at her lake house away from the city. She introduced me to comedy music, musicals, and root beer. I had even inherited my red hair from her. When I had talked with her on our birthday, she had just been diagnosed with stage four cancer.

"I'm not going to take the radiation," she said in a calm voice. "I want to enjoy the time I have left. And I don't want anyone to be sorry for me. I've made peace with God. I'm old. I've lived a good life." She was so matter-of-fact.

"You're a good dad, Thom. I'm sorry I couldn't come up for Amy's service." I understood. She was in her late eighties and she'd lost a lot of her strength and energy. "I don't want a service myself. I told Colleen I didn't want people making a fuss." She had wanted us to all commemorate her on our own time and in our own way. We did. My Aunt Colleen still collected as many of the family as possible to celebrate Grandma's life. I was sad I could not attend, but I knew I could mourn without being in attendance.

Getting the call seven months after our birthday, even though I knew it was coming, was still difficult. I felt like another piece of me was gone.

> A little over 43 years ago, at 5:30ish in the morning on October 1, 1973, Laureen Edison found out her first grandson was born. It was her birthday. I've felt close to Grandma since we shared this unique bond. I have some amazing memories of birthday skirmishes and outings throughout the years. When each of my boys were born, we made sure to get a four generation picture taken while sitting on a couch together at different family gatherings. Sadly, I haven't seen her since July 2008 (when we shared a 2-hour lunch at the Phoenix airport), but we've talked on the phone many times.
> 
> Last night, around 10:00 p.m., I got the news that Jesus stopped by her bed and took her home. She'd fallen Thursday night, and

the doctors gave us grim news: she wasn't expected to survive the night...but she did. Three of her five children and her husband were able to be near in her final hours. I'm so glad she returned to her faith in the last few years. She and Amy should be having a great time right about now.

I'll miss you, Grandma.[93]

In the third week of May, standing in front of my class as I led a discussion on the book, *The Outsiders*, one of my students raised his hand and said, "Mr. Johnson, shouldn't Ponyboy be past his grief? It's been eight months since his parents died."

I simply began speaking from experience, talking about the experiences of my boys. Wow! Emotion can surprise you! I didn't really think about the consequences of what I was about to say, I just opened my mouth and let it pour forth. Often, I take a moment before answering a student's question, especially if it's with a personal experience. Not that day. I think it was a God moment.

"Grief is not an easy or short emotion. You can't simply turn it on or off. And there is no set amount of time it takes for a person to grieve, especially a young boy grieving over the death of his parents. My boys are still struggling with different things related to my wife's passing. My oldest is graduating in a couple weeks, and his mama won't..." I was suddenly unable to speak. I knew if another word departed from my lips, it would be amidst sobs. Panic began creeping up my throat. I was with my most difficult class. Seconds seemed like an eternity. You could have heard a pin drop on carpet. After a long *awkward* silence, I was finally able to recover.

"As kids grow up, they look forward to their parents being a part of the big events and even the everyday. Ponyboy is still in grief after eight months, yes, and he will probably revisit that grief when he's an adult, when he gets married, and even when he has children." I think I made my point, even though I was trying to do so in a much different way.

The bell rang shortly after my comments. I was thrilled my lunch break and prep period were next so I could reset. When I posted about the experience that night, I was pretty frustrated with myself. Almost every year I've taught, I've broken down crying in front of a class...at least once. When I taught Holocaust literature, it was expected. But teaching *The Outsiders*? I thought I had been very unprofessional. I felt that I had manipulated my classroom with my own emotional baggage. But my post was met differently.

A dear friend said, "Thanks for being real with your students and allowing the Lord to minister to them through your journey of healing." I chuckled at the epiphany. Maybe God wanted to help my students and their journey through grief (or some other difficult issue) by allowing them to see my brokenness. My principal even chimed in on this Facebook post.

> And in the moment, as tough as I can only imagine it was, you gave to your students a deeply personal moment that taught them something about what this thing we call 'being human' is. Those are the moments that make for exceptional teaching. Thank you Thom for being a teacher and for being human![94]

I no longer felt unprofessional. At the end of the school year, it was clear that my students needed to know how to be human and feel.

When June arrived, I was overwhelmed and getting very numb to emotion. On the first of June, the realization I would have a high school graduate living in the house for a final summer before "entering adulthood" and going off to college left me plummeting to the depths with a millstone tied around my feet. It felt like time was accelerating to breakneck speed. I didn't feel like I had time to ponder or to even be sentimental...much.

Gabriel's school musical was performing the weekend before and the weekend of Micah's graduation. I was running from one event to the next. On opening night of Gabriel's play, his godparents came to watch. Both brothers and I were also in the audience. After the performance, his face beamed. I remember thinking, *Amy would have loved this!*

On Friday, June 9, 2017, I took the whole day off work. Micah's senior awards ceremony happened that morning. Seeing him in his graduation tassels brought me a mixture of happiness and sadness. It was really happening. That night, the family piled into the audience, as did Pastor Todd and his wife Julie. Todd's connection with Gabriel has always been strong since Gabe was in the fourth grade and Todd began working at the church. Gabriel's performance was faultless; he even pulled off the prescribed emotional facial cues! That evening, when I tucked him into bed, he was exhausted. I lay in bed awake, also exhausted. I couldn't process it all.

The next day was Micah's graduation. Since his school was an option school, he was only issued a small number of tickets. They held graduation in the school's state of the art theatre instead of another school's football stadium. When we got to the school, I pinned a white rose to Micah's shirt to signify his mama. I snapped a picture of him in his cap and gown and tassels, hugged my gentle giant, and then made my way into the theatre seats. I sat in the audience grinning from ear to ear. I was so proud of him. At one point, I turned to my left to tell Amy something, and then realized she wasn't there. I had a pang of guilt. Amy was always by my side, for nearly twenty years. Now, almost a year after her death, I was still looking for her. I didn't tell anyone what had just happened. I didn't want to bring anyone else down with me.

After graduation, we celebrated with the family at Olive Garden, Micah's favorite restaurant. It was a great day…I just kept wishing my bride was with me. By the end of the night, I was so exhausted from the emotional yo-yo. I lay in bed that night wishing I could rewind the day so that I could feel differently, so that I could just be filled with joy for my son.

The following Tuesday—the day before Amy's birthday—was a particularly difficult day at school. Micah and I weren't getting along, and I didn't know why. He'd been upset with me since Monday after work. Gabriel had two emotional meltdowns of epic proportions on Sunday and Monday. Both centered on Micah graduating and going to college. Isaiah had been sticking to the shadows again, pulling away from everyone like he had when Amy died. All I wanted to do was go to sleep. Each time I was in a quiet room alone, I'd begin thinking of the many things I had to get done before Amy's family came to the house on Wednesday evening to commemorate her birthday. Even in thinking about the party, I was focused on cleaning the house and getting the food done on time. I put my feelings in a box and threatened them to stay put.

> I've been numb since Saturday morning. I hugged my graduate, took a picture of him, teared up, then sent him on to his graduation ceremony. Amy's birthday is tomorrow. I've tried to feel, but I just fall asleep. I don't know if this feeling has to do with one or both of the issues. I'm just numb.[95]

My aunt's wisdom came a day later. As I read it, I began to let go of the guilt.

I think numbness ~ at least temporary numbness ~ has its place in the coping scheme of things. Don't fight it. You know the tears will fall, the feelings will feel, unbidden. Emotions cannot be corralled and harnessed and given orders on when or how to appear or disappear. They have a spirit of their own and will express themselves in ways and at times that may surprise us. God gave us emotions, feelings, and the wisdom to let them do their work. Love you![96]

I found out after the party that Micah was wrestling with his mom's death, having wished she was at his graduation.

"I didn't want to go to a stupid birthday party for Mom!" he loudly informed me.

"Why?"

"She's dead, Dad. I didn't want to celebrate a birthday she wouldn't be able to celebrate with us. It didn't seem right."

"Why didn't you tell me?"

"Because I didn't want to hurt your feelings." I felt guilty. I had organized the birthday party because I didn't know what else to do. Rather than know everyone would be at their own homes missing Amy on her birthday, I figured it would be better if we had cake and ice cream and reminisced about the things we missed—the happy memories. That did happen, but at the expense of Micah. I felt guilty for having not picked up on his pain.

School the next day was the final day of *The Outsiders* unit. I was enjoying the unit. My students were really getting into it. They loved the novel and everything I threw at them, including both of the interpretive art projects. The end of the unit called for a "Narrative Conflict Speech." We'd looked at conflict in the novel, in politics, and in the world around us. For the speech, students were required to reflect on a personal conflict. The speech had to explain "how the conflict was created" and "how the conflict was perpetuated." The speeches took three days. There were many funny and witty speeches. The last day, however, held a few astounding speeches. I broke. The shell holding back my emotions began to crack.

Because of confidentiality, I can't share specifics, but know this: there were stories of abuse (physical and emotional), abandonment, neglect, anxiety, death, and a few "un-imaginables." I never dreamed students would share what they did. When I was growing up, I didn't want anyone in my middle school knowing what was happening at home. My students were different. They had watched me deal with pain throughout the year. They'd seen me cry. They'd seen me laugh. It was the perfect end to a very emotional year.

There's no human way to stay numb through the stories my students told on those final days. There were a few humorous speeches, but I'm still haunted by the pain of the kids I taught that year. I made a mental note to not wait until the end of the year to do *The Outsiders* in the future. I'd plan it right after Christmas. The joy of the holidays should help balance the conflict.

I had only one more day with my wonderful students. That night I prayed I could look at the faces of my students on the last day and smile and joke and sign yearbooks without crying—not because it was the end of the year, but because of the pain these "too young kids" were enduring daily. I got through the school day compartmentalizing my personal conflict of late—I even dressed up in the outfit Amy loved seeing me wear, but, I wasn't really ready for the gut punch that punted me out of Numb. Suffice it to say, the students whose speeches were slated for the last day of school held even more gut-wrenching conflict only God could heal.

## CHAPTER 28

# Lessons from Camp

As I sat down to write this chapter, I was sitting in the manor at summer camp, the first camp after Amy's passing. For five years, she had been the head of Hospitality, taking care of the nutrition needs for campers and staff. She had been in charge of the mess hall, the candy cabin, and the staff lounge.

Three months before camp began, I was preparing myself, steeling my heart to go back and face camp without my better half. I was ready, very ready, to go and not feel. Then came the first camp staff meeting. I walked into the room, and on stage was the Christmas gift I'd given Todd, one of our Children's Pastors, who is also the fourth and fifth grade camp director.

I had taken Amy's lanyards and camp t-shirts from the past five camps to my very crafty friend, Miss Chris. I had this idea of framing the shirts in a way that the logos would show. I found a black shadow box that could stand alone, or hang on the wall, and my friend and I began to think, move, cut, and create. What came of the endeavor was beautiful; it was the perfect gift to a great friend who walked through the darkest days, weeks, and months with us. It was to stand in his office or at his house as a memorial of my wonderful wife and the five years she'd worked with/for him.

Todd's Thank You Gift

There, in the front of the room on the stage, the memorial frame stood atop a small table. The room, which could seat 90 staff around round tables, suddenly became the size of a phone booth. I couldn't breathe. My vision blurred. The silence began to scream. In a panic, I began to search for an exit. A rolling cart with empty pitchers waiting to be filled with ice water stood next to the exit. I took my leave, fleeing with the pitchers and something to do. When I returned, fifteen minutes later, with pitchers full of ice and water, my heart was still racing, but I was able to breathe again, and I could see things as they were. I hid in the back, taking up my usual assignment at camp meetings: manning the computer, lights, and soundboard.

As camp grew closer, I was sure I was ready to go. I'd reminisced—purposely. I'd looked through pictures and videos from previous years. I'd intentionally talked about the memories to get the tears out—in order to dry out the ducts. However, the day to go to camp and set up arrived with a terrifying urge to quit. *'Todd, I just can't. I'm sorry.'* No. *'Todd, I'm sorry, but this is too hard.'* No. *'Todd...'* The varied versions kept fighting in my head, but alas, out of a sense of responsibility and knowing what Amy would say, I bit down, pulled on every ounce of strength I could muster, and determined my way to camp, begging Jesus—as each mile passed—to give me strength.

Camp set-up was thrown off as one of the hospitality team members was pulled away for a family emergency, one and a half hours before all staff were expected to show up at camp. I found myself stepping into her role to help as I'd helped Amy in the past. Later, beginning to settle in, I kept "seeing" Amy around the camp. The first night was rough.

> Camp started today. During staff worship we sang No Longer Slaves (which we sang at Amy's memorial)…It was Amy's hospitality that made her famous at camp. Watching the kids de-bus, I flashed to my first year at camp (Amy's second). She was standing at the end of the line cheering the kids on. Then I flashed to last year; she was standing near the front of the line cheering kids on. I thought I had come through all the emotional flashes yesterday during set-up, but alas, I was wrong. I miss you, Honey. You are not forgotten.[97]

Being at camp made the grief all the more tangible. Her loss all the more real. The pain leveled out and I noticed it dissipating slightly after a day of surprise emotions.

That year's hospitality team had ordered signs long before camp began, re-naming the staff lounge and candy cabin after Amy. I knew about the signs before I arrived at camp. I'd even seen both signs. But seeing them actually at camp, in place, was very different. I smiled, warmed that Amy was being honored and remembered by more than just me and the boys, but I worried that the new team wasn't getting the credit they deserved.

On the third night of camp as I was standing in the staff lounge talking with a few of my oldest son's friends, a new—and very young—camp counselor motioned to the sign and sneered, "Who is *this Amy* and why does she think so much of herself to name the staff lounge after herself?" I was standing less than an arm's reach from this young girl and I had a decision to make. Pulling everything together, fighting to stay calm, I turned to the young woman and quietly said, "Amy was my wife. She was in charge of hospitality here at camp for the last five years. She passed away shortly after camp last year, so Todd and the new hospitality team named this room after her to honor her leadership and memory at camp." Then I turned to leave, trying to keep it together when my son's college age friends tackled me with multiple hugs, sweeping me into the next room.

I've thought about that incident a few times, praying and forcing myself to remember that not everyone knows…that not everyone realizes the damage their uninformed words can wreak.

I've been trying to recall when I've possibly made the same error—hurting people with my words, words of judgement, words of justification, words of uneducated idiocy.

> "Seventeen and pregnant? Well, she should have waited like the Bible and common sense tells her."
>
> "Did you know she was raped and doesn't believe abortion to be an option…ever?"

Excuse me while I get surgery to extract my rather large foot from my mouth.

> "I wish Sheila would discipline that child instead of just letting him run all over the church causing such a ruckus! Doesn't she know this is a house of worship we are supposed to respect? Even our children?"
>
> "Did you know he has autism and she's been working with a counselor and behavioral psychologist for over two years? He's much better than he used to be."

This one happened before my son with autism was born. Having to deal with similar issues over my son's life, this memory was a rather painful sin to acknowledge, especially since I don't know whatever became of "Sheila" (not her real name).

As Christians, we often think we can be judgmental and condescending because *we're* living correctly—why isn't everyone else? I've learned this lesson from the receiving end in a powerfully painful way.

After Amy had given birth to our second son, twelve and a half weeks early, and she'd returned to church, a lady she had known since childhood stopped her after service one Sunday.

"This trial in your life must be due to sin, and your son will have to pay the price for your sin. I've given birth to six children and *never* had any problems. I guess I'm just a baby making machine. God might heal your son or prevent something from happening to your next child if you confess your sin and stop throwing your life away."

To this day I still have to remind myself that I chose to forgive this woman, and whenever I think of this incident, I pray for her. I don't know what became of the woman. My hope and prayer is that she's learned to focus on her issues with God and sin and has stopped digging for potential issues in others around her.

Another time I learned this lesson came while Amy was hospitalized, before Gabriel was born. She was on three times daily monitoring, while nurses made sure that the little life growing in her had the best possible chance to survive birth. One day, while lying in the hospital bed, hooked up to the baby monitoring machine, the phone rang. Amy answered and was met by an unfamiliar voice. The woman introduced herself and told her she had been praying for her.

"I completely understand where you're at, Amy," the unfamiliar voice said, "I lost a set of twins at your current gestation. You can do this."

"But I haven't lost this pregnancy," Amy replied.

"But you probably will. Most pregnancies in your situation end without a live birth."

Amy hung up the phone. She didn't say another word. A few hours later, a twenty-something, unmarried, young lady showed up to visit Amy. This young woman was expecting to stay, talk, and pray with Amy for at least an hour. Her expectations were severely cut short after her opening bid.

"Amy, you don't know me," she began as she shouldered through the closed hospital room door without knocking. A nurse was inspecting Amy's baby bump monitor, sheets askew. "I'm from the church and just joined the Hospital Visitation team." She didn't even acknowledge that Amy was not modestly covered, nor did she recoil from entering the room interrupting such a private moment. "I completely understand the pain you're in and I wanted to pray with you and give you scriptures I found to help you keep a hold of your faith."

After a pregnant pause, in which the nurse quickly covered Amy and then exited the room post haste, Amy said, "Really? You understand what it's like to possibly be losing a child?"

The young woman stammered, "Well, no, I've never been in your situation exactly, but I still understand the feelings you're having and the pain you're in."

"Have you ever been married?"

A simple head shake side to side was the only response.

"Have you ever been pregnant?" The tenor of Amy's voice was growing quickly and there was no ceiling to it.

Flustered, the young woman replied, "No...I...I've never...I've never even been with a man in my life." Her tone was indignant and pained. It's ironic to me to know this woman was feeling emotional pain from Amy's words (which she took for accusations) rather than understanding her own words were causing unnecessary pain in this hospital room.

"Then how can you stand there and tell me you understand my pain? That you understand my feelings? Sure, you expect that I'm in pain and probably have mixed emotions, but you've never felt the wonder and joy from a baby growing inside of you. You don't know the bliss that comes from telling your husband that he's going to be a father again. You don't know the feeling of brokenness when you have to look at your husband and tell him that the pregnancy, which is nearly twenty weeks along might not make it to a live birth!" Amy's voice was elevated and growly. "And you can't begin to imagine the terror of knowing that one wrong movement could turn that joy into sorrow that may NEVER go away!" By this point in Amy's tirade, the young woman had backed up nearly to the door. "And there is NO WAY you could understand the guilt I'm wrestling with because it's *my body* that's failing my unborn child. It's *my body* that's failing my husband. *My body*! Not yours!"

"Um...I think...I should just go," the young woman whispered.

"Your intention is appreciated," Amy was able to say evenly, "but your words are empty and hurtful. Yes, I agree, you *should* leave."

Now, you may think Amy was unkind in this situation. Yes, the young woman may have been well intentioned. My point, however, is that Christians, even well-intentioned Christians, can say some of the must hurtful things to people who are suffering. It's so easy to say, "I understand," or "You'll get through this with God's help," or "Don't lose faith." Many Christians simply do not evaluate their words *before* they speak.

James, the brother of Jesus, penned tremendous insight in his letter to the churches:

> ...the tongue is a small part of the body, but it makes great boasts. Consider what a great forest is set on fire by a small spark. The tongue is also a fire, a world of evil among the parts of the body. It corrupts the whole body, sets the whole course of one's life on fire, and is itself set on fire by hell.
>
> All kinds of animals, birds, reptiles and sea creatures are being tamed and have been tamed by mankind, but no human being can

tame the tongue. It is a restless evil, full of deadly poison. (James 3:5-8, NIV)

With the words of James in mind, we as Christians must weigh everything we are going to say *before* the words spill out or are spat out of our mouths, only to cause irreparable damage and strife within the Church, or even with unchurched children of God who will never darken the door of a sanctuary again if their life depended on it. Grace and forgiveness play a large part in our lives as believers. I'm not implying that they cannot be applied in these painful situations. What I am saying, however, is words hurt more than broken bones, skinned knees, or sticks and stones.

I've witnessed many Christians—myself often the leader of the pack—stumble upon a person in pain. The initial reaction is to "help" because that is what a good Christian should do: help. But many do not know *what* will help, let alone *how* to help. What I've learned from my experience on both sides of the tongue wars boils down to something extremely simple, yet profound, that might be a bit *awkward*, at least at first. What most hurting people are feeling in the midst of their significant pain is an acute loneliness. *No one understands this kind of pain. I'm sure I'm the only one who's ever gone through this situation, or at least it doesn't happen very often to other people.* Sometimes the one in pain may even think, *Where is God in all of this?* What many hurting people desperately want, need, even crave, is someone to sit quietly with them, to listen to them, and to silently share their pain...and maybe hand out tissues.

Yes, I realize some may gasp with frustration at my direction in painful circumstances. *Share their pain? How?* Sit next to them. Offer your shoulder. Lend your ears and lock your lips. "Set a guard over my mouth, Lord; keep watch over the door of my lips" (Psalm 141:3, NIV). Cry *with* them. Silent tears, shed while listening to someone else's pain, or even shed while those in pain silently cry too, are tears that bring healing faster than crying done in solitude. God made Adam and Eve not just as sexual partners who could procreate; He made Adam and Eve because man was not created to be alone.[98] God created Adam and Eve as partners, to live life together, and to help carry each other's burden.

Many wounded people go off by themselves to hide. They hide from people around them who *couldn't possibly understand me* or who *would never find themselves in a situation like this*. They try to hide from the pain altogether.

Some even find themselves hiding from the shame of their pain. My question is this: Why should pain always come with shame? It shouldn't!

I met one of my favorite writers during Christmas Break of 1992 as a freshman in college. I was in a lot of pain, pain stemming from my childhood sexual abuse trauma, pain stemming from the sexual confusion caused by that abuse, and pain stemming from the lack of love and parental involvement in my life. It was very late one night and I was staying with a friend off campus for a couple of days before heading to my hometown for Christmas festivities. I was deep into *No Wonder They Call Him the Savior: Chronicles of the Cross*, when Max Lucado blew a hole in my theology...big enough for God to fit through. The book speaks of the Cross and is divided into three sections: "Its Words," "Its Witnesses," and "Its Wisdom." The chapter responsible for blasting the aforementioned hole gives the account of the final witnesses of the cross. It has haunted me, helped me, and healed me many times.

> Before we bid goodbye to those present at the cross, I have one more introduction to make. This introduction is special.
>
> There was one group in attendance that day whose role was critical. They didn't speak much, but they were there. Few noticed them, but that's not surprising. Their very nature is so silent they are often overlooked. In fact, the gospel writers scarcely gave them a reference. But we know they were there. They had to be. They had a job to do...
>
> Their prime role...was with that of the Messiah. With utter delicacy and tenderness, they offered relief to his pain and expression to his yearning.
>
> Who am I describing? You may be surprised.
>
> Tears.
>
> Those tiny drops of humanity. Those round, wet balls of fluid that tumble from our eyes, creep down our cheeks, and splash on the floor of our hearts. They were there that day. They are always present at such times. They should be, that's their job. They are miniature messengers; on call twenty-four hours a day to substitute for crippled words. They drip, drop, and pour from the corner of our souls, carrying with them the deepest emotions we possess. They tumble down our faces with announcements that range from the most blissful joy to darkest despair.

> The principle is simple; when words are most empty, tears are most apt.[99]

How do I know Lucado is on the right track? After hearing of one of his closest friend's death, Jesus went to the town to minister to Mary and Martha, Lazarus's sisters. How did He minister to them? In front of many who had come to pay their respects, "Jesus wept" (John 11:35, NIV). He wasn't afraid to show emotion. He wasn't raised that "men don't cry." He knew the power of healing in those "tiny drops of humanity." He was setting an example. He wept for his friend, with his friends.

About a year or so after Gabriel's birth, very close friends of ours who had walked through the scariest days of our pregnancy with us found themselves in a wholly unexpected, and altogether excruciatingly painful situation. At twenty weeks pregnant, the check-up was normal. The pregnancy was doing well—except however, for the mother's extreme nausea. At twenty-one weeks, something was not right. Our friends went to the doctor's office only to find that their son, their third child yet to be born, had died in-utero. The mother had to endure induced labor and the pain of birth only to be met with unknowable and unbearable agony. After naming their son, holding his lifeless body in their arms, and weeping together, our friends buried their son in a private service, in a special "babies only" cemetery behind the hospital. We reached out to them often. We saw them weekly. One night, when they needed to talk, we sat with them and listened…and cried. We didn't tell them, "We understand." We were blessed to bring our boy home. We didn't tell them, "God's going to take care of this." Although it's true, in the heat of the moment, at the pinnacle of the pain, that is a hurtful utterance, not a helpful salve. We simply listened, held hands, and cried. We've been through other painful situations that these friends have simply sat with us, listened, held our hands, and cried with us. Afterward, the weight of the pain seemed bearable. And it was because God was giving us/them someone to help carry the backpack.

In early 2014, while driving home after work almost a year after Amy's diagnosis, an incredible interview on the radio arrested my attention. Jason Gray was being interviewed about his "controversial" new song, "Not Right Now." I was driving down a fairly busy thoroughfare while listening. I quickly needed to find a place to park, cry, and heal.

*Don't tell me when I'm grieving
That this happened for a reason...*

*...You don't even have to speak
Just sit with me in the ashes here
And together we can pray for peace...*

*I know someday, I know somehow
I'll be okay, but not right now*[100]

    This song spoke words I had felt when I myself had a scary diagnosis in college, when Amy's pregnancy with Gabriel went awry, and when she was diagnosed with kidney failure. There is wisdom here. Want to be the "for a lifetime" friend? Sit, hold hands, hug or just put an arm around your friend. Silently weep…with them. Pray *for* and *with* them—possibly silently too (it's not easy to know before hand; when in doubt, silence is golden). Wipe away tears or offer tissues. Rinse and repeat as needed. When you find yourself in a dark situation, where *Not Right Now* rings in your heart and ears, you will have friends to sit with you. *The principle is simple; when words are most empty, tears are most apt.*[101]

## CHAPTER 29

# From 5 to 3 in 12

We left Portland in a rental car on a Tuesday bound for Southern California and college. The week prior had been stuffed with planned and un-planned events, starting with a mysterious "Date with Dad." I took Micah to a local Shari's Restaurant for pie. I knew if we went somewhere public, I would be less inclined to cry. Boy, was I wrong.

Micah and I were seated in the back of the restaurant, offered drinks and menus, and then left in silence. Micah looked worried. He knew something "was up." It wasn't often I invited him out for pie, especially when there was so much at home still to do.

"Dad, is everything okay?"

"Yes." I was being a little mean. I knew that inviting him out to a restaurant without telling him why would drive him nuts. I also needed Micah to understand he was special, important, and that this *moment* was special, important. I still waited though, trying to find the words. It's ironic that the writer in the family was short on words. I got the giggles sitting at the table pondering that irony.

Without the *right* words, I dove into a different conversation. We talked about the Graduation/Going Away party happening at the house the very next day. We talked about the trip to California. We ordered pie. I ordered the chocolate peanut butter pie, the kind Amy and I would always split when we were dating. It seemed appropriate since her memory was with us for that *moment*. One bite and my eyes were full. Micah noticed.

"Dad, why are we...here, really here?" he asked.

"Well," I began, holding a small, wrapped package beneath the table. I'd snuck it in without him seeing it. "Um...This moment is one of the last moments I get to have with you, just you, before you head out on your own. Years ago, I had planned this to be a celebration of three, not two." Tears began to roll. I paused. "But, because Mom's not able to be here..." I trailed off, setting the package on the table in front of him.

"What's this?" I'm not sure why people ask that question when a gift is set in front of them. It's something I've always pondered. It brought me out of the moment enough to not completely lose my dignity. I simply nodded at the package.

Micah opened it very slowly, as if he were trying to save the paper, then shredded the paper after taking it off the package. It's a family joke. I chuckled. He grinned. I can always count on Micah, with his Tigger-like personality, to bring a smile to my face. He opened the box then stared at the contents, unable to speak. He looked up at me, then back in the small box. I couldn't tell if he was confused or overwhelmed.

"Before your mom was cremated, the mortuary captured her fingerprints. Then they gave me a brochure that I've kept hidden for a long time, knowing this day was coming. I haven't done anything for your brothers because they get to have Mom's fingerprints all around them every day. But, since you were going so far away, I thought you'd like to take one of her fingerprints with you."

The box contained a single dog-tag on a chain with Amy's fingerprint on the front. The inscription was simply "Mom – 6/14/74-9/06/16."

"Turn it over."

The back of the dog-tag contained a quote from Micah's favorite musical, *Wicked*: "Because I knew you, I have been changed, For good."[102]

"Do you like it?" There were no words, just nods. My heart was full. Sending my boy over 600 miles away without a touchstone or Ebenezer[103] was something I could not do. The dog-tag would keep him grounded and connected to his family, to his mom. I wanted it to remind him that her fingerprints were all over his life, that he couldn't get too far away from her, that she was with him in his memories, his thoughts, and his foundation.

Micah's Memorial Dog Tag

    The following day over 100 people came to the open house bar-b-que, all to say goodbye to an inspirational young man. Family and friends from all aspects of life came to bless Micah and send him off with joy. I set up a gallon jar for people at the party to write encouragements to Micah so that when he was in college, missing home or discouraged, he could dip into the jar and read the words of those he loved challenging him to keep going. After all, it was only because of my faith and the encouragement of those around me that I was still standing, still moving forward.

    After a week of cleaning up from the party, watching the eclipse, and packing, we set off toward Southern California. It was a Tuesday. I had to be back in Portland by 8:30 a.m. Friday to begin the new school year. Micah and I would drive together to the university and then I would fly back alone. On the way down, we caught up with Bob and Susie and their kids. They were taking Nate, their son, to college in another part of California. We caravanned, ate dinner together at In-N-Out Burger in Medford, Oregon, and then stopped at the "Welcome to California" sign to document the boys' next stage in life. It was a lot of fun.

    About an hour after separating from our friends on the road, our conversation turned solemn.

    "Dad, you and Mom have referred to something God told you about me, about loneliness, when I was born. I'd like to know the whole story if you don't mind."

I told him.

When Amy was pregnant with Micah, God told us that our unborn child would have a special calling in the ministry. God also said, *He will battle with loneliness.* I can't count the many times I asked God to take this from Micah. I offered to go back into full-time ministry if Micah could have a "normal job." But I knew I was wasting my breath. As Micah grew up, we witnessed the loneliness at many different stages of his life. When he got to high school we agonized over his loneliness. He seemed to be the kid everyone wanted around, but no one remembered to invite. During his Freshman year, Micah caught mono and spent a little over three months at home without the strength to go to school. During that time, he bonded with his mother at a much deeper level. Amy had already been diagnosed with kidney failure. They spent time together talking about life, about sickness, about death, about C.S.I. and Matlock. They played Gin Rummy and Cribbage. Their bond became very strong and very precious. When we decided to move Micah out of the Christian high school he was attending during the middle of his junior year, the loneliness reared its head worse than we'd ever seen it. As we prayed, God reassured us that He was in control.

When I finished the story, I could hear Micah's sniffles. It was pitch dark outside. I could not see Micah's face. I could not look at him and see if he was alright. I had to use my dad intuition, something I had exercised more in the past twelve months than I had ever used in the past.

We arrived at Biola University on Thursday morning around 10:00 a.m. We moved Micah into the dorm, raced to the nearest office store to pick up cords that weren't included with the new printer we'd brought with us, and had a final meal together. It was a whirlwind of a trip. Standing in his room, just he and I, I gave Micah a bear hug and a final blessing. It was all I could do to walk out of that room, down the hall, and get in the rental car. Micah walked me to the rental car. It was much easier to walk that lonely road with him. He jumped into the passenger seat of the car.

"Drop me off at the gate, Dad," he said to my quizzical look.

I made the drive down the hill to the front gate as slowly as possible.

"You're going to have an incredible time," I said.

"Call me when you get home," he said as he climbed out of the car.

"It'll be almost 2:00 a.m. I'm not going to call you. You can call me tomorrow after I get off work. I love you. You're going to have a great time. You've got this." The door closed. The car lurched forward. Micah was in the rearview mirror...until he wasn't. That's when the tears really started. I felt like another death was happening in my family. Another piece of my heart was torn from me.

About fifteen minutes from LAX, I switched on the radio. One of my favorite Christian comedians was talking about saying goodbye. She had lost her husband to a stroke. Her mother died shortly before her husband. For the life of me, I can't remember what she said, but what I heard brought me to a place of peace, and then I was laughing.

*I've got him right where I want him.*

*I know, Abba. I know. It's just hard sometimes. I'm going to miss him.*

My conversation with God continued.

*When my plane touches down, my house will feel pretty empty and quiet.* It was a worried statement, not a complaint *Our slightly larger than average family will have gone from five to three living together in twelve months.* That had been a pretty profound realization. We had come a long way during Micah's last year in high school. We had all hit the wall—at one time or another. We had all stumbled through varying stages of grief: Denial, Anger, Betrayal (sometimes it was more Bargaining than Betrayal), Depression, and Acceptance. Some of us stayed in one or more of the stages for longer than others. Some of us had vacillated between steps going back and forth between anger and betrayal and back to anger. Others took a different path. We knew we were healing together. We had all been told that no one walks through the five stages of grief the same way as another person.

Nearly sixteen hours after waking up with Micah that Thursday morning, I was sitting aboard the plane heading home from Los Angeles International Airport very conflicted. We had raced through the day having had to be up since about 6:30 that morning. It was surreal. I had just dropped my oldest off at Biola University for the next stage of his life...without me. At least, without me being "right there" with him. I was immediately thankful for modern technology and video chat! Micah had never known life outside our home. Yes, he had stayed the night with friends and family, had been to summer camps, and had taken a family vacation or two with us, but he had never lived somewhere else consistently where he could make all his own choices, pay his own bills, and go where he wanted without having to ask, or check-in, or even bring a tag-a-long. I was very proud of him, but I was also very aware of the grief I was feeling for "losing" another family member.

In January before Micah turned eighteen, I told him that my job as his parent was helping him move to a new stage in life. I relinquished all decisions to him. He no longer had a curfew. He no longer needed to check with me before making plans. He no longer had to ask permission about how he spent his time. He did agree to continue doing his chores while at home to help the family continue to function smoothly. And he did agree to let me know where he was going to be, simply because if there had been an Olympic event in worrying, I would be the all-time gold medalist with many tokens to prove it.

It was hard for Micah to move into that role for himself, but he learned. He also learned how to take conflict by the horns and deal with it, instead of hiding. By the time August came around, I was not worried about him going off to college. So why was I sitting on that plane worried?

A year prior, our family had consisted of five members. Things looked rather promising. Amy was able to get the much needed dental work completed so she could be officially placed on the kidney donor list. It had been over a two-year process, fighting insurance all the way. Who would have thought that someone needing a kidney transplant would need to meet with specialists in gynecology, ophthalmology, cardiology, neurology, and dentistry? September 2, 2016, marked the last tooth extraction appointment. The dentist and oral surgeon both signed off on the last requirements. Amy called the list coordinator that afternoon. She would have her official intake interview at 10:00 a.m. on September 7, 2016. When we went bowling on Labor Day, we were celebrating not just my new job, we were celebrating the completion of the requirements.

Amy never lived to make that appointment. Her Freedom Day, as Kymra named it, was September 6, 2016, one day before the appointment, a few hours after our bowling celebration.

When I went off to college, I didn't return home to live. Ever. I visited, but I never wanted to live in my hometown ever again. My heart knew that Micah has been raised in a different home than I, but I guess that's why I was worried. Would he come home? Or would my house continue to be as quiet as it would inevitably be when I arrived home from that flight?

*I've got him right where I want him.*

*I know, Abba. I know. It's just hard sometimes. I'm going to miss him.* Sometimes my conversations with God are very short. Hardly are they ever full of *thee* or *thou* or much of the formal, flowery stuff I learned from listening to others pray when I was a kid.

*He's going to be fine. You're going to be fine. This is the plan I have for both of you.*

*I know, God. I trust you. Please help the boys and me learn a new new-normal.*

God has answered that prayer many times over in ways I never dreamed.

Just days after returning home, Micah used the video chat feature in Facebook to call me.

"Dad, you're not going to believe what happened!" He was excited and bouncy. Very Tigger-like. I could tell his news was something big.

"What?"

"I visited a college life group last night with one of the guys who helped us move me into the dorms. During prayer, the college pastor came over to talk with me. 'God told me you've been wrestling with loneliness.' I just looked at him stunned. Then he said, 'and He wants you to know that your loneliness is going to come to an end.'"

The silence helped me process what he'd said.

"Dad, I haven't said anything to anybody down here about that!"

It was an answer to prayer. Joy began to bubble in my heart. Micah was going to do well at school!

Gabriel, Isaiah, and I had some challenges learning how to live as just three, two of whom were young teenage boys in the middle of puberty's lovely grip. But God had been right beside each of us, sometimes carrying us, every step of the way. We still found ourselves surrounded by prayer warriors, trusted family and friends.

Days before we left for California, my grandmother called. "We're going to have a birthday party for Grandpa," she had said. "I know he's very sick, but he's still here, so we're going to celebrate." We made the trip. It was a very tight itinerary, especially for Micah. There had been still so much to do.

"I don't want you to look back and regret not going," I told him the night before we made the trip.

"I know, but there's so much still to do."

"It'll get done," I reassured him.

When we arrived at the farm, the mood was a little more somber than a birthday party should be. Grandpa—or Pa as I called him growing up—had been battling cancer for a few years. We all thought he would not live past Summer 2016. There it was August of 2017. Looking at him in his hospital bed, I could tell his days were numbered. It was really difficult for me to wrap my head around yet another imminent death. Pa and Grandma Nancy had pretty much stepped in and raised me, often times acting in place of one of my parents. Pa taught me much about being a man, an honest, hard-working, reliable man. So much of who I am today can be traced back to the many lessons he taught me throughout my childhood.

Each of my boys got to spend a minute wishing Pa a "Happy Birthday."

"I love you, Pa," Gabriel said, "and Jesus does too. I'm going to miss you." I cringed a bit, then I remembered Gabriel's purpose since birth—to be a bearer of Good News. I hugged him and he ran into the other room to talk with his cousins.

Micah and Isaiah each got a moment with Pa as well. Both were a little nervous. I think it is harder to "prepare" for death when one is staring it in the face. Talking without addressing it is a bit awkward as well. Both boys wished him a "Happy Birthday" and both said "I love you." Both boys also stood next to the bed trying to listen to what Pa was saying to them. Neither of them could understand him. I was happy they knew to stay and listen, but sad it was so difficult for Pa to communicate. After they left, I sat down next to my grandfather's bed.

"Do you need anything, Pa?" I started.

"Water," he whispered with a scratchy voice. I helped him get a drink. As I sat the cup down, he motioned me to come closer. He tried to say something, but I didn't hear him.

"Pa, I'm sorry. I couldn't hear you." I leaned in even closer.

"You have really good boys, Thom. You raised them well."

"I learned a lot from you," I answered.

"I didn't do much."

But he had. Pa was one of my heroes. For much of my childhood, I was on the farm. He clothed me when my mother could not. He came to my high school plays, to my graduation, and my wedding to celebrate life with me. When we told my grandparents we were pregnant with Micah, they were happy with us. Then, when I then told Pa my son would carry his name (Micah Gene), it was the first time I ever saw him tear up (not cry—he was a good ole cowboy). Sitting there next to Pa, I wanted him to be pleased at the life I had chosen to live. Pa was a man of few words, but he had always had time for me. I tried to be on the farm as much as I could, both growing up and as an adult.

It was clear that he was proud of me.

August 30, 2017, just 6 days after dropping Micah off at college, I received the phone call that my hero had died. Calling Micah was difficult. It was nearly the anniversary of his mother's death. Although he was not as close to Pa as I had been, I didn't know how the news would settle with him. I was surprised at how upset he was. He asked to fly home for the memorial service. As it turned out, Grandma Nancy had asked me to perform the memorial service at the farm like I had done six years prior when my Aunt Carrie had died. I needed Micah's help with his brothers once again.

On the one-year anniversary of Amy's death, I took the day off work. I did not think it wise to try and power through the day, not knowing what my boys might encounter, especially with Micah in southern California. Gabriel and Isaiah both went to school. I didn't make a big deal about reminding them of the day as it approached. After dropping Isaiah off at school, I stopped at Starbucks and ordered Amy's signature drink: a Grande, nonfat, two pump pumpkin, two pump white mocha, and two pump cinnamon dolce steamer.

When they asked for a name, I said, "Amy." I texted a picture of the cup to Kymra.

"Amen," she replied.

"Happy Freedom Day," was the message I attached. "Thanks for all your help, prayer, and support this past year."

"You are welcome. But it's not over, is it? This day is one day—365 days after, but does it mean more than that? The mending of your hearts goes on." Then she sent a prayer. I smiled. I had expected the day to be an extremely painful one, full of tears. It was painful, but it was also peaceful.

"Nope," I started typing, "I'm learning that God sends His people to be His hands and feet, but mostly His expression of love to His children who need their Daddy. I know the help, prayers, and support will continue; I just pray I'll be that expression of God's love to someone when He needs me to be." I hit *send* and then another thought came to me. "Thank you. His gift to me last July was to experience His true joy. He keeps filling me with it this year."[104]

From Starbucks I headed to a store, picked up a bottle of Diet Coke and a large bag of Peanut M&M's. I drove to the church knowing Todd would be in his office. As I walked into the conference room, Todd saw me and waved. As I entered his office, Todd saw the gift I'd brought. He stood, took the gift, and wrapped his arms around me. I needed that hug.

"Thank you," I managed. "I could not have done this last year without your help and support."

"I love you, Thom. You know that. She was an amazing lady," he said, motioning to the memorial gift I'd given him at Christmas. It was sitting on a shelf in his office.

Within a couple months of Amy's death, I stepped into her Sunday morning role in Children's Ministry, working under Todd. He was one of the few who saw up close how God had pieced me back together.

I spent most of that day at home outlining this book, at peace, knowing God was working on some incredible miracles of healing in my life, in the lives of my boys, and in the lives of the army of help surrounding us. When the boys arrived home from school, they were surprised to see me. That was when I reminded them what day it was. Both had tried to forget. We ate dinner out that night.

For days after I continued to ponder what God had been teaching me about trust, healing, and joy. One night I watched the recording of Amy's memorial service. I was struck by a few things and found myself writing another post. It happened to be the one-year anniversary of Amy's memorial service.

> It's almost unbelievable that one year ago today, my boys, our family, and our friends gathered to celebrate the life of a truly Amy-zing woman, whom a dear friend called "both Mary and Martha, taking care of people while sitting at the feet of Jesus."
>
> This year has held much grief, many firsts, and an astounding number of accomplishments in our home. We couldn't be where we are at without God's love, support, and direction, which often showed up in the hearts and hands of those He sent to minister to us, to help us, and to cry with us. From feeding us, to cleaning our house, to clothing us in attire that honored Amy at her service, God showed up in BIG and little ways. Our hearts are full of the love of God, our family, and friends.
>
> We lost a tremendously strong, fierce, godly warrior in our home. But God filled that void with the Mom Mafia—a group of fierce warrior women who have pulled together and picked up where Amy left off—giving wisdom, baking goodies, acting as taxi, celebrating achievements, teaching, encouraging, and praying with

the conviction and fervor only a mother could. I lived in fear of being a single father since Amy was hospitalized for a month with her second pregnancy. God delivered me from that fear the summer before she passed away. Although single parenting is hard (very hard), the Mom Mafia (and my close male friends whom I bounce ideas off) has made it so much easier. For each of you ladies—godmothers and a few godly ladies God specifically chose and placed in my boys' lives many years ago—I am so grateful, blessed, and honored for your help. Amy would be honored and proud of each set of capable hands into which she "handed off the baton of mothering."[105]

The realization did not end with that post. The very next day, while driving to work, I received a staggering "download from God" (as a very close friend of mine calls them).

Driving to work this morning, worship music playing, Pastor Randy's sermon came quickly to mind, crashing into truths that I knew separately, but had never realized were hand-in-hand concepts.

As many of you may know, I've struggled with fear (soul-crushing, growth-inhibiting fear). July 2016 marked the end of that battle when I was able to accept God's gift of Joy...not happiness... Joy, true, uninhibiting, soul-releasing, Peace-filled JOY!

Pondering this past year, especially the spiritual battle my household has been fighting these past [few] weeks, and the markedly different battle-plan I've learned from the Mom Mafia, all lights blinked on and I could see what God's been trying to teach me since college (maybe even before).

It's a simple message really, yet one that radically is changing my morning habits, my afternoon slump, and is permeating the late evening darkness: "Worship keeps our eyes on God...[giving us] a big God and a little devil." In other words, when we worship—and truly worship—there is no space for fear, because "to worship" means we are filling our vision with the face of God.

This will be the beginning to a whole new chapter in the book I'm writing![106]

As God always does, He showed up mightily and changed my plan. Within a few days I received an email from a friend.

Thom,

I've been having an on-going conversation with God about healing. Mostly it's me thanking Him for His specific healing or care- regularly. Within that conversation is a deepening realization of just HOW much and HOW often He intervenes with care- and health. And the result is me- just choosing to be acutely observant of this part of His nature....HE IS HEALER.

All this to say- there was something that you said on Facebook last week- that bowled me over.

I know God heals. He heals sometimes before we realize that we are sick. He heals sometimes through the many blessings of modern medicine. He heals sometimes very, very slowly (so that treasures that only [we] and our closest loved ones see, are developed and revealed). And sometimes He chooses to heal us in His presence in Eternity. And I'm very aware- and very grateful for all of His healing.

But Thom, you shared that from the first time that Amy had to be hospitalized (with Gabe) that you feared being a single parent. And that God healed you of that last summer.

THOM, I may not express my wondderment and amazement well in an email.......BUT GOD HEALED YOU BEFORE YOU WERE HURT.

I didn't know that this kind of healing existed!

Thank you! Thank you! For revealing a NEW and exciting TRUTH about our Heavenly Father. It means A LOT to me.

Love, Kymra[107]

I was blown away by the concept within Kymra's email, and, after pondering both my posts and her email, God made it very clear that this issue was to be "near the end" of the book. It was also at that time that I realized that the book I was writing—this book—was truly a piece of worship to God. I didn't want to write this book at first, but He coaxed me using the love, friendship, and encouragement of my family and friends.

Realizing this writing was to be an act of worship led me back to the throne room of Heaven. I was in awe as I pondered everything that had happened. God had seen to it to remove from me the specific fear I had wrestled with for thirteen years and the general fear of death I had wrestled with since I was twelve. He re-introduced me to His joy. And although the years that followed Amy's death were hard, full of pain and tears, they were not absent of joy. I was not afraid of being a single dad. Mind you, I never looked forward to it, but the thought no longer held me frozen in a screaming vacuum of silence. I had never thought of God healing *before* a person was injured, and I'm still running the concept through my Bible college theology class. At present, I don't think Kymra's wrong.

CHAPTER 30

# Returning to Spring

After autumn is finished, life turns to the coldness of winter and the strength of the soul is tested. In these pages, I have given an account of the hard work of autumn, sometimes painfully showing the work that needed to be accomplished all the while looking at the beauty and majesty of God's miracles and the memories surrounding my boys and me through the death of my wife. The work associated with autumn is hard work, and often seems unending. Some days, the yard is empty because the leaves were dealt with and the flower beds are put to rest for the winter. Some days, the winds of life have shaken the trees so much that the memories and pain are littered all around and the raking must begin once again. Some days are much worse than others, but the fact still remains, the season of autumn brings with it much hard and time consuming work.

About six months after I "finished" writing the book, I entered the darkest season I'd ever faced without Amy. It seemed as if things couldn't get any worse, but they did. My autumn had ended. The dark days and nights of cold, when the soul seems to be hibernating, was a test I was not anticipating. Amy and I had diligently tried to raise our boys the way we felt Abba God was calling us to lead them. The stark landscape of my winter of grief literally began in the winter, over two years after Amy had passed away. One of my boys was in severe trauma, having convinced himself that he *needed* to be *taking care* of the rest of us, not himself. He'd seen me at my worst and believed he needed to be the strength of the family since I had been falling apart. He went so far as to refuse to do any more work of grieving for himself. Another son was highly emotional and melting down any and everywhere—especially at school. He was pushing me away and anger began to creep back into his heart, anger at his mother and me for "allowing her to die." The third son was dealing with his own barren winter-scape of the soul and slowly, but surely, pulling away from the family. The entire time his mother was ill, this son was wrestling with stepping away completely from the family. He was hurting and didn't want to hurt anymore. To God's credit, He spared me from more grief and kept my son safe, intervening in ways only God could the time my son was more than considering making plans to take his life.

I was holding my own…very well, I might add…well, pretty well, depending on whom you asked. Actually, the truth was I was in a canoe without a paddle, traveling down the raging river of Denial, headed for the rockiest and roughest part of the journey.

I *thought* I was holding my own until it became very clear I was not. Just days after New Year's 2019, two of my boys had the biggest emotional blowout I had ever witnessed between them. One was ready to "go play in traffic." I stood up to fight the devil for the soul and the body of my broken boy. It was a long night, ending in the early morning of the next day at the hospital. Two days later, I went into my school to learn of a terrible threat of violence that was supposed to have taken place just a few days later at my place of work. The administrators of my school were investigating and the facts were dire and downright terrifying. That was when I hit the wall. That was when, while struggling with my own humanity, and the realization that my children could have become orphans, I reached out for help and companionship. But the help I sought was not from my friends and family, neither was the companionship. I had convinced myself that after three years of grief I had already asked *too much* of my circle of friends. The darkness and solitude I was feeling had been increasing exponentially.

I reached out to find someone to date, but it was not God's timing. I knew I was playing with fire, that I wasn't healthy enough for a relationship, but I reached out anyway. I wanted someone with whom I could share my life. I wanted to laugh again. I wanted to feel again. I struck up a friendship that I knew from the start would go nowhere...but I pursued it anyway because I was so very much alone.

When I realized how dark things had become, I finally reached out for pastoral care and counseling. I ended a brief online relationship. Then I began to actively and directly work on me. In the hands of God's anointed, I found myself slowly beginning to heal. Every other week I was meeting with a professional counselor who was delving to the root of the pain, unearthing stuff I had tried to ignore. The opposite weeks, I was regularly checking in with two close friends who also happened to be pastors at my church. The realization of God's biggest lesson to me, from the time I had been a little boy—through all the physical, emotional, and sexual abuse I'd endured—landed pretty heavily in my lap. The irony of the simplicity and profundity of it all was not lost on me. We were not made to do life alone! God made Adam AND Eve because we were not meant to *do life* alone! My friends, whom I had pushed away out of guilt, were still near me, battling in the spiritual realm for the safety of me and my boys. A few (who have later confessed) had also been petitioning God, praying for lightning to strike twice. They saw how alone I was and they knew I was not meant to live life for another forty years...alone. I, however, had resigned myself to just that.

When my dear friend and senior pastor looked me in the eye and told me, "God has someone for you, Thom. He's preparing her for you," I refused to believe him. I refused to even let my heart begin to hope. The pain of losing Amy nearly cost me my boys and everything else in my life.

As March turned into April, April turned into May, and the end of the school year turned into summer, I began to seek God about the vast loneliness with which I had been struggling. It was a prayer for the whole summer. The darkness my boys had been under had passed, and although life was not "easy," it was clear God was moving and they were securely in His hand.

In mid-July, I had a brief encounter with an intriguing acquaintance who puzzled me. I knew her parents very well. I had also known her brother and sister-in-law for over twenty-five years. She and I had never truly met outside of a random post on Facebook. The face-to-face encounter lasted for less than ten minutes and I was puzzled by her, but, at the time, I was also sure I was called to live a life of obedience...alone.

By late August, I was elbows deep preparing for a new school year. As the school year began, God reminded me of the path to finding *true joy* that

He'd had me on three years prior. I needed to return my focus to seeking Abba God's peace and joy.

Days before my birthday, God challenged me to focus on gratitude. Slightly offended, because I felt I was very grateful, I asked God, "What are You trying to tell me?" And for the next few days, I listened and tried to push my offense out of the way. On my birthday that year, October 1, 2019, I vowed to begin each day by telling Abba God *specifically* why I was grateful for at least two things in my life. The joy wasn't immediate, but my frozen heart from the winter of my soul began to thaw. The *Numb* I thought I'd grown past was finally leaving.

The hard strength that is proved through what can sometimes seem like the hibernation of the soul through the dead of winter, brings with it the promise of spring. New life. New beauty. New adventures.

Seven weeks—to the day—after my birthday, I was standing in a Starbucks, purchasing a painting from the same person I'd had the awkward encounter with in mid-July. As I stood talking with her, my heart knew immediately what God was doing. He had led me to the single woman He'd been preparing specifically for me and my boys. Spring in the Johnson home was finally beginning!

A few weeks later while standing in church, I was reminded of Moses's final words to the nation of Israel: "Only be careful, and watch yourselves closely so that you do not forget the things your eyes have seen or let them fade from your heart as long as you live. Teach them to your children and to their children after them" (Deuteronomy 4:9, NIV).

This book is in response to Moses's direction, to not forget the things God has shown me and taught me...with the intent to teach not only my children, but also the many people connected to the legacy Amy left behind when God called her Home.

As the years increase, I know there will still be more adjusting, grieving, and growing for each of us. The memories of our loved ones stay with us. March 20, 2020, was the day God set aside for a second strike of lightning; I married the incredible Carolyn Walker. It was a glorious day. The whirlwind that culminated on March 20, 2020, is the focus of another book God is already at work writing on my heart. Someday soon, there will be a move to a different house and another child heading off to college. A *New Normal* will have to be determined once again. There will be days when I miss Amy (and the others I've lost) a great deal. But through it all, I get to remember that the incredible, timely, omnipotent Father in Heaven—whom I sometimes call *Abba* or *Daddy*—is walking next to me and my new bride. God is good. Autumn will happen again in my life, but I will not forget that spring is on its way. I pray I never lose sight of His hand nor His joy. I also pray this book brings healing and hope to people wrestling with fear and overwhelmed with grief. May you find hoy at the side of our Savior too.

# ABOUT THE AUTHOR

**Thomas Michael Johnson** holds an M.Ed. in Educational Leadership and an MAT in Secondary Education. Known by most as Thom, he lives near Portland, Oregon, with his new bride, three sons, and the family dog. He spends his time adventuring with his wife, gaming with his boys, teaching language arts with middle schoolers, and saving the world with his superheroic imagination. Previously published in a national magazine, this is Johnson's first book.

# END NOTES

## Chapter 6

1. Thom Johnson, "Susan K. Standley" (eulogy, Beaverton Foursquare Church, Beaverton, OR, September 29, 2007).
2. Ibid

## Chapter 9

3. Carol McLeod, "A Jolt of Joy," Read the Bible. A free Bible on your phone, tablet, and computer, YouVersion, July 29, 2016, https://my.bible.com/users/TJthojo/reading-plans/228-a-jolt-of-joy/subscription/512934106/day/13/segment/0.
4. Point of Grace, "Jesus Is," written by Connie Harrington, produced by Brown Bannister, August 4, 1998, track 4 on *Steady On*, Word and Epic Records, compact disc.
5. Kari Jobe, "I Am Not Alone" written by Marty Sampson, Ben Davis, Kari Jobe, Austin Davis, Mia Fieldes, Grant Pittman, and Dustin Sauder, produced by Sparrow Records for Sony/ATV Music Publishing LLC, March 25, 2014, track 9 on *Majestic*, Essential Music Publishing, Capitol Christian Music Group, and Music Services, Inc., compact disc.
6. Bethel Music, "No Longer Slaves," written by Jonathan David Helser and Melissa Helser, produced by Bobby Strand, Chris Greely, and Matthew Wilcox, January 26, 2015, track 4 on *We Will Not Be Shaken (Live)*, Bethel Worship, compact disc.
7. Ibid
8. Matt Redman, "10,000 Reasons (Bless the Lord)," written and performed by Matt Redman, produced by Sparrow Records, July 12, 2011, track 4 on *10,000 Reasons*, Kingsway Music, compact disc.
9. Ibid.

10  Hillary Scott and the Scott Family, "Thy Will," written by Bernie Herms, Hillary Scott, and Emily Weisband, produced by Ricky Skaggs, July 29, 2016, track 4 on *Love Remains*, EMI Nashville, compact disc.

## Chapter 11

11  Andrea Low, September 7, 2016 (1:39 p.m.), comment on Facebook, "It is with mixed joy, sadness, and pain that I announce the passing of my Amy-zing wife," https://www.facebook.com/thom.johnson.9/posts/10209996700175296.

12  Marisa Merritt Coleman, September 7, 2016 (11:18 a.m.) comment on Facebook, "It is with mixed joy, sadness, and pain that I announce the passing of my Amy-zing wife," https://www.facebook.com/thom.johnson.9/posts/10209996700175296.

## Chapter 12

13  Thom Johnson, "30 hours as a single dad and widower," Facebook, September 7, 2016 (12:00 a.m.), https://www.facebook.com/thom.johnson.9/posts/10210005452154090.

14  Meal Train accounts can be set up at www.mealtrain.com.

## Chapter 13

15  Thom Johnson, "This morning I took Isaiah to school," Facebook, September 12, 2016 (1:34 p.m.), https://www.facebook.com/thom.johnson.9/posts/10210052401967806.

## Chapter 15

16  Michelle Watson, January 14, 2017 (5:51 p.m.), comment on Facebook, "Why did she have to leave ME, DAD?," https://www.facebook.com/thom.johnson.9/posts/10211277573076318.

17  Thom Johnson, January 14m 2017 (6:48 p.m.), comment to Michelle Watson's comment on Facebook, "Why did she have to leave ME, DAD?," https://www.facebook.com/thom.johnson.9/posts/10211277573076318.

## Chapter 16

18  Thom Johnson, "In about 12 hours, the service for my beautiful bride, my Amy-zing wife, my perfect counterpart, will be coming to a close." Facebook,

September 17, 2016 (12:49 a.m.), https://www.facebook.com/thom.johnson.9/posts/10210090613683075.

19  Vickey Thivierge, "Invocation" (Memorial Service for Amy Johnson, Beaverton Foursquare Church, Beaverton, OR, September 17, 2016).
20  Michelle Watson, "Worship" (Memorial Service for Amy Johnson, Beaverton Foursquare Church, Beaverton, OR, September 17, 2016).
21  Watermark, "My Heart, Your Home," written by Nathan and Christy Nockels. July 2, 2000, Rocketown Records, compact disc.
22  Natalene Aaberg, "What did I love about Amy?" (Memorial Service for Amy Johnson, Beaverton Foursquare Church, Beaverton, OR, September 17, 2016).
23  Eric Aaberg, "What did I love about Amy?" (Memorial Service for Amy Johnson, Beaverton Foursquare Church, Beaverton, OR, September 17, 2016).
24  Kim Tienken, "Every life tells a story" (Memorial Service for Amy Johnson, Beaverton Foursquare Church, Beaverton, OR, September 17, 2016).
25  Kymra Mercer, "Amy was both Mary AND Martha" (Memorial Service for Amy Johnson, Beaverton Foursquare Church, Beaverton, OR, September 17, 2016).
26  Ibid
27  Isaiah Johnson, "What my mom taught me" (Memorial Service for Amy Johnson, Beaverton Foursquare Church, Beaverton, OR, September 17, 2016).
    *Isaiah wrote his own speech, with only one grammar check from his English Teacher father.
28  "Let It Go" is from the soundtrack of the Disney movie *Frozen*, performed by Idina Menzel, July 21, 2014.
29  "Single Ladies (Put a Ring on It)" is from Beyoncé's *I Am...Sasha Fierce* album, October 13, 2008.
30  "Hit Me With Your Best Shot" is from Pat Benatar's *Crimes of Passion* album, September 15, 1980.
31  "Something To Believe In" is from the soundtrack of Disney's *Newsies*: The Musical (Original Broadway Cast Recording) album, performed by Jeremy Jordan and Kara Lindsay, April 10, 2012.
32  "Proud of Your Boy" is from the soundtrack of Disney's *Aladdin* (Original Broadway Cast Recording) album, performed by Adam Jacobs, May 27, 2014.
33  "I Want the Good Times Back" is from the soundtrack of Disney's *The Little Mermaid*: The Musical (Original Broadway Cast Recording) album, performed by Sherie Rene Scott, Tyler Maynard, & Derrick Baskin, February 26, 2008.
34  "That Would Be Enough" is from the soundtrack of the Broadway Musical *Hamilton*, performed by Phillipa Soo and Lin-Manuel Miranda, September 25, 2015.
35  "Blow Us All Away" is from the soundtrack of the Broadway Musical *Hamilton*, performed by Anthony Ramos, Ariana DeBose, Sasha Hutchings, Ephraim Sykes, and Lin-Manuel Miranda, September 25, 2015.

36 "For Good" is from the soundtrack of the Broadway Musical *Wicked*, performed by Kristin Chenoweth and Idina Menzel, September 4, 2006.
37 "Goodbye Until Tomorrow/I Could Never Rescue You" comes from the soundtrack of the original motion picture *The Last Five Years*, performed by Anna Kendrick and Jeremy Jordan, February 10, 2015.
38 Micah Johnson, "Goodbye until tomorrow" (Memorial Service for Amy Johnson, Beaverton Foursquare Church, Beaverton, OR, September 17, 2016).
    Micah wrote his own speech, without help. The quotations are the song titles he used when referencing his life with his mother.
39 Randy Remington, "Sermon" (Memorial Service for Amy Johnson, Beaverton Foursquare Church, Beaverton, OR, September 17, 2016).
40 Gabriel Johnson, "Amy was my mom" (Memorial Service for Amy Johnson, Beaverton Foursquare Church, Beaverton, OR, September 17, 2016).
41 Ibid
42 Michelle Watson, "Re: Michelle's Endorsement for *Good Grief*," email to Thom Johnson, February 25, 2020.
43 Isaiah Johnson, "What my mom taught me" (Memorial Service for Amy Johnson, Beaverton Foursquare Church, Beaverton, OR, September 17, 2016).
44 Micah Johnson, "Goodbye until tomorrow" (Memorial Service for Amy Johnson, Beaverton Foursquare Church, Beaverton, OR, September 17, 2016).
45 Gabriel Johnson, "Amy was my mom" (Memorial Service for Amy Johnson, Beaverton Foursquare Church, Beaverton, OR, September 17, 2016).
46 Todd Crist, "How amazing was Amy?: A benediction" (Memorial Service for Amy Johnson, Beaverton Foursquare Church, Beaverton, OR, September 17, 2016).

## Chapter 17

47 Thom Johnson, "Today was 2 weeks," Facebook, September 20, 2016, 10:08 p.m., https://www.facebook.com/thom.johnson.9/posts/10210126672024511.
48 Thom Johnson, "I've spent much of my free time since Wednesday evening in tears, for one reason or another," Facebook, October 15, 2016, 9:38 a.m., https://www.facebook.com/thom.johnson.9/posts/10210350003967670.

## Chapter 18

49 Casting Crowns, "Just Be Held," written by Mark Hall and Matthew West, produced by Mark A. Miller, January 28, 2014, track 3 on Thrive, Beach Street/Reunion Records.
50 Ibid

51  Ana Nunez, November 22, 2016 (9:53 p.m.), comment on Facebook, "Tomorrow will be the 19th Anniversary of the day I married Amy," https://www.facebook.com/thom.johnson.9/posts/10210722215432724.
52  Thom Johnson, November 22, 2016 (10:24 p.m.), reply on Facebook to Ana Nunez's comment "Tomorrow will be the 19th Anniversary of the day I married Amy," https://www.facebook.com/thom.johnson.9/posts/10210722215432724.
53  Twila Paris, "The Warrior is a Child," written and performed by Twila Paris, June 15, 1995, track 1 on *The Warrior is a Child*, Benson Records, compact disc.
54  A similar retelling of the same story can be found in Luke 18:16b-17.

## Chapter 19

55  Todd Agnew, "Did You Know?," written and performed by Todd Agnew, produced by Provident, October 3, 2006, track 5 on Do You See What I See, Ardent//INO Records, compact disc.

## Chapter 20

56  Thom Johnson, "2017 – Day 1 – I think I passed the dad test," Facebook, January 1, 2017, 9:10 p.m., https://www.facebook.com/thom.johnson.9/posts/10211147390821843.
57  Debbie Wood, January 2, 2017 (7:49 p.m.), comment on Facebook, "2017 – Day 1 – I think I passed the dad test," https://www.facebook.com/thom.johnson.9/posts/10211147390821843.

## Chapter 21

58  Thom Johnson, "Here was the plan," Facebook, February 14, 2017, 7:20 p.m., https://www.facebook.com/thom.johnson.9/posts/10211570949810553.
59  Kendra Magee, February 15, 2017 (4:04 p.m.), comment on Facebook, "Here was the plan," https://www.facebook.com/thom.johnson.9/posts/10211570949810553.
60  Dan Stevens, "Evermore," written by Tim Rice, March 10, 2017, track 14 on *Beauty and the Beast: Original Motion Picture Soundtrack*, Walt Disney Records, compact disc.
61  Kevin Kline, "How Does a Moment Last Forever (Music Box)," written by Tim Rice, March 10, 2017, track 6 on *Beauty and the Beast: Original Motion Picture Soundtrack*, Walt Disney Records, compact disc.
62  Michelle Watson, March 17, 2017 (10:48 p.m.), comment on Facebook, "My day began with an accidental find," https://www.facebook.com/thom.johnson.9/posts/10211570949810553.

63. Thom Johnson, "I have hated Valentine's Day since high school," Facebook, February 16, 2018, 8:20 a.m., https://www.facebook.com/thom.johnson.9/posts/10214910288731939.
64. Mindee Hardin, February 16, 2018 (10:55 a.m.), "I have hated Valentine's Day since high school," Facebook, https://www.facebook.com/thom.johnson.9/posts/10214910288731939.

## Chapter 22

65. Thom Johnson, "Why is it always in the shower lately that I completely lose my composure and break down sobbing?," Facebook, December 21, 2016, 9:35 a.m., https://www.facebook.com/thom.johnson.9/posts/10211041495974538.
66. Mandisa, "Prove Me Wrong," written by Mandisa Hundley and Cindy Morgan, May 19, 2017, track 3 on *Out of the Dark*, Sparrow Records, compact disc.
67. Ibid.
68. Ibid.
69. The Armor of God is found in Ephesians 6:10-18.
70. Thom Johnson, "Last night, in preparation for today, I started picking up my bedroom and looking through drawers that haven't been opened since September," Facebook, March 28, 2017, 12:50 p.m., https://www.facebook.com/thom.johnson.9/posts/10211969827582248.
71. Thom Johnson, "The mystery continues," Facebook, September 21, 2017, 11:31 p.m., https://www.facebook.com/thom.johnson.9/posts/10213689632096286.

## Chapter 23

72. "From a Distance" is from *Some People's Lives* album by Bette Midler, September 4, 1990.
73. "One of Us" was originally recorded by Joan Osborne in 1995 on her album *Relish*, produced by Relish Records. It was later covered by Prince—who changed the word "slob" into "slave"—a year later (1996) on his *Emancipation* album, on NPG Records.
74. The story of the Prodigal Son can be found in Luke 15:11-32.
75. The story of the Syrophoenician woman can be found in Mark 7:24-40.
76. Michelle Watson, September 23, 2016 (6:29 a.m.), comment on Facebook, "It's important that I share with you the newest member of my Superhero Club," https://www.facebook.com/thom.johnson.9/posts/10210144946921372.
77. C.S. Lewis, *The Complete Chronicles of Narnia* (New York: HarperCollins Publishers, 1998), 99.
78. The story of Mary Magdalene can be found in Luke 7:36-50.

79  The calling of the disciples who were fishermen can be found in Matthew 4:18-22.
80  Genesis 2:24; Matthew 19:5; Mark 10:8; and Ephesians 5:31
81  Micah tweaked the song "She Used to be Mine," from *What's Inside: Songs from Waitress* album written and recorded by Sara Bareilles, November 6, 2015, The lyrics printed were the ones Micah had written based on the original song.

## Chapter 24

82  Micah Johnson, "A really honest post about my 18th birthday," *In Constant Search: The Pursuit of Joy, Jesus and Attention* (blog), May 21, 2017, https://inconstantsearchblog.wordpress.com/2017/05/21/a-really-honest-post-about-my-18th-birthday/.

## Chapter 25

83  Thom Johnson, "Yesterday, in the middle of a storm I didn't think would end," Facebook, September 16, 2016, 7:52 a.m., https://www.facebook.com/thom.johnson.9/posts/10210084486729905.
84  "Exceptional" students are often referred to as TAG students. TAG stands for *Talented and Gifted Students*.
85  Talented and gifted students who also have another Special Education identification: i.e. Autism, Downs Syndrome, Attention Deficit Hyperactive Disorder, etc.
86  "The Abominable Snow Rabbit (1961) Quotes", IMDb.com, retrieved April 3, 2018, https://www.imdb.com/title/tt0054593/?ref_=ttqt_qt_tt.
87  Thom Johnson, "Dad, you don't look like an idiot to me," Facebook, February 28, 2017, 8:46 p.m., https://www.facebook.com/thom.johnson.9/posts/10211699855513115.
88  The story of the Fall of Man can be found in Genesis 3.
89  Thom Johnson, "It's Amy-zing what a week and 2 apply placed questions can do!," Facebook, November 19, 2017, 12:10 p.m., https://www.facebook.com/thom.johnson.9/posts/10214165088102389.

## Chapter 27

90  Rhonda Gill, "I read my mom the sweet cards I received from your kind, handsome, brave, strong sons on Mother's Day," Facebook, May 19, 2017, 7:37 a.m., https://www.facebook.com/thom.johnson.9/posts/10212469332549560.
91  Susie Sirovatka, "Words cannot express the depth of love and beauty that I was shown this afternoon," Facebook, May 14, 2017, 9:30 p.m., https://www.facebook.com/susie.sirovatka/posts/10155422758588534.

92  Mindee Hardin, "CONFESSION: My most cherished gift yesterday was not from my family," Facebook, May 15, 2017, 9:38 a.m., https://www.facebook.com/mindeehardin/posts/10211265891021816.
93  Thom Johnson, "A little over 43 years ago," Facebook, May 8, 2017, 9:01 p.m., https://www.facebook.com/thom.johnson.9/posts/10212373004701424.
94  Kevin Crotchett, May 18, 2017 (10:10 p.m.), comment on Facebook, "I'm currently teaching 'The Outsiders'," https://www.facebook.com/thom.johnson.9/posts/10212466859247729.
95  Thom Johnson, "I've been numb since Saturday morning," June 13, 2017, 8:21 a.m., https://www.facebook.com/thom.johnson.9/posts/10212705714218954.
96  Kathy Johnson, June 14, 2017 (4:15 p.m.), comment on Facebook, "I've been numb since Saturday morning," https://www.facebook.com/thom.johnson.9/posts/10212705714218954.

## Chapter 28

97  Thom Johnson, "Camp started today," Facebook, July 11, 2017, 5:17 p.m., https://www.facebook.com/thom.johnson.9/posts/10213015986695572.
98  The story of Creation can be found in Genesis 1-2, while the specific reference can be found in Genesis 2:18.
99  Max Lucado, "Miniature Messengers," in *No Wonder They Call Him the Savior: Chronicles of the Cross* (Portland, Oregon: Multnomah Press, 1986), 105-106.
100  Jason Gray, "Not Right Now," written by Jason Jeffrey Gray and Joshua David Wilson, produces by Jason Ingram and Cason Cooley, March 4, 2014, track 3 on *Love Will Have the Final Word* by, Centricity/Capitol Christian Music Group, compact disc.
101  Max Lucado, "Miniature Messengers," in *No Wonder They Call Him the Savior: Chronicles of the Cross* (Portland, Oregon: Multnomah Press, 1986), 106.

## Chapter 29

102  Kristin Chenoweth & Idina Menzel, "For Good" written, composed, and produced by Stephen Lawrence Schwartz, December 16, 2003, track 18 on Wicked: 2003 Original Broadway Cast, Verve Records, compact disc.
103  From 1 Samuel 7. The Philistines were beating the nation of Israel. The Israelites asked Samuel to pray on their behalf. He did. At the end of the battle, "Samuel took a stone and set it up between Mizpah and Shen, and called its name Ebenezer, saying, 'Thus far the Lord has helped us'" (vs. 12, NIV).
104  Kymra Mercer, text to Thom Johnson, September 6, 2017.
105  Thom Johnson, "It's almost unbelievable that one year ago today, my boys, our family, and our friends gathered to celebrate the life of a truly Amy-zing

woman," Facebook, September 17, 2017, 12:21 p.m., https://www.facebook.com/thom.johnson.9/posts/10213628219321005.
106 Thom Johnson, "Driving to work this morning, worship music playing, Pastor Randy's sermon came quickly to mind, crashing into truths that I knew separately," Facebook, September 18, 2017, 8:27 a.m., https://www.facebook.com/thom.johnson.9/posts/10213634280672535.
107 Kymra Mercer, "Re: Healing," email to Thom Johnson, September 22, 2017.